T0181642

IFIP Advances in Information and Communication Technology 649

IFIP – The International Federation for Information Processing

IFIP was founded in 1960 under the auspices of UNESCO, following the first World Computer Congress held in Paris the previous year. A federation for societies working in information processing, IFIP's aim is two-fold: to support information processing in the countries of its members and to encourage technology transfer to developing nations. As its mission statement clearly states:

IFIP is the global non-profit federation of societies of ICT professionals that aims at achieving a worldwide professional and socially responsible development and application of information and communication technologies.

IFIP is a non-profit-making organization, run almost solely by 2500 volunteers. It operates through a number of technical committees and working groups, which organize events and publications. IFIP's events range from large international open conferences to working conferences and local seminars.

The flagship event is the IFIP World Computer Congress, at which both invited and contributed papers are presented. Contributed papers are rigorously refereed and the rejection rate is high.

As with the Congress, participation in the open conferences is open to all and papers may be invited or submitted. Again, submitted papers are stringently refereed.

The working conferences are structured differently. They are usually run by a working group and attendance is generally smaller and occasionally by invitation only. Their purpose is to create an atmosphere conducive to innovation and development. Refereeing is also rigorous and papers are subjected to extensive group discussion.

Publications arising from IFIP events vary. The papers presented at the IFIP World Computer Congress and at open conferences are published as conference proceedings, while the results of the working conferences are often published as collections of selected and edited papers.

IFIP distinguishes three types of institutional membership: Country Representative Members, Members at Large, and Associate Members. The type of organization that can apply for membership is a wide variety and includes national or international societies of individual computer scientists/ICT professionals, associations or federations of such societies, government institutions/government related organizations, national or international research institutes or consortia, universities, academies of sciences, companies, national or international associations or federations of companies.

More information about this series at https://link.springer.com/bookseries/6102

Luis M. Camarinha-Matos (Ed.)

Technological Innovation for Digitalization and Virtualization

13th IFIP WG 5.5/SOCOLNET
Doctoral Conference on Computing,
Electrical and Industrial Systems, DoCEIS 2022
Caparica, Portugal, June 29 – July 1, 2022
Proceedings

 Springer

Editor
Luis M. Camarinha-Matos ⓘ
Universidade Nova de Lisboa
Monte da Caparica, Portugal

ISSN 1868-4238   ISSN 1868-422X   (electronic)
IFIP Advances in Information and Communication Technology
ISBN 978-3-031-07522-3   ISBN 978-3-031-07520-9   (eBook)
https://doi.org/10.1007/978-3-031-07520-9

This Springer imprint is published by the registered company Springer Nature Switzerland AG
The registered company address is: Gewerbestrasse 11, 6330 Cham, Switzerland

Preface

This proceedings, which collects selected results produced in engineering doctoral programs, focuses on research and development in technological innovation for digitalization and virtualization. The ongoing 4th industrial revolution is characterized by an intense digitalization and digital transformation of all sectors of society. This encompasses the adoption and integration of a variety of new information and communication technologies to develop more efficient, flexible, agile, and sustainable solutions. Furthermore, the recent pandemic forced millions of people to work or study from their homes, which created an immediate challenge for organizations unprepared for this scenario. This led to a fast virtualization of daily interactions and the work environment. As a result, to effectively support digitalization and virtualization many different knowledge areas are coming together leading to the creation of various innovative technologies and tools, while also motivating new research directions.

The 13th Advanced Doctoral Conference on Computing, Electrical, and Industrial Systems (DoCEIS 2022) aimed at providing a venue for sharing and discussing ideas and results from doctoral research in various interrelated areas of engineering, while promoting a strong multidisciplinary dialogue. Furthermore, the conference aimed at creating collaborative opportunities for young researchers as well as effective ways of collecting valuable feedback from colleagues in a welcoming environment. As such, participants were challenged to look beyond the specific technical aspects of their research question and relate their work to the selected theme of the conference, namely, to identify in which ways their research topics can contribute to technological innovation for digitalization and virtualization. Furthermore, current trends in strategic research programs point to the fundamental role of multidisciplinary and interdisciplinary approaches in innovation. More and more funding agencies include this element as a key requirement in their research agendas. In this context, the challenge proposed by DoCEIS contributes to the process of acquiring such skills, which are mandatory in the profession of a PhD [1].

DoCEIS 2022, which was sponsored by SOCOLNET, IFIP, and IEEE IES, attracted 48 paper submissions from a good number of PhD students and their supervisors from 15 countries. This book comprises 22 works selected by the International Program Committee for inclusion in the main program and covers a good spectrum of application domains. As such, research results and ongoing work are presented, illustrated, and discussed in the following areas:

- Smart Systems Thinking
- Cyber-physical Systems
- Health-related Digitalization
- Electric Systems and Machines
- Smart Devices
- Control and Digital Platforms

We hope that this collection of papers will provide readers with an inspiring set of new ideas and challenges, presented in a multidisciplinary context, and that by their diversity these results can trigger and motivate richer research and development directions.

We would like to thank all the authors for their contributions. We also appreciate the efforts and dedication of the DoCEIS International Program Committee members, who both helped with the selection of articles and contributed valuable comments to improve the quality of papers.

April 2022   Luis M. Camarinha-Matos

Reference

L. M. Camarinha-Matos, J. Goes, L. Gomes, P. Pereira (2020). Soft and Transferable Skills Acquisition through Organizing a Doctoral Conference. *Education Sciences* 10 (9), 235. DOI: https://doi.org/10.3390/educsci10090235.

Organization

13th IFIP/SOCOLNET Advanced Doctoral Conference on COMPUTING, ELECTRICAL AND INDUSTRIAL SYSTEMS
Monte Caparica, Portugal, 29 June – 1 July 2022

Conference and Program Chair

Luis M. Camarinha-Matos   NOVA University of Lisbon, Portugal

Organizing Committee Co-chairs

Luis Gomes   NOVA University of Lisbon, Portugal
João Goes   NOVA University of Lisbon, Portugal
Pedro Pereira   NOVA University of Lisbon, Portugal

International Program Committee

Antonio Abreu   Polytechnic Institute of Lisbon, Portugal
Vanja Ambrozic   University of Ljubljana, Slovenia
Luis Bernardo   NOVA University of Lisbon, Portugal
Frede Blaabjerg   Aalborg University, Denmark
Xavier Boucher   Ecole Nationale Superieure des Mines de Saint Etienne,
                            France
Giuseppe Buja   University of Padua, Italy
Ana Cabrera   Universitat Politècnica de Catalunya, Spain
Luis M. Camarinha-Matos   NOVA University of Lisbon, Portugal
Wojciech Cellary   WSB University in Poznan, Poland
Noelia Correia   University of Algarve, Portugal
José Dominguez Navarro   Universidad de Zaragoza, Spain
Filipa Ferrada   NOVA University of Lisbon, Portugal
Florin G. Filip   Romanian Academy of Sciences, Romania
Maria Helena Fino   NOVA University of Lisbon, Portugal
Adrian Florea   'Lucian Blaga' University of Sibiu, Romania
José M. Fonseca   NOVA University of Lisbon, Portugal
Paulo Gil   NOVA University of Lisbon, Portugal
João Goes   NOVA University of Lisbon, Portugal
Luis Gomes   NOVA University of Lisbon, Portugal
Juanqiong Gou   Beijing Jiaotong University, China
Paul Grefen   Eindhoven University of Technology, The Netherlands

Michael Huebner	Brandenburg University of Technology, Cottbus, Germany
Tomasz Janowski	UNU Unit on Policy-Driven Electronic Governance, Poland
Vladimir Katic	University of Novi Sad, Serbia
Srinivas Katkoori	University of South Florida, USA
Asal Kiazadeh	NOVA University of Lisbon, Portugal
Matthieu Lauras	IMT Mines Albi, France
Marin Lujak	Universdad Rey Juan Carlos, Spain
João Martins	NOVA University of Lisbon, Portugal
Rui Melicio	University of Évora, Portugal
Paulo Miyagi	University of São Paulo, Brazil
Eric Monmasson	CY Cergy Paris Université, France
Filipe Moutinho	NOVA University of Lisbon, Portugal
Luis Oliveira	NOVA University of Lisbon, Portugal
Rodolfo Oliveira	NOVA University of Lisbon, Portugal
Angel Ortiz	Universitat Politècnica de València, Spain
Peter Palensky	Delft University of Technology, The Netherlands
Luis Palma	NOVA University of Lisbon, Portugal
Nuno Paulino	NOVA University of Lisbon, Portugal
Pedro Pereira	NOVA University of Lisbon, Portugal
Paulo Pinto	NOVA University of Lisbon, Portugal
Armando Pires	Polytechnic Institute of Setubal, Portugal
Ricardo J. Rabelo	Federal University of Santa Catarina, Brazil
Alberto Reatti	Università degli Studi di Firenze, Italy
Luis Ribeiro	Linkoping University, Sweden
Enrique Romero-Cadaval	University of Extremadura, Spain
Carlos Roncero	University of Extremadura, Spain
Ioan Sacala	Politehnica University of Bucharest, Romania
Eduard Shevtshenko	University of Tartu, Estonia
Catarina Silva	Polytechnic Institute of Leiria, Portugal
Thomas Strasser	Austrian Institute of Technology, Austria
Zoltán Ádám Tamus	Budapest University of Technology and Economics, Hungary
Kleanthis Thramboulidis	University of Patras, Greece
Damien Trentesaux	Université Polytechnique Hauts-de-France, France
Theo Tryfonas	University of Bristol, UK
Zita Vale	Polytechnic Institute of Porto, Portugal
Oleksandr Veligorskyi	Chernihiv National University of Technology, Ukraine
Manuela Vieira	Polytechnic Institute of Lisbon, Portugal
Ramon Vilanova	Universitat Autònoma de Barcelona, Spain
Valery Vyatkin	Luleå tekniska universitet, Sweden
Lai Xu	Bournemouth University, UK
Soufi Youcef	University of Tebessa, Algeria

Local Organizing Committee (PhD Students)

Behrooz Saeidi, Portugal/Iran
Daniel Almeida, Portugal
David Leonardo, Portugal
Diogo Pereira, Portugal
Florindo Canas, Portugal
Fábio Oliveira, Portugal
Jorge Calado, Portugal
João Madeira, Portugal
Leandro Filipe, Portugal

Luis Lourenço, Portugal
Masoud Ardestani, Portugal/Iran
Miguel Lourenço, Portugal
Rafael Rodrigues, Portugal
Sepideh Kalateh, Portugal/Iran
Shuai Liu, Portugal/China
Sonia Hosseinpour, Portugal/Iran
Terrin Pulikottil, Portugal/India

Technical Sponsors

   Society of Collaborative Networks

   IFIP WG 5.5 COVE
Co-Operation Infrastructure for Virtual Enterprises
and Electronic Business

Organizational Sponsors

Organized by

PhD Program in Electrical and Computer Engineering

Contents

Smart Systems Thinking

Modelling Mutual Influence Towards Sustainable Energy Consumption

Kankam O. Adu-Kankam[1,2(✉)] and Luis M. Camarinha-Matos[1]

[1] School of Science and Technology, and UNINOVA - CTS, Nova University of Lisbon,
Campus de Caparica, 2829-516 Monte Caparica, Portugal
kankamadu@gmail.com, cam@uninova.pt
[2] School of Engineering, University of Energy and Natural Resources (UENR), P. O. Box 214,
Sunyani, Ghana

Abstract. The notions of Collaborative Virtual Power Plant Ecosystem (CVPP-E) and Cognitive Household Digital Twin (CHDT) have been proposed to contribute to the efficient organization and management of households within Renewable Energy Communities (RECs). Both ideas can be represented by digital twins, which complement each other. CHDTs can be modelled as software agents, designed to possess some cognitive capabilities which could enable them to make autonomous decisions, based on the preferences or value system of their owner. Due to their cognitive and decision-making capabilities, these agents could exhibit some behavioural attributes such as engaging in collaborations, mutually influencing one another and the ability to adopt some form of social innovation. These behavioural attributes are expected to promote collaboration which are envisioned to increase the survivability and sustainability of the CVPP-E. This study therefore seeks to demonstrate the capability of CHDTs to mutually influence one another towards a common goal - thus promote sustainable energy consumption. We adopted a multi-method simulation technique that involves the integration of multiple simulation paradigms such as System Dynamics, Agent-Based, and Discrete Event simulation techniques on a single simulation platform. The outcome of the study shows that mutual influence could enhance the sustainable consumption in the ecosystem.

Keywords: Mutual influence · Collaborative networks · Sustainable consumption · Digital twins · Renewable energy communities

1 Introduction

It was claimed in a recent study that buildings consume nearly 40% of global energy, 25% of global water and 40% of global resources [1]. The study further advanced the argument that one-third of global greenhouse gases are emitted by residential and commercial buildings. Other similar studies such as [2] have also affirmed that energy consumption in households (HHs) is in the rise and this could partially be attributed to the increasing demands for comfort and its consequent requirement for larger HH equipment. This has

L. M. Camarinha-Matos (Ed.): DoCEIS 2022, IFIP AICT 649, pp. 3–15, 2022.
https://doi.org/10.1007/978-3-031-07520-9_1

also been attributed to higher purchasing power and improvement in the standard of living of occupants [2].

Generally, it is known that the Earth´s resources are depleting rapidly. This depletion can partly be ascribed to the global surge in energy demand, of which HHs play a key role. The adverse effect of depleting the earth resources is currently resulting in the problem of climate change. This phenomenon poses severe threats to the survivability and sustainability of planet earth and its entire occupants. To help address this immense concern, several studies have suggested diverse approaches that can help reduce energy consumption at the HH levels. One of such approaches, as described in [3, 4] and [5], involves the notions of Collaborative Virtual Power Plant Ecosystem (CVPP-E) and Cognitive HH Digital Twin (CHDT). These are a pair of concepts that are proposed to complement each other and can be conceptualized as digital twin representation of (a) a Renewable Energy Community, which is hereby represented as the CVPP-E, and (b) the constituent HHs of the community, also represented as CHDTs. According to the authors of [5], CHDTs can be designed and modelled as software agents that can possess some cognitive capabilities which could enable them to make autonomous and rational decisions based on the preferences of their owners. Furthermore, it is claimed that CHDTs could exhibit some behavioural attributes such as engaging in collaborations and mutually influencing one another towards collective decision-making. In this study we attempt to demonstrate "Mutual Influence" capabilities of these CHDTs, and further endeavour to show how such influence can be adopted to alter the decision making of CHDTs. The study is therefore guided by the following research questions:

RQ-1. In the context that "influencer" CHDTs could convey either positive or negative influence on "infuencee" CHDTs in a CVPP-E, how can the aggregation of these influences over time be used to determine the overall behaviour of a CHDT?

RQ-2. How can the overall behaviour of a CHDT be used in decision-making?

RQ-3. Considering that CHDTs could be influenced to alter their decisions, how can "mutual influence" be used to alter the decisions of CHDTs towards sustainable energy consumption.

2 Relationship with Technological Innovation for Digitalization and Virtualization

Advances in digitalization and virtualization are helping to gradually bridge the divide between the physical and virtual worlds. The coupling of these two worlds unveils the possibility of mirroring the real world in its equivalent form within the virtual space [6]. These concepts represent facets of a major transformation that is currently ongoing in industry and services, often referred to as industry 4.0. They encompass the adoption and integration of a variety of new information and communication technologies for the development of more efficient, flexible, agile, and sustainable solutions [7]. In the domain of energy, these concepts are helping to facilitate the integration of intelligence in the form of software agents for optimum grid management and operation. In this context, this study proposes the virtualization of Renewable Energy Communities (RECs) and their constituent HHs into a form of Digital Twins (DTs). Furthermore, the study suggests the digitalization of energy use preferences of the constituent HHs of these RECs, in a form of delegated autonomy, which is assigned to their DT counterparts. It is perceived that these DTs could possess some cognitive or intelligent attributes that could enable them to make rational and autonomous decisions on behalf of their owners. This could help to provide flexible and sustainable energy consumption within these virtualized RECs. In view of the above, the scope of this work aligns well with the ongoing trend in the digital transformation.

3 Theoretical Framework and Related Works

We derived the Collaborative Virtual Power Plant Ecosystem concept by merging principles and concepts from the disciplines of Collaborative Networks (CNs) [8], and Virtual Power Plants (VPP) [9]. The central theme for the concepts of CNs is the idea of collaboration, where multiple entities come together with the primary objective of achieving a common goal. In studies such as [10] and [11], CN concepts are well elaborated. Conversely, VPPs are virtual entities that involve the interaction between multiple stakeholders and are comprised of decentralized multi-site and heterogeneous technologies, formed by aggregating deferrable and non-deferrable distributed energy sources [3]. The mix of these two concepts resulted in the proposed hybrid concept called Collaborative Virtual Power Plant Ecosystem (CVPP-E). This idea was first introduced in [3]. A CVPP-E can be perceived as a Digital Twin (DT) model of a REC, such as described in [12]. Other relevant studies described a CVPP-E as a form of a business ecosystem or a community of practice where members approach energy generation, consumption, and conservation from a sustainability point of view using collaboration as a key technique. The governing structure is claimed to be polycentric and decentralized with a manager who plays a coordinating role and promotes collaborative behaviours. Our current work extends previous developments by focusing on the effects of mutual influence among CHDTs and how such influence can be channelled to promote more sustainable energy consumption.

4 Modelling Framework

Modelling the CVPP-E and CHDTs: According to [13], a REC is a community that is formed based on open and voluntary participation. It is usually owned, managed, and controlled by shareholders or members who are autonomous and located within the proximity of the projects. Essentially, members of a REC can generate renewable energy for their own consumption, and may store, sell, or share excess with community members. In this context, the study, attempt to replicate the REC concept by aggregating several autonomous software agents into a population of CHDTs. Each CHDT represents a unit of HH within the community. In the model, we categorized the constituent HHs (CHDTs) into 5 different categories. The categorization and related data was sourced from [14]. The considered categories are: (a) HHs with single pensioner (b) HHs with single non-pensioner (c) HHs with multiple pensioners (d) HHs with children (e) HHs with multiple persons with no dependent children.

A key aspect of the CHDTs concept is their cognitive capabilities. In this study, CHDTs are modelled at three abstraction levels. The upper-level is used to model the community status and decision making processes, while the mid-level is used to model the different behavioural attributes of the CHDT. At the low-level is where energy assets such as HH appliances, energy storage devices, as well as the PV systems are modelled. Although it is acknowledged that the physical layer involves the integration of diverse energy assets, it is expected that several technical factors should be taken into consideration as far as the organization and efficient management of these energy assets are concerned. However, the emphasis of the study was focused primarily at the upper and mid layers where decision-making and varied behavioural attributes occur. Therefore, the lower level technical factors are not addressed in this work. This is because this study hinges around two key principles: (a) collaborations which is based on some common goals, and (b) the notion of community. Currently, the literature on energy communities suggests that members usually form a cohesive union around the energy infrastructure, due to the notion of "community membership", "sense of belonging", "common identity", etc. Furthermore, it is claimed that members of these communities are usually expected to conform to community norms, practices, and rules. Therefore, the behavioural traits as well as the decision-making attributes of members is what we deem paramount in this work.

In modelling a CHDT, we first consider its community status, which defines a CHDTs long-term characteristics which enables it to play some specific roles in the community. For instance, being a prosumer, consumer, influencer, or influencee. Thus, the status of a CHDT is modelled using a "composite state" as shown in Fig. 1, and is assumed at the model initialization stage, and is remembered and maintained as an "active state" by the agent throughout the model run. The behavioural attribute at the mid-level includes behaviours such as the ability to convey influence (influencer) or being the recipient of an influence (influencee). These behavioural attributes are also modelled as internal states, using "simple states" which are embedded inside the "composite state" as shown in Fig. 1.

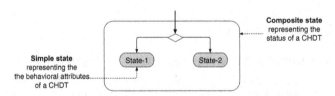

Fig. 1. A composite and simple states of a CHDT

At the low-level, prosumer CHDT are modelled to possess a Photovoltaic (PV) unit for energy generation, a local energy storage system, and nine (9) HH appliances. An Anylogic [17] model of the nine considered appliances as shown in Fig. 2. The Anylogic enables the integration of multiple simulation paradigms such as system dynamics, agent based, and discrete event techniques on a single platform. The considered appliances are: (a) Washing machine, (b) Dishwasher, (c) Tumble/clothes dryer, (d) Audio-visuals, (e) Microwave, (f) Cooker, (g) lighting, (h) Oven, and (i) Refrigerator. The consumption priority of a prosumer is firstly from the PV system, then the local storage, followed by the community storage, and finally the grid. Prosumers can share excess energy with the community through a common community storage system as shown in Fig. 3. Consumers are also modelled to possess nine HH appliances. Their primary energy source is the grid, however, when community storage is found to be available, they switch sources to utilize the storage until it runs out, then they revert to the grid.

In the model, the consumption of each HH appliance per CHDT is continuously aggregated throughout the period of the model run. The data from these aggregated values form the load profile for each appliance per household. Furthermore, the consumption for all appliances per household are also aggregated to form the load profile for that HH. Finally, the consumption for all the households in the community is also aggregated to form the global load profile of the entire community. The anylogic simulation platform has a built-in graphical analysis tool that enables these data be plotted. In Sect. 6 of this study, the data collected at the global level is used in the analysis of the global behaviour of CHDTs in the community.

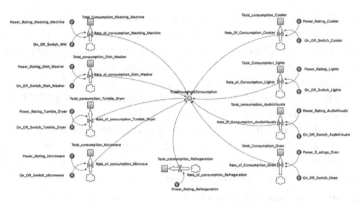

Fig. 2. Anylogic model of the nine HH appliances.

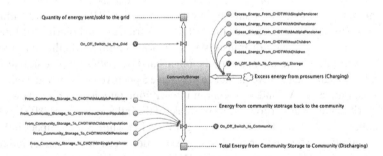

Fig. 3. Anylogic model of the community storage

An active state, as mentioned earlier, defines the aspects of the CHDT that are functional. An inactive state, on the contrary, describes attributes that are dormant. As shown in Figs. 4 and 5, active states are depicted using unshaded regions with continuous boundary lines. Inactive states on the other hand are shown as shaded regions with dotted boundary lines. In Fig. 4 as an example, we elucidate an active CHDT (CHDT-1) whose status as a prosumer is active and a state describing this CHDT as an influencer is also active. Likewise, in Fig. 5, we show an active CHDT (CHDT-2) whose status as a consumer is active and a state describing this CHDT as an "influencee" is also shown active.

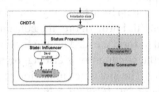   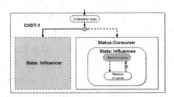

Fig. 4. A CHDT with active prosumer status, active influencer state and active "send influence" state

Fig. 5. A CHDT with active consumer status, active "influence" state and active "receive influence" state

Additionally, Influencer CHDTs also have an active internal state labelled "send influence" which contains algorithms responsible for the conveyance of influence.

Similarly, influences CHDTs have an active "receive influence" states which also contain algorithms responsible for the reception of influence. In this described scenario, it is assumed that influencer CHDTs do not receive influence and influencee CHDTs also do not convey influence. Generally, when the status or state of a CHDT is active it executes algorithmic instructions that are associated with that particular status or state, and this enables the CHDT to behave according to the embedded instructions. Having knowledge of all active states (both composite and simple) as well as the accompanying algorithmic instructions, and making basic rational decisions based on this knowledge is what gives the CHDT its cognitive capabilities.

Modelling Influences and Decision-Making: In this study we consider two types of endogenous influences. These are positive and negative influences. Endogenous influence refers to influences that are of external origin relative to a CHDT. These influences could originate from the CVPP manager or other influential CHDTs that are within the ecosystem. Each influence possesses the following attributes (a) Polarity (b) Intensity (c) Impact and (d) Frequency of transmission. Polarity signifies whether an influence is positive or negative. The intensity on the other hand describes the magnitude of the influence. For instance, a positive influence may have a positive polarity and a minimum intensity/magnitude of "X" and a maximum intensity/magnitude of "Y". Likewise, the impact describes the severity (how strong or weak) of the influence on the CHDT. A high-impact influence affects the CHDT for a longer duration while a low-impact influence has a short duration. The frequency of transmission describes how often an influencer CHDT convey influence to the community. CDHTs make decision based on a predefined threshold called the "decision constant" which is represented by "$\propto$". This parameter is a positive value and can be reached when the aggregated impact of all influences acting on the CHDT equals this constant. A negative constant could also be adopted and used to determine when a CHDT makes a negative decision such as refusal to participate in collaborations. Additionally, influences are conveyed and received in the form of "pulses" that are transmitted sporadically from several sources (i.e., from the various influencer CHDTs) to random destination (influencee CHDTs). The pulsating characteristics of the influences are modelled using a probability distribution functions. These functions are expressed as follows: (a) Positive influence: *Uniform distribution (+a, + b)*, (b) Negative influence: *Uniform distribution (-c, -d)*, (c) Frequency of transmission:

Uniform distribution (e, f) times per hours, days, weeks, months, or years. (d) Impact: *Uniform distribution (g, h) hours, days, weeks, months, or years, (g) Decision threshold* $= \alpha$. Where $+ a, -c, e$, and g are the possible lower limits, and $+ b, -d, f,$ and h are the possible upper limits for each related elements of the influence.

5 Demonstration of the Modelling Technique Using Selected Scenarios

Scenario for Modelling CHDT Population: In Table 1, we define the population size for each category of HH within the CVPP-E. This population shall be maintained throughout the demonstration.

Table 1. CHDT population considered for each category of HHs

Item	Category of CHDT	Population size
1	CHDT with single pensioner	10
2	CHDT with single non-pensioner	10
3	CHDT with multiple pensioners	10
4	CHDT with children	10
5	CHDT with multiple persons with no dependent children	10
Total population size		**50**

Scenario for Modelling Installed PV Systems: For the prosumers population, four different capacities of PV systems are considered. Each prosumer CHDT can inherit any one of them. The PV systems and their respective capacities are: (a) BainSystem = 6.930 kW, (b) BrainSystem = 1.950 kW, (c) Helius = 3.99 kW, and (d) DaSS = 3.22 kW. All PVs are located in the Great Britain [15]. Data from these real-life systems are used to model the PV generation aspects of the model. The aspects of the energy storage is modelled as following: (a) State of charge $= M$, (b) the storage capacity $= N$, and (c) depth of discharge $= K$. Condition for discharging storage is when $M > = 70\%$ of N. Condition for charging is when $M < = 30\%$ of N.

Scenario for the Modelling of Influences and Decision-Making: The defined parameters for this scenario are as follows: *(a). Positive influence: Uniform distribution (0, 2), (b) Negative influence: Uniform distribution (-2, 0), (c) Frequency of transmission: Uniform distribution (0, 3) times per week, (d) Impact: Uniform distribution (0, 5) hours* *from the moment of receiving the influence, (e) Decision threshold* (α) *= 50. Community Storage capacity (N$_C$) = 300 Kwh. Local storage capacity (N$_L$) = 20 kwh for Brain-System, 15 kwh for helious, 12 kwh for DaSS, and 10 kwh for BainBridge. Finally, the depth of discharge for all storage was 70% of N.*

Scenario for Modelling Embedded HH Appliances: The parameters that were used to model the use-behaviours of all the nine (9) HH appliances are shown in Table 2. The parameters were obtained from [14] and [16]. The data from [14] was sourced from the Household Electricity Survey: A Study of Domestic Electrical Product Usage (Intertek Report R66141) [14]. The report is a comprehensive and extensive one that covers several aspects of household's energy use. The data was collected from 251 households in England spanning the period May 2010 to July 2011. For each category of HH, the survey captured the HH size i.e., the number of occupants per HH. For instance, Table 2, shows the number of HH per each category, that was used for that survey. For each HH, the number of occupants or household size was different. Therefore, the data that was used to model the appliance's consumption, which was borrowed from this report captures the different occupants per household.

Table 2. Parameters used to model the use-behaviour of the considered appliances

Type of inhabitant	Number of HH
Single pensioner households	34
Single non-pensioner household	35
Multiple pensioner household	29
Household with children	78
Multiple person household with no dependent children	74

Table 3. Parameters used to model the use-behaviour of the considered appliances.

Type of Appliance	DoU *(hrs)*		APR (kW)		FoU/ week		
	min	*max*	*min*	*max*	*min*	*ave*	*max*
Wash. Mach	0.50	3.00	0.500	1.000	0.00	4.00	8.00
Tumble dryer	0.50	3.00	1.000	3.000	4.38	6.00	5.38
Dishwasher	0.50	3.00	1.000	1.500	4.19	6.19	5.19
Audio-visuals	0.50	6.00	0.025	0.148	1.00	11	21.0
Microwave	0.16	1.00	0.600	1.150	1.00	7.00	14.0
Electric Cooker	0.50	3.00	2.000	4.000	1.00	7.00	14.0
Lighting	0.16	8.00	0.015	0.165	1.00	7.00	21.0

(continued)

Table 3. (*continued*)

Type of Appliance	DoU *(hrs)*		APR (kW)		FoU/ week		
	min	*max*	*min*	*max*	*min*	*ave*	*max*
Refrigeration	24.0	24.0	0.011	0.091	–	–	–
Oven	0.50	2.00	2.000	4.000	1.00	7.00	14.0

Table 3 shows the Duration of Use (DoU), Appliance Power Rating (APR), and Frequency of Use (FoU).

Scenario for Testing Collective Decision Making: As shown in Table 4, two different cases, constituting of different population sizes, were considered. In all cases, the influencer CHDTs attempt to influence the "influencee" CHDTs towards the Delegation of Deferrable Loads (DDL), i.e., suspend the use of loads whose utilization can be deferred to a later time without causing much inconvenience to the user. The appliances that were considered for DDL are (a) washing machines, (b) dish washers and (c) tumble dryers. DDL appliances avoid consumption from the grid and wait until local storage or community storage is available. To help test these cases, the Anylogic simulation platform [17] was adopted.

Table 4. Two cases with varying population sizes are used to test collective decision making.

Cases	Population (%)					
	Influencer population "A"	Influencee population	Positive Influencer Population	Negative Influencer population	Prosumer population	Consumer population
Case-1a	90% of 50	10% of 50	90% of A	10% of A	20% of 50	80% of 50
Case 1b	90% of 50	10% of 50	10% of A	90%of A	20% of 50	80% of 50
Case-2a	10% of 50	90% of 50	90% of A	10% of A	80% of 50	20% of 50
Case-2b	10% of 50	90% of 50	10% of A	90% of A	80% of 50	20% of 50

6   Results and Discussion

RQ-1 & RQ-2: In this section, we attempt to answer research questions 1 & 2. After running the simulation model for a period of 728 h (30 days) the following sample behaviours were extracted from some selected CHDTs. In Figs. 6a & 6b we show the characteristics of the modelled influence that was received by two different CHDTs, i.e., CHDT-1 and CHDT-2. The pulses that appear below the x-axis represent negative influences whilst the ones above the x-axis are positive influences. Attributes such as polarity, intensity, impact, and frequency of transmissions can be observed in both Figs.

In Figs. 7a to 7d, we show how the aggregation of influences over time, can be used to determine the overall behaviour of a CHDT. We also demonstrate how the overall behaviour can be used in decision-making. For instance, Figs. 7a, 7b and 7c, show CHDTs 3, 4 & 5 that initially behaved negatively. However, the duration of their negative behaviour lasted differently. It lasted longer with CHDT-4 than CHDTs 3 & 5. Eventually, all three CHDTs changed behaviour from negative to positive. However, CHDT 3 changed behaviour faster than CHDT 4 & 5. This was because CHDT 3 was highly influenced positively than CHDTs 4&5. For this reason, CHDT-3 exceeded the decision threshold " α" and therefore was able to decide within the simulated period (30 days) but CHDT 4 and CHDT 5 were unable. Finally in Fig. 7d, CHDT 6 behaved positively right from the beginning of the model execution and it was also able to decide much quicker than CHDTs 3, 4 and 5.

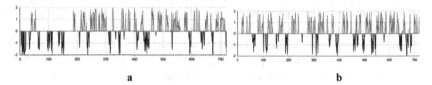

Fig. 6. **a.** Influences received by CHDT-1. **b.** Influences received by CHDT-2

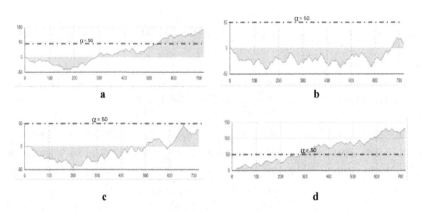

Fig. 7. **a.** CHDT-3. **b.** CHDT-4. **c.** CHDT-5. **d.** CHDT-6

RQ-3: Also in this section, we attempt to answer research question 3. By referring to Table 4, we hereby consider cases 1a &1b. The outcome of the model for these cases are shown in Fig. 8a & 8b. For this case, the population of prosumers, consumers, influencers, and influencees were maintained the same. The difference between the two scenarios is the number of positive and negative influencers. In case1b, 10% of the influencer population were positive influencers and 90% were negative influencers. For this reason, the majority of the CHDTs were influenced negatively and this resulted in few decisions-making causing high proportion of energy to be consumed from the grid, (about 69%). Furthermore, it is observed that consumption from the community storage was also low (about 13%). By comparing case 1b to case 1a, where the population of positive influencers was high, thus, 90% and the population of negative influences was low, thus, 10%, it can be seen that the majority of the CHDTs were influenced positively resulting in more decision making, hence a reduction in the consumption from the grid, thus, 51%, and an increase in the consumption from the community storage thus, 24%.

a   b

Fig. 8. **a.** Case-1a. 90% positive influencers. **b.** Case-1b. 10% positive influencers.

Referring to Table 4 and Figs. 9a and 9b, we hereby consider cases 2a and 2b. In case 2a we consider 90% of the influencer population to be positive influencers and 10% to be negative influencers. On the contrary, in case 2b, we consider 10% of the influencer population to be positive influencers and 90% to be negative influencers. It can therefore be observed that in case 2a where the number of positive influencers was high, the use of the grid is relatively low, about 53%, as compared to case 2b where the use of the grid is relatively high, about 60% due to the rather low population of positive influencers (i.e., high population of negative influencers). The use of PV and local storage also appreciated significantly in case 2a as compared to case 2b. The difference in both cases resulted from the population difference between negative and positive influencers.

a   b

Fig. 9. **a.** Case-2a. 90% positive influencers. **b.** Case-2b. 10% positive influencer

There are several techniques that can be used to help spread influence in a social system or network. In particular, the power of online information diffusion is one effective method that has been utilized to positively influence citizens in many ways. For instance, in the response to natural or man-made disasters [18] and the Hotmail phenomenon in the early 1990s [19]. This effect, which is often referred to as the "viral phenomenon" or "viral marketing" has been adopted by companies to encourage sharing between individuals with social connections, because it is known that social recommendations can help increase traffic to websites of businesses, resulting in higher engagement and revenue. In this study, positive influencers in the ecosystem could utilize the power of viral marketing and social recommendation. When combined with incentives (monetary incentives or social recognition incentives) it is possible to increase the number of influencers and thus help spreading their influence out to other members of the ecosystem.

7 Conclusion and Future Work

This study has enabled the furtherance of the notions of CHDTs by demonstrating the decision-making and mutual influence capabilities of these software agents. Firstly, we showed how influence is exchanged between influencer and influence CHDTs. Furthermore, we illustrated how the aggregation of influences over time can help to determine the overall behaviour of a CHDT. Again, the study has shown how CHDTs are able to make influence-induced decisions using the principle of thresholds. This work has further helped to establish the fact that CHDTs could engage in collective actions that could result in the global achievement of some common goals. It has further been shown that a high population of positive influencers can help influence the community positively and a high population of negative influencers could also influence the community negatively, subsequently affecting the sustainability of the ecosystem. In future studies, we shall consider the use of incentives to help increase the number of positive influencers and thus leverage the positive effect. Finally, we draw the conclusion that the notion of CVPP-E and CHDTs are feasible concepts. In terms of possible implementation, IoT, sensors, and smart HH devices could be adopted as interfaces between the various HH appliances and the respective CHDT. For the software aspect, a CHDT could have the form of smart software agents or a HH energy management system which could be used to initiate the exchange of information between energy assets, the community manager, and other CHDTs. A local area network with network devices like routers, edge servers, and IoT gateways on top of the physical layer could also surface for the communication aspects.

Acknowledgment. We acknowledge project CESME (Collaborative & Evolvable Smart Manufacturing Ecosystem and the Portuguese FCT program UIDB/00066/2020 for providing partial financial support for this work.

References

1. Aversa, P., Donatelli, A., Piccoli, G., Luprano, V.A.M.: Improved thermal transmittance measurement with HFM technique on building envelopes in the mediterranean area. Sel. Sci. Pap. J. Civ. Eng. **11**(2), 39–52 (2016)
2. IDEA: Analyses of the energy consumption of the household sector in Spain (2011). www.cros-portal.eu/sites/default/files/SECH_Spain.pdf%5Cn
3. Adu-Kankam, K.O., Camarinha-Matos, L.M.: Towards collaborative virtual power plants: trends and convergence. Sustain. Energy, Grids Networks **Segan.2018**, 217–230 (2018). https://doi.org/10.1016/j.segan.2018
4. Adu-Kankam, K., Camarinha-Matos, L.: Towards collaborative virtual power plants. In: Camarinha-Matos, L.M., Adu-Kankam, K.O., Julashokri, M. (eds.) DoCEIS. IAICT, vol. 521, pp. 28–39. Springer, Cham (2018). https://doi.org/10.1007/978-3-319-78574-5_3

5. Adu-Kankam, K., Camarinha-Matos, L.: Towards a hybrid model for the diffusion of innovation in energy communities. In: Camarinha-Matos, L.M., Ferreira, P., Brito, G. (eds.) DoCEIS. IAICT, vol. 626, pp. 175–188. Springer, Cham (2021). https://doi.org/10.1007/978-3-030-78288-7_17

6. Shevtshenko, E., Mahmood, K., Karaulova, T., Raji, I.O.: Multitier digital twin approach for agile supply chain management. In: Proceedings of the ASME International Mechanical Engineering Congress and Exposition, vol. 2B-2020, no. April 2021, pp. 0–11 (2020)

7. Raji, I.O., Shevtshenko, E., Rossi, T., Strozzi, F.: Modelling the relationship of digital technologies with lean and agile strategies. Supply Chain Forum 22(4), 323–346 (2021)

8. Camarinha-Matos, L.M., Afsarmanesh, H.: Collaborative networks: a new scientific discipline. J. Intell. Manuf. 16(4–5), 439–452 (2005)

9. Rouzbahani, H.M., Karimipour, H., Lei, L.: A review on virtual power plant for energy management. Sustain. Energy Technol. Assessments 47, 101370 (2021)

10. Ferrada, F., Camarinha-Matos, L.M.: A modelling framework for collaborative network emotions. Enterp. Inf. Syst. 13(7–8), 1164–1194 (2019)

11. Graça, P., Camarinha-Matos, L., Ferrada, F.: A Model to assess collaboration performance in a collaborative business ecosystem. In: Camarinha-Matos, L.M., Almeida, R., Oliveira, J. (eds.) DoCEIS. IAICT, vol. 553, pp. 3–13. Springer, Cham (2019). https://doi.org/10.1007/978-3-030-17771-3_1

12. Adu-Kankam, K.O., Camarinha-Matos, L.M.: Emerging community energy ecosystems: analysis of organizational and governance structures of selected representative cases. In: Camarinha-Matos, L.M., Almeida, R., Oliveira, J. (eds.) DoCEIS. IAICT, vol. 553, pp. 24–40. Springer, Cham (2019). https://doi.org/10.1007/978-3-030-17771-3_3

13. The European Parliament and the Council of the European Union, "Directive (EU) 2018/2001 of the European Parliament and of the Council on the promotion of the use of energy from renewable sources. Official Journal of the European Union (2018). https://eur-lex.europa.eu/legal-content/EN/TXT/PDF/?uri=CELEX:32018L2001&from=fr. Accessed 07 Mar 2022

14. Zimmermann, J.-P., et al.: Household Electricity Survey: A study of domestic electrical product usage. Intertek Report R66141 (2012). https://www.gov.uk/government/uploads/system/uploads/attachment_data/file/208097/10043_R66141HouseholdElectricitySurveyFinalReportissue4.pdf. Accessed 18 Feb 2022

15. "PVOutput." https://pvoutput.org/. Accessed 08 Oct 2021

16. Wattage & Power Consumption of Typical Household Appliances - 106 Appliances in All - Lets Save Electricity. https://letsavelectricity.com/wattage-power-consumption-of-household-appliances/. Accessed 12 Mar 2021

17. Mahdavi, A.: The Art of Process-Centric Modeling (2020). https://www.anylogic.com/resources/books/the-art-of-process-centric-modeling-with-anylogic/

18. Chen, W., Lakshmanan, L.V.S., Castillo, C.: Information and Influence Propagation in Social Networks. In: Özsu, M.T. (ed.) Synthesis Lectures on Data Management, vol. 5, no. 4, pp. 1–177. Morgan & Claypool Publishers series (2013)

19. Hugo, O., Garnsey, E.: "The emergence of electronic messaging and the growth of four entrepreneurial entrants. New Technol. Based Firms New Millenium 2, 97–123 (2002)

Assessing the Benefits of Renewable Energy Communities: A Portuguese Case Study

Humberto Queiroz[1,2]([✉]), Rui Amaral Lopes[1,2], João Martins[1,2], Luís Fialho[3], João Bravo Dias[4], and Nuno Bilo[5]

[1] NOVA School of Science and Technology (FCT NOVA), Caparica, Portugal
h.queiroz@campus.fct.unl.pt, {rm.lopes,jf.martins}@fct.unl.pt
[2] Centre of Technology and Systems (CTS UNINOVA), Caparica, Portugal
[3] Renewable Energies Chair, University of Évora, Évora, Portugal
lafialho@uevora.pt
[4] EDP LABELEC, Sacavém, Portugal
joao.bravodias@edp.pt
[5] Câmara Municipal de Évora, Évora, Portugal
nuno.choraobilo@cm-evora.pt

Abstract. The new European legislation regarding self-consumption from local renewable energy sources, and the following Portuguese transposition, define new structures to the self-consumption process, namely the Storage Installation and the Production Installation. It also brings the concept of Renewable Energy Community (REC), defining how it can be formed and how to manage its energy consumption and generation. Regarding this management, there is the possibility to share the generated energy locally, among REC members, by the application of sharing coefficients. This paper analyses the benefits introduced to a group of buildings, in terms of electricity costs, when they operate as a REC. Additionally, it analyses the impact of battery storage systems on renewable energy sources self-consumption, when the referred buildings operate individually or as a REC.

Keywords: Renewable energy community · Self-consumption · Energy storage

1 Introduction

According to Directive (EU) 2018/2001 of the European Parliament and of the Council on the promotion of the use of energy from renewable sources [1], the increase of renewable energy usage is one of the goals of the European Union energy policy. The increase of renewable energy sources also plays a role on the energy security framework, along with the environmental benefits. However, the natural intermittence of some technologies commercially available (e.g., solar Photovoltaic (PV) systems) and high reverse power flows might introduce problems during the operation of electrical grids [2]. Non-hydro renewables (geothermal, solar, wind, ocean, biofuel and waste) were responsible for up to 11% of all electricity generation in 2019 [3] but this figure is expected to increase to 40–70% by 2050.

© IFIP International Federation for Information Processing 2022
Published by Springer Nature Switzerland AG 2022
L. M. Camarinha-Matos (Ed.): DoCEIS 2022, IFIP AICT 649, pp. 16–25, 2022.
https://doi.org/10.1007/978-3-031-07520-9_2

Given the importance of the building sector, which is responsible for the consumption of 48% of all electricity generated [3] one of the innovations brought by Directive 2018/2001 refers to the possibility of aggregating buildings as a Renewable Energy Community (REC). Among other objectives, RECs aim to enable renewable energy sharing among its members with the overall goal of improving the development of the renewable energy market, while contributing to the promotion of energy efficiency at building and cluster levels, and to the decrease of energy poverty through electricity costs reduction. RECs are also a tool, as an added value, to increase both local acceptance of renewable energy sources, and citizen participation on energy transition [1]. Additionally, existing energy flexibility can be aggregated and used at community level to mitigate the referred challenges imposed to the operation of electric grids by the introduction of energy conversion systems based on renewable energy resources [4].

In this context, the contributions of this paper are twofold: firstly, a comparison with individual and collective self-consumption is conducted in order to analyse the impacts of both configurations on the electrical energy import and resulting electricity costs. The second major contribution refers to the assessment of the Storage Installation impact on both self-consumption configurations (individual and collective). Regarding the collective self-consumption, the recent published European and Portuguese legal framework are considered in this study, with special attention to the association of buildings into a renewable energy community and the energy sharing procedure among its members.

2 Relationship to Technological Innovation for Digitalization and Virtualization

The "World Energy Outlook 2021", published by the International Energy Agency [5], states that there is a need to increase the capacity of distribution lines, to handle the growing distributed solar PV capacity, which is predicted to increase four-fold by 2030. To comply with this increasing share of distributed renewable energy sources into the distribution grids, there is a need to manage locally how this energy is used. The concept of Renewable Energy Community is created by the Directive 2018/2001 of the European Council [1] in order to address this need. However, for a proper energy management within the borders of a REC there is a need to virtualize the energy sharing process, since it is impossible to drive the generated energy to a given user when it is needed. Furthermore, REC members might be distant from each other, which makes unfeasible the physical management of the energy trading among them. In this case, the distribution grid is used, and grid fees are charged. These fees are virtually calculated, based on the net values of energy import and export of each community member. Thus, the energy sharing is made at energy meter level, and the result is charged to every REC member.

Through simulation, the case study presented in this paper addresses the impacts introduced by a REC on a group of real buildings in Évora, Portugal, in terms of electricity costs, when comparing to their individual operation. These buildings are, in fact, detached from each other and physically separated by hundreds of meters. However, it is possible to manage the energy import, sharing and export of these buildings by virtualizing the process at energy meter level. Additionally, this paper aims to assess the impact introduced by Storage Installations (SIs) on PV self-consumption at building and community level. The presented case study is carried out under the scope of European POCITYF H2020 project [6], which, among other objectives, aims to create a REC that will integrate the referred buildings.

3 Renewable Energy Community

At European level, the concept of Renewable Energy Community is described by Directive 2018/2001 of the European Council [1]. This document defines a REC as a legal entity, formed by the association of electricity consumers, which has the main objective of providing environmental, economic, and social benefits to its members and to the surroundings entities, both private and public. Renewable Energy Communities have the rights to generate, store, use and export energy to the grid. They also have the right to share part of the generated energy among its members.

Considering the Portuguese context, the definition of Renewable Energy Communities has been updated by Decree-Law 15/2022 [7], which states that energy sharing among REC members must be conducted using sharing coefficients whose values are agreed by all members. The complete regulation of REC operation is described by Regulation 373/2021, published by the Portuguese Energy Services Regulatory Authority (ERSE) [8]. This regulatory document also brings two new concepts for the self-consumption topic: i) the Storage Installation, an electrical installation licensed on the terms of the Decree-Law 15/2022, for storage of renewable electrical energy, static or by using electric vehicles batteries, which can be installed on private network or in the public grid; and ii) the Production Installation (PI), an electrical installation licensed under the terms of the Decree-Law 15/2022, for production of renewable energy on one or more Units for Self-Consumption Production (USCP), which is connected to the public grid, directly or by a local network. Regarding the energy sharing coefficients, the Portuguese regulation [8] states that they must be sent to the distribution system operator prior to the start of the sharing process.

Studies on energy communities have been recently increasing, given the importance for meeting strategic objectives in terms of responding to the climate emergency by, for instance, promoting the use of renewable energy resources. Botsaris et al. [9] address the business case scenario and the market players involved in a virtual REC composed of different types of buildings in Greece. Results show that the community implementation on a low-income housing context must be followed by promotion schemes due to the initial cost of adapting existing buildings and installing new equipment. On another context, Ceglia et al. [10] analysed the environmental performance of a simulated REC composed of two office buildings, implemented considering European regional directives [1] together with the Italian legal framework. Results show that the share of consumed electricity which is locally generated rises to 79% when considering collective self-consumption. The user's intention to participate on a REC, assessed by the analysis of their attitude, the norms and the possible behavioural control that might be perceived by them, is described in [11]. This survey shows that, when people are previously informed of the benefits related to a REC, both economic and environmental, their interest to participate increases.

One of the main features of a Renewable Energy Community refers to the energy sharing process. Under the Portuguese context, sharing is made by the definition of sharing coefficients (according to Decree-Law n° 15/2022 [7]), which can be static or time dependent. Static coefficients might have distinct values for different days (e.g., weekdays and weekends), while variable coefficients might follow any criteria, such as energy consumption and generation during a specific period. According to this second type, the sharing coefficients used in this case study vary throughout the day (15-min resolution) following the power needs of each member relative to the entire REC, as described by Eq. (1), where ESC_i refers to the value of the energy sharing coefficient attributed to member i at time-step n, Pd is the power demand and N is the number of REC members.

$$\mathrm{ESC}_i(n) = \left(\frac{Pd_i(n)}{\sum_{j=1}^{N} Pd_j(n)} \right) \tag{1}$$

The literature also shows that the energy sharing process is normally associated with peer-to-peer energy transactions in microgrids with local energy sources. Liu et at. [12] developed an energy sharing model, to be used with a price-based demand response mechanism, applied to an energy community formed by residential, commercial and office buildings. Hutty et al. [13] also applied an energy sharing model to a residential microgrid, on a community formed by 50 residences. However, in this case, along with the PV systems used as local energy source, electric vehicles are also an asset, which can play as loads, when charging, or as an energy source when discharging. The business model proposed by Fioriti et al. [14] takes into consideration rewards distribution within the community together with strategies to add or remove members, and a reward mechanism to a possible aggregator entity. They concluded that the grid dependence, when the community operates in a cooperative way, decrease by 54%. They also conclude that a collective implementation of local energy sources is cheaper than the individual purchasing of needed assets to turn self-consumption possible. Lastly, the increase of PV self-consumption by the community members is up to 46% when they operate collectively.

4 Case Study

This case study assesses the benefits introduced to a group of four public buildings by the implementation of a REC. These buildings are located in Évora, Portugal, and belong to the local municipality. Additionally, this case study addresses the impact of energy storage systems on PV self-consumption, when the referred buildings operate individually or as a REC. These buildings are used for distinct activities, resulting in different electricity needs, as presented in Fig. 1, which shows the normalized daily average demand profiles for 2019 (real data collected with 15-min resolution). In more detail, Building #1 is a multipurpose pavilion, used for concerts, sports tournaments and other events (see the increased power demand during the night due to shows), Building #2 is a public market, Building #3 is a public school and Building #4 is the City Hall. The annual peak power demand, the electrical energy needed to comply with users' necessities, and the associated electricity costs are presented in Table 1. Currently, none of the buildings is equipped with PV systems although the installation is foreseen during the POCTIYF H2020 project, where these buildings will integrate a Positive Energy Block in Évora historic centre.

For this case study, two distinct scenarios are considered for the future PV systems installation. In the first one, the four buildings operate individually and therefore self-consumption is carried out at building level. In the second scenario, a REC is implemented in order to allow the collective self-consumption, as regulated by [8], where local generation, by the same Production Installations mentioned before, is shared among REC members according to the energy sharing coefficient described in Sect. 3 (Eq. 1). In both scenarios the impact of installing Storage Installations is assessed. These energy storage installations are controlled to only charge when PV surplus is available and to discharge whenever power demand is higher than generation. The overall power demand and generation (four buildings) is considered at community level.

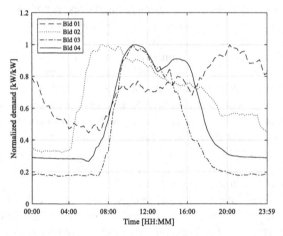

Fig. 1. Normalized daily average load diagram of the considered buildings.

Table 1. Buildings' energy related metrics.

Building	Peak power (kW)	Demand [kWh/y]	Cost [€/y]
#1	78	37,904	4,876.80
#2	21	33,289	4,305.70
#3	43	36,486	5,051.10
#4	136	236,350	32,064.00
Total	–	344,029	46,297.60

The PV production is estimated using real irradiance data acquired during 2019 from a local weather station. Figure 2 presents the average daily profile of the global horizontal irradiance (15-min resolution), which was computed by averaging the corresponding 365 daily profiles. Table 2 summarizes the considered PV peak power for each building and the associated yearly energy output. The rated power of the buildings to be installed, in the POCITYF project context, are a result of a survey conducted on the early stages of the project. The real values to be installed may differ from the ones used in this study. The generation profile of each building was obtained using the model described in [15] without modifying the inclination of the PV modules relative to the horizontal plan. Regarding the Storage Installations, it is assumed that each building uses the 10 kWh/5kW system described in [16] when the individual self-consumption is carried out. For the scenario where the REC is formed, the SI is considered to be installed directly in the public grid, with the same total storage capacity as in the individual self-consumption scenario.

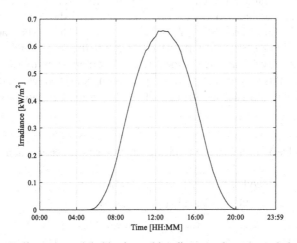

Fig. 2. Daily average global horizontal irradiance at the case study location.

Table 2. PV systems specifications.

Building	Rated power [kWp]	Generation [kWh/y]
#1	7.2	10,801
#2	15.7	23,552
#3	40.6	60,904
#4	85.5	128,260
Total	–	223,517

5   Results and Discussions

The results presented in this section focus on the energy imported from the distribution grid by each building and the corresponding costs, considering that PV generation is primarily used for self-consumption and that no revenue is received from injecting PV surplus into the grid. For both scenarios, energy is priced considering two tariffs. The first one, with a value of 0.15 €/kWh, is observed from 08:00 to 22:00. The second one (0.09 €/kWh) is registered during the remaining period. The periods are based on a daily cycle billing, while the prices are adapted from the values considered for the Low-Voltage billing for 2019 [17].

5.1 Individual Self-consumption (ISC)

When operating individually, buildings use their PV systems to satisfy part of the daily consumption profiles and therefore reduce energy imports from the grid. However, given the mismatch between demand and generation profiles, part of the generation is still exported to the grid. Table 3 presents the energy imported from the distribution grid by each building and the corresponding costs. This table also shows the impact of using a Storage Installation (10 kWh/5 kW) at each building. These SIs leads to a better performance regarding energy import and, consequentially, costs. Total energy imports and costs decreased by 4% and 5%, respectively, when comparing to a scenario without storage. However, this improvement is not equal among all buildings, since Building #2 and Building #3 have a better use of their SI due to the higher share of energy locally generated.

Table 3. Buildings' performance – Individual self-consumption.

Building	Import [kWh/y]			Cost [€/y]		
	w/o SI	w/ SI	Variation (%)	w/o SI	w/ SI	Variation (%)
#1	29,757	27,955	−6%	3,678.40	3,408.20	−8%
#2	20,748	18,482	−11%	2,473.20	2,133.30	−14%
#3	16,217	14,207	−12%	2,068.10	1,766.50	−15%
#4	140,090	137,800	−2%	17,890.00	17,547.00	−2%
Total	206,812	198,444	−4%	26,109.70	24,855.00	−5%

5.2 Collective Self-consumption (CSC)

The main difference of this scenario to the previous one regards the use of the locally generated energy. When the buildings implement a REC and take advantage of collective self-consumption, the four generation and consumption profiles are added and seen as a single entity before sharing the PV generation to reduce the imports of each member. The total generation is therefore computed for each 15-min time-step and shared among REC members applying the sharing coefficient previously defined (Eq. 1). The SI, if considered, is seen as another generator when discharging and as a load when on charging, as defined in [8]. Table 4 shows the results obtained for the REC scenario (with and without energy storage systems).

Table 4. Buildings' performance – Collective self-consumption.

Building	Import [kWh/y]			Cost [€/y]		
	w/o SI	w/ SI	Variation (%)	w/o SI	w/ SI	Variation (%)
#1	22,165.00	21,761.00	−1.9%	2,591.00	2,530.30	−2.4%
#2	15,269.00	14,997.00	−1.8%	1,747.70	1,707.00	−2.4%
#3	11,201.00	10,981.00	−2.0%	1,324.30	1,291.20	−2.5%
#4	80,564.00	79,010.00	−2.0%	9,291.70	9,058.60	−2.5%
Total	129,199.00	126,749.00	−1.9%	14,954.70	14,587.10	−2.5%

The SIs have a positive impact on the energy import and associated costs. However, this impact is lower than on the individual self-consumption operation. On average, the SIs lead to a 1.9% improvement on the energy import and to a 2.4% cost reduction. However, even without them, the performance of the collective self-consumption operation is considerably better than the operation based on an individual self-consumption, with total imports and costs decreasing by 37% and 42%, respectively.

5.3 Discussion

As described in the previous sections, the collective self-consumption leads to a better performance comparing to the individual self-consumption process of each building considering both assessment metrics (i.e., energy import and cost). Additionally, total peak load also decreases when operating as a REC, which can have a significant impact on the energy bill due to its cost on the price formation. Results also show that energy storage devices have higher positive impact when considering the individual operation. The reason for this is related with the lower PV surplus of the entire community, which decreases the use of all storage systems.

In terms of grid interaction, Fig. 3 presents the daily average demand profiles for all buildings, considering their original operation (no PV) and the two scenarios (individual self-consumption and REC). This figure shows that the average peak load decreases for all building except Building #1, due to its peak demand during the evening. The impact of collective self-consumption is evident, reducing grid interaction in terms or energy and power for all buildings when the solar resource is available.

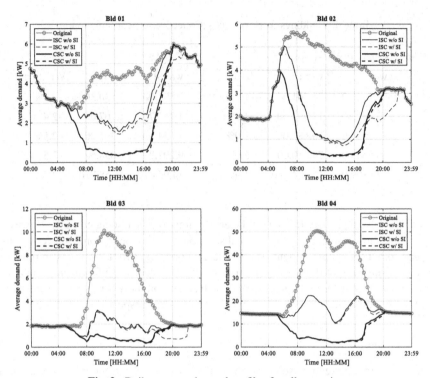

Fig. 3. Daily average demand profiles for all scenarios.

6   Conclusions and Future Work

This paper analyses the benefits of implementing a Renewable Energy Community (in terms of electrical energy imports and associated costs) on a group of four buildings from the municipality of Évora, Portugal. The considered case study also addresses the impact of including battery energy storage systems at building and community levels to increase PV self-consumption. The collected results shows that the electrical energy imports and costs are 36% and 41% lower, respectively, for the four buildings when they operate as a Renewable Energy Community (comparing to the individual operation). Previous results [18] also show that the installation of battery energy storage systems would not be profitable in any of the considered scenarios given the yearly annual savings and the required initial investment.

The work presented in this paper leaves open the opportunity to further study the impact of different types of energy sharing coefficients on REC members benefits. Additionally, further studies should be carried out regarding the possibility and feasibility of energy flexibility tools integration on a REC operation with energy sharing since there is a lack of studies joining energy flexibility concepts and energy sharing on a REC context.

Acknowledgements. This research was partly funded by European Union's H2020 programme as part of the POCITYF project (a positive energy city transformation framework), Grant agreement ID 864400 and by the Portuguese "Fundação para a Ciência e a Tecnologia" (FCT) in the context of the Center of Technology and Systems CTS/UNINOVA/FCT/NOVA, reference UIDB/00066/2020.

References

1. European Parliament and Council of The European Union: DIRECTIVE (EU) 2018/2001 of the European Parliament and of the Council of 11 December 2018 on the promotion of the use of energy from renewable sources (recast) (2018)
2. Amaral Lopes, R., Magalhães, P., Gouveia, J.P., Aelenei, D., Lima, C., Martins, J.: A case study on the impact of nearly Zero-Energy Buildings on distribution transformer aging. Energy **157**, 669–678 (2018). https://doi.org/10.1016/j.energy.2018.05.148
3. IEA: Key World Energy Statistics 2021, pp. 1–82 (2021)
4. Amaral Lopes, R., Grønborg Junker, R., Martins, J., Murta-Pina, J., Reynders, G., Madsen, H.: Characterisation and use of energy flexibility in water pumping and storage systems. Appl. Energy. **277**, 115587 (2020). https://doi.org/10.1016/j.apenergy.2020.115587
5. IEA: World Energy Outlook 2021 (2021)
6. POCITYF Project. https://pocityf.eu/
7. Ministério da Economia e da Inovação: Decreto-Lei n.o 15/2022 (2022)
8. ERSE: Regulamento ERSE 373/2021. Diário da República (2021)
9. Botsaris, P.N., Giourka, P., Papatsounis, A., Dimitriadou, P., Goitia-Zabaleta, N., Patsonakis, C.: Developing a business case for a renewable energy community in a public housing settlement in Greece—the case of a student housing and its challenges, prospects and barriers. Sustainability **13**, 3792 (2021). https://doi.org/10.3390/su13073792
10. Ceglia, F., Marrasso, E., Roselli, C., Sasso, M.: Small renewable energy community: the role of energy and environmental indicators for power grid. Sustainability. **13**, 2137 (2021). https://doi.org/10.3390/su13042137
11. Conradie, P.D., De Ruyck, O., Saldien, J., Ponnet, K.: Who wants to join a renewable energy community in Flanders? Applying an extended model of Theory of Planned Behaviour to understand intent to participate. Energy Policy **151**, 112121 (2021). https://doi.org/10.1016/j.enpol.2020.112121
12. Liu, N., Yu, X., Wang, C., Li, C., Ma, L., Lei, J.: An energy sharing model with price-based demand response for microgrids of peer-to-peer prosumers. IEEE Trans. Power Syst. **32**, 3569–3583 (2017). https://doi.org/10.1109/TPWRS.2017.2649558
13. Hutty, T.D., Pena-Bello, A., Dong, S., Parra, D., Rothman, R., Brown, S.: Peer-to-peer electricity trading as an enabler of increased PV and EV ownership. Energy Convers. Manag. **245**, 114634 (2021). https://doi.org/10.1016/j.enconman.2021.114634
14. Fioriti, D., Frangioni, A., Poli, D.: Optimal sizing of energy communities with fair revenue sharing and exit clauses: value, role and business model of aggregators and users. Appl. Energy. **299**, 117328 (2021). https://doi.org/10.1016/j.apenergy.2021.117328
15. Duffie, J.A., Beckman, W.A.: Solar Engineering of Thermal Processes, 4th edn. Wiley, Hoboken (2013)
16. HUAWEI: Smart String Energy Storage System LUNA2000–5/10/15-S0 - Technical Specification
17. ERSE: Diretiva n° 5/2019 - Tarifas e preços para a energia elétrica e outros serviços em 2019. Diário da República (2019)
18. Queiroz, H., Amaral Lopes, R., Martins, J.: Automated energy storage and curtailment system to mitigate distribution transformer aging due to high renewable energy penetration. Electr. Power Syst. Res. **182**, 106199 (2020). https://doi.org/10.1016/j.epsr.2020.106199

Open Innovation Association with Feeling Economy

Sepideh Kalateh[1,2]([✉]), Sanaz Nikghadam Hojjati[1,2], Luis Alberto Estrada-Jimenez[1,2], Terrin Pulikottil[1,2], and Jose Barata[1,2]

[1] Centre of Technology and Systems, UNINOVA Instituto Desenvolvimento de Novas Tecnologias, Caparica, Portugal
{sepideh.kalateh,sanaznik,lestrada,tpulikottil,jab}@uninova.pt
[2] NOVA University of Lisbon, Caparica, Portugal

Abstract. Innovation and technology have always worked together to accelerate human evolution and society's development. However, emerging technologies including Artificial Intelligence (AI), Collaborative Networks (CN), Innovation Platform, automation, etc., leapfrogged this process to a new level. Through AI, Machines perform tasks related to recognition and control better than human. On the other hand, in near future "thinking"-based skills will not grantee employment and wage creation, however, considering machine lack in automating human feeling, the feeling related skills which are "soft" aspects of job could define human tasks. Current review paper aims to study the association of Open Innovation (OI) Platform as a type of CNs with Feeling Economy as a future trend of emerging economy. In view of importance of collaborative and innovative network's role in smooth and sustainable transition from a thinking-based economy to an emotion-based economy, this work provides a clear understanding of OI and Feeling economy concepts and their inline transition and requirements based on a systematic review.

Keywords: Open innovation · Feeling economy · Creativity · Soft skills · Artificial intelligence · Collaborative networks · Human-centered

1 Introduction

The increasing complexity and dynamism of markets, growing availability of private venture capital, number of knowledge workers and their mobility level and technology development has pushed business owners to accept the consequences of adapting a new paradigm which was opposed to their closed and private traditional research labs [1, 2].

Businesses that use high-tech AI-based solutions in their life cycle, get courage to open their doors to the flow of knowledge, innovations and ideas to survive and create competitive advantage. By accessing to the internal data of the business, AI empowered OI solutions provide better understanding of its business issues, weaknesses, and strengths. By gathering and analyzing external data and resources, they provide optimal solutions and possible opportunity for business challenges.

© IFIP International Federation for Information Processing 2022
Published by Springer Nature Switzerland AG 2022
L. M. Camarinha-Matos (Ed.): DoCEIS 2022, IFIP AICT 649, pp. 26–34, 2022.
https://doi.org/10.1007/978-3-031-07520-9_3

Despite the role of technology in improving business, its impact on jobs cannot be ignored. There are three perspectives to the impact of technology on employment rate:

- Doomsayer's perspective considers technology as a factor to improve efficiency in human labour by tasks automation [3].
- Optimist's perspective, suggests that many types of labour may be replaced by technology, but the benefit and efficiency that achieve from technological empowerment outweigh transition costs [4, 5].
- It indicates, by developing automated technologies, workers may require more social skills, as automating this type of skills is hard [6]. Unifying Perspective, suggests that multiple assets will accompany technological changes and create uncertainty about future works [7] and technology directly will influence the demands for special skills [8, 9], therefore, it results in increasing demands in jobs, which typically require non-repetitive and soft skills and as a consequence rising salary in related jobs [10].

Each of these different perspectives motivate changes in current economic trends and skills requirement for human resources to have a successful career in near future. However, accuracy of a forecast is highly depending on accurate understanding of past and present situations and most commonly by analysing the trends. Facing the need for future transformation processes worldwide regarding to changes on the job nature and emergent skills, the challenges for labour productivity, employment and mobility, the quality and new forms of work, and how technology can help to create this ambitious and human feelings centered environment, requires huge studies and research [11–13].

The present systematic review paper aims to study the role of OI in association and accelerating the economy of feeling as a possible future trend for economy. The main novelty is that the paper assesses and validates the analysis outcomes and propositions of previous works regarding the relation between OI and feeling economy with a look at skills needs necessary for the new job content in emerging era. This will trace the baseline to understand, analyze and discuss the soft skill factors that can have a direct influence in the OI platform success and also the impact of OI in moving toward more feeling oriented working environment. At the end of this paper a set of recommendations will be elaborated to guide the further development of the work.

2   Methodology

2.1   Objectives and Research Questions

This section will provide a clear understanding of the research trends in relationship between soft skills and OI in the world of smart industry and digitization. The Systematic Review Methodology is used as a baseline to structure my work. Interested readers can have a detailed description of such methodology at [14, 15].

A summary of the objectives of this research paper can be described in the following research questions:

1. Does OI based CNs has relationship with feeling economy trend?
2. What are the current trends and deviations in relation between soft skills and OI?

3. What will be the future trends for soft skills' necessity in OI based on paper review?

Following section will describe the methodology used to fulfill the objectives of this paper to answer the questions.

3 Methodology

For the search and selection of the adequate articles, Scopus database was used. It is one of the most well-known and large academic article databases. Various terms were used recursively and combined to conduct literature review part. However, the most important and final terms are composed of keywords "Open Innovation" and "soft skill" and "Feeling Economy" without any further criteria on all fields.

Totally 172 papers have been suggested by the Scopus database which have been refined in different steps as are shown in Fig. 1 and reached to 71 relevant papers.

4 Open Innovation and Necessity of Soft Skills' Presence

In the past decades, innovation and creativity illustrated a critical role in the successful performance of organizations in the long and short term. It acts as an influential tactic for organizations to obtain competitive advantages by inventing new products, services and processes to underserved or unserved customers [16].

Previous researches show that innovations and CNs create added value for involved partners by lowering the costs of services or existing products, improving their quality, introducing innovative products or services which there is enough demand in the target market, or delivering improved business models [17, 18].

Furthermore, it has been observed that extreme innovations transform, destroy or create new markets by introducing new solutions to existing challenges. Therefore, researchers are interested in addressing innovation and innovation flows as a key factor on companies' financial success and markets economy [19, 20]. It has been considered as an effective remedy for difficult and complicated global situations such as Covid-19 pandemic [21, 22].

The emphasis on openness of knowledge and innovation flows within and outside the companies' boundaries has played a key role to the evolution of OI and generation of novel methods of collaboration networks [1, 23]. OI indicates, companies demand innovation and knowledge flows whether inside or outside their boundaries to empower flow of innovation, while at the same time looking for external markets and partners to commercialize their internal knowledge assets, technologies and innovation [24]. OI also results in an uneven growth in productivity and prosperity which has direct impact on economy [25]. OI aids in a shift to produce greater openness for knowledge and innovation sharing. This process occurs from the inside to the outside of the company and vice versa [1]. Wide-spread collaboration and communication networking are critical factors of this platform.

Based on reviewed papers [26], effective performance in OI platform demands high efficiency of communication, leadership, collaboration, Critical thinking and Flexibility and Agility. Simultaneously, significant required soft skills in OI platform can be summarised as below:

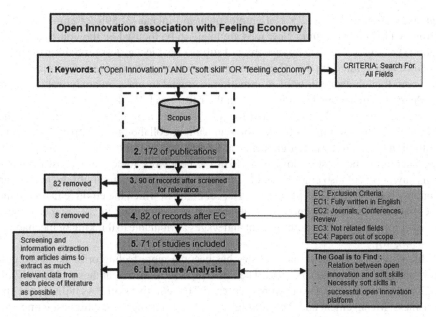

Fig. 1. Systematic review methodology, from [14, 15]

- Collaboration
- Leadership
- Communication
- Flexibility and Agility
- Critical thinking

Soft skills are essential to empower the smooth outflows and inflows among various sectors inside and outside the companies' boundaries [27–30]. Employees' soft skills have become critical factor in evaluating their value to a company [31]. Companies are looking for new training and recruitment methods to increase their employees' soft skills alongside the hard skills to guaranty their successful performance in OI [32, 33]. In next section we will dig more in the added value of soft skills and the new era of economy based on feeling.

5 Economy Based on Feeling

Contemporary industry is facing dramatic changes. It is experiencing different way of producing products, providing services, business processes, and chain management [34, 35] alongside the changes in required skills and training for the workforce [36]. Based on world economic world 50% of employees will need reskilling by 2025, 40% of skills are expected to change in the next 5 year [37].

New digital technologies such as AI, machine learning and internet of things are affecting the nature of work spaces and jobs [38]. Related studies have proved the important role of tasks automation on workforce and companies across Europe showing that automation will affect 35% of employment in Finland [3] 59% of employment in Germany [12] in near future. New jobs are likely to be focused on the non-routine and emotive tasks which require higher-order of soft skills which are less probable to be automated in near future [39, 40]. Furthermore, some experimental evidence demonstrates that, even though availability of information is crucial to make an analytical decision, people tend to make the decision based on their feelings [39, 41, 42].

This also leads to higher demand for jobs that are more difficult to automate and need high quality of soft skills like communication, collaboration, empathy and critical thinking that are essential elements of toady's successful business nature [37, 43, 44]. Therefore, the most important skills of the new work force are not just technical skills anymore, but also emotive and interpersonal ones, which highlight the need of an economy based on feelings [45]. This is an economy in which the emotive tasks are the essential tasks and employment with higher soft skills are more likely to receive more wages comparing the total employment and wages attributable to thinking or mechanical tasks [40, 46].

Many researches show that Industry has become more feeling oriented in the past years and it is a sustainable process. The Fig. 2 represents the researches within 2012 till 2022 years from Scopus for keywords "soft skill" or "emotive skill". As it illustrates, the "Business, Management and Accounting" area represents the second highest number of publications by field, which shows the significant role of soft skills in this area.

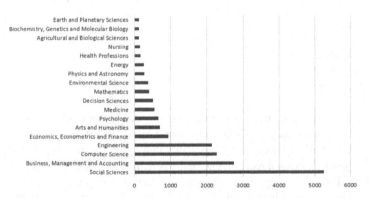

Fig. 2. Research trends toward the importance of"soft skill" in "Business" area.

Openness of innovation and knowledge flows happens when the required tools with the necessary skills are presented, in the next section we will discuss feeling economy and OI association and convergence.

6   Results and Discussion

In recent years, OI research has advanced on different aspects. The studies that focus on multiple perspective of influential factors on OI provide valuable insights on a whole range of essential required factors that shape OI processes flow which result in a platform of innovations in collaborative and interactive network [47].

Earlier we asked about Feeling economy and OI association and discussed their significant features. The Fig. 3 illustrates the OI and feeling economy inline interactions.

OI needs to fulfill essential factors to accelerate the outflow and inflow of innovation. One of the required factors is soft skills [45, 48]. At the same time smart industry tends to delegate more thinking and repetitive tasks to new technologies which provide even more apace for human workforce to focus on what is their advantages, soft skills. Emerges of soft skills, create an environment which people are well-trained or eager to educate in emotive skills, and they can communicate and collaborate in productive way in CNs.

OI by providing an innovative environment alongside the open exchange of knowledge beyond company boundaries and proactive networking provide a high potential environment for human soft skills to be expressed and trained. OI association with feeling economy provides a proactive platform for industries successful growth and establishment.

New era is emerging, era of feeling economy and the recent advancements in smart industry along the companies' needs to establish a concrete network whether inside or outside their boundaries in order to be successful in globalization markets [49]. Although, innovative technologies and tools are making it easier and more convenient, this cannot be achieved without the presence of soft skills [50].

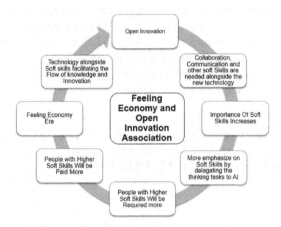

Fig. 3. OI and feeling economy association.

7 Conclusion

Current research has critically analyzed association of OI with Feeling Economy and importance of soft skills in near future and in future industrial revolution (Industry 5.0). However, emerging technologies like AI and machine learning may help us in accelerating and improving thinking tasks, but they are still straggling support human societies and work place in emotive and creative related tasks as good as human beings which lead us to the new economical trend which is based on human feeling.

This study highlighted that successful launch and maintenance of innovative networking platform like OI is in high association with soft skills. By showing the future trends, it illustrates the path, required skills and education for innovative CNs. This study showed the trends toward more emotive networking by the usage of smart industry tools therefore it enables the companies to plan with clearer vision to train their workforce, change their business vision and recruitment strategies and be ready to tackle the changes of emerging era of Feeling Innovative CNs to perform successfully in near future.

The results of this research put light on a deep research gap which could be addressed in future studies, including, developing knowledge, tools, methodologies and technologies which future workforce could apply to develop their skills and position in Feeling economy-based societies and Industry 5.0. Also, according to the finding of this study, there is a high expectation that future innovative ecosystems and business developments will be based on CNs particularly OI, which lead to the conclusion that current and future businesses require more attention in this type of platforms and networks to guarantee their business sustainability alongside the feeling skills which are the foundation of OIs ecosystem. However, there should be more in-depth study regarding the characteristic of feeling oriented working process and Feeling oriented innovation process to provide better understanding of the emerging new era of feeling and openness.

It is important to have a better understanding regarding the different aspects of CNs and OI, the skills required for working in such an environment, technologies that could help us to facilitate our communication such as affective computing or computational creativity, methodologies and assessment tools, regulation, ethics and data privacy, etc. Due to the reality that women traditionally considered as humans which has better soft skills, a question will be raised based on this study is, how gender equality could play a role in an economy which is based on feeling, and what will be association between these two.

Acknowledgement. This work was supported in part by the FCT/MCTES (UNINOVA-CTS funding UID/EEA/00066/2019) and the FCT/MCTES project CESME - Collaborative and Evolvable Smart Manufacturing Ecosystem, funding PTDC/EEIAUT/32410/2017.

References

1. Nambisan, S., Siegel, D., Kenney, M.: On open innovation, platforms, and entrepreneurship. Strateg. Entrep. J. **12**(3), 354–368 (2018)
2. Frosch, R.A., Gallopoulos, N.E.: Strateg. Manuf. Sci. Am. **261**(3), 144–153 (2009)
3. Pajarinen, M., Rouvinen, P., Ekeland, A., et al.: Computerization threatens onethird of Finnish and Norwegian employment. Etla Brief. **34**, 1–8 (2015)
4. Frase, P.: Four Futures: Life After Capitalism. Verso Books (2016)
5. Avent, R.: A world without work is coming–it could be utopia or it could be hell. The Guardian **19**, 2016 (2016)
6. Deming, D., Kahn, L.B.: Skill requirements across firms and labor markets: evidence from job postings for professionals. J. Law Econ. **36**(S1), S337–S369 (2018)
7. Autor, D.H., Levy, F., Murnane, R.J.: The skill content of recent technological change: an empirical exploration. Q. J. Econ. **118**(4), 1279–1333 (2003)

8. Autor, D., et al.: The polarization of job opportunities in the us labor market: implications for employment and earnings. Center Am. Prog. Hamilton Proj. **6**, 11–19 (2010)

9. MacCrory, F., Westerman, G., Alhammadi, Y., Brynjolfsson, E.: Racing with and against the machine: changes in occupational skill composition in an era of rapid technological advance (2014)

10. Tidd, J., Bessant, J.R.: Managing Innovation: Integrating Technological, Market and Organizational Change. Wiley, Hoboken (2020)

11. Goos, M.: The impact of technological progress on labour markets: policy challenges. Oxf. Rev. Econ. Policy **34**(3), 362–375 (2018)

12. Brzeski, C., Burk, I.: The robots are coming. Consequences of automation for the German labor market. INGDiBa Econ. Res. **30** (2015)

13. Bessen, J.E.: How computer automation affects occupations: technology, jobs, and skills. In: Boston Univ. School of Law, Law and Economics Research Paper, pp. 15–49 (2016)

14. Snyder, H.: Literature review as a research methodology: an overview and guidelines. J. Bus. Res. **104**, 333–339 (2019)

15. Xiao, Y., Watson, M.: Guidance on conducting a systematic literature review. J. Plan. Educ. Res. **39**(1), 93–112 (2019)

16. Huston, L., Sakkab, N.: Connect and develop. Harv. Bus. Rev. **84**(3), 58–66 (2006)

17. Hauser, J., Tellis, G.J., Griffin, A.: Research on innovation: a review and agenda for marketing science. Mark. Sci. **25**(6), 687–717 (2006)

18. Camarinha-Matos, L., Fornasiero, R., Ramezani, J., Ferrada, F.: Collaborative networks: a pillar of digital transformation. Appl. Sci. **9**, 5431 (2019)

19. Badir, Y.F., Frank, B., Bogers, M.: Employee-level open innovation in emerging markets: linking internal, external, and managerial resources. J. Acad. Mark. Sci. **48**(5), 891–913 (2019). https://doi.org/10.1007/s11747-019-00674-6

20. Zheng, Z., Huang, C.Y., Yang, Y.: Inflation and growth: a non-monotonic relationship in an innovation-driven economy. Macroecon. Dyn. **25**(5), 1199–1226 (2021)

21. Chesbrough, H.: To recover faster from covid-19, open up: managerial implications from an open innovation perspective. Ind. Mark. Manag. **88**, 410–413 (2020)

22. S'a, M.J., Santos, A.I., Serpa, S., Ferreira, C.M.: Digitainability—digital competences post-covid-19 for a sustainable society. Sustainability (Switzerland) **13**(17) (2021)

23. Nikghadam Hojjati, S., Barata, J.: Computational creativity to design cyberphysical systems in industry 4.0, pp. 29–40 (2019)

24. Chesbrough, H., Vanhaverbeke, W., West, J.: Open Innovation: Researching a New Paradigm. Oxford University Press on Demand, Oxford (2006)

25. Bogers, M., Chesbrough, H., Moedas, C.: Open innovation: research, practices, and policies. Calif. Manag. Rev. **60**(2), 5–16 (2018)

26. Sopa, A., et al.: Hard skills versus soft skills: which are more important for Indonesian employees innovation capability. Int. J. Control Autom. **13**(2), 156–175 (2020)

27. Lazaro-Mojica, J., Fernandez, R.: Review paper on the future of the food sector through education, capacity building, knowledge translation and open innovation. Curr. Opin. Food Sci. **38**, 162–167 (2021)

28. Al Amri, T., Puskas Khetani, K., Marey-Perez, M.: Towards sustainable i4.0: key skill areas for project managers in GCC construction industry. Sustainability **13**(15) (2021)

29. Schneider, S., Kokshagina, O.: Digital transformation: what we have learned (thus far) and what is next. Create. Innov. Manag. **30**(2), 384–411 (2021)

30. Wehrle, M., Birkel, H., von der Gracht, H.A., Hartmann, E.: The impact of digitalization on the future of the PSM function managing purchasing and innovation in new product development – evidence from a Delphi study. J. Purchasing Supply Manag. 100732 (2021)

31. Florek-Paszkowska, A., Ujwary-Gil, A., Godlewska-Dziobon', B.: Business innovation and critical success factors in the era of digital transformation and turbulent times. J. Entrepreneurship Manag. Innov. **17**(4), 7–28 (2021)
32. Bello-Pintado, A., Bianchi, C.: Consequences of open innovation: effects on skilldriven recruitment. J. Knowl. Manag. (2020)
33. Oh, M., Choi, S.: The competence of project team members and success factors with open innovation. J. Open Innov. Technol. Mark. Complex. **6**(3), 51 (2020)
34. Pulikottil, T., Estrada-Jimenez, L.A., Nikghadam-Hojjati, S., Barata, J.: Predictive manufacturing: enabling technologies, frameworks and applications. In: Camarinha-Matos, L.M., Ferreira, P., Brito, G. (eds.) DoCEIS 2021. IAICT, vol. 626, pp. 51–61. Springer, Cham (2021). https://doi.org/10.1007/978-3-030-78288-7_5
35. Wang, D., Han, H., Zhan, Z., Xu, J., Liu, Q., Ren, G.: A problem solving oriented intelligent tutoring system to improve students' acquisition of basic computer skills. Comput. Educ. **81**, 102–112 (2015)
36. Dhanpat, N., Buthelezi, Z.P., Joe, M.R., Maphela, T.V., Shongwe, N.: Industry 4.0: the role of human resource professionals. SA J. Hum. Resourc. Manag. **18**(1), 1–11 (2020)
37. Forum, W.E.: The future of jobs report 2020. https://www.weforum.org/reports/the-future-of-jobs-report-2020/infull/infographics-e4e69e4de7. Accessed Feb 2022
38. Borges, A.F., Laurindo, F.J., Sp'ınola, M.M., Gonc‚alves, R.F., Mattos, C.A.: The strategic use of artificial intelligence in the digital era: systematic literature review and future research directions. Int. J. Inf. Manag. **57**, 102225 (2021)
39. Ra, S., Shrestha, U., Khatiwada, S., Yoon, S.W., Kwon, K.: The rise of technology and impact on skills. Int. J. Train. Res. **17**(suppl.), 26–40 (2019)
40. Kalateh, S., Estrada-Jimenez, L.A., Pulikottil, T., Hojjati, S.N., Barata, J.: Feeling Smart Industry, pp. 1–6 (2021)
41. Bandelj, N.: Emotions in economic action and interaction. Theory Soc. **38**(4), 347–366 (2009)
42. Gruber, M.J., Gelman, B.D., Ranganath, C.: States of curiosity modulate hippocampus-dependent learning via the dopaminergic circuit. Neuron **84**(2), 486–496 (2014)
43. Heffernan, O.: They say they want a revolution. Nature **453**(7193), 268 (2008)
44. Margherita, E.G., Bua, I.: The role of human resource practices for the development of operator 4.0 in industry 4.0 organisations: a literature review and a research agenda. Businesses **1**(1), 18–33 (2021)
45. Miranda, J., Lo'pez, C.S., Navarro, S., Bustamante, M.R., Molina, J.M., Molina, A.: Open innovation laboratories as enabling resources to reach the vision of education 4.0, 1–7 (2019)
46. Huang, M.H., Rust, R., Maksimovic, V.: The feeling economy: managing in the next generation of artificial intelligence (AI). Calif. Manag. Rev. **61**(4), 43–65 (2019)
47. West, J., Salter, A., Vanhaverbeke, W., Chesbrough, H.: Open Innovation: The Next Decade (2014)
48. Gunawan, K.: Peran studi kelayakan bisnis dalam peningkatan umkm (studi kasus umkm di kabupaten kudus). BISNIS: Jurnal Bisnis dan Manajemen Islam **6**(2), 101–115 (2019)
49. Rios, J.A., Ling, G., Pugh, R., Becker, D., Bacall, A.: Identifying critical 21st century skills for workplace success: a content analysis of job advertisements. Educ. Res. **49**(2), 80–89 (2020)
50. Lavrynenko, A., Shmatko, N., Meissner, D.: Managing skills for open innovation: the case of biotechnology. Manag. Decis. (2018)

Creating Meaningful Intelligence for Decision-Making by Modelling Complexities of Human Influence: Review and Position

Paulo Pina[1,2]([✉]) and Rui Neves-Silva[3]

[1] inknow Solutions, Rua Adriano Correia de Oliveira 4 A, 1600-312 Lisboa, Portugal
pina@inknow.pt
[2] UNINOVA CTS, NOVA University of Lisbon, 2829-516 Monte Caparica, Portugal
[3] Faculty of Sciences and Technology and UNINOVA CTS, NOVA University of Lisbon, 2829-516 Monte Caparica, Portugal

Abstract. Strategic decision-making still struggles to cope with the interference of people in its proposed plans, creating a gap between idealised and real-world versions. Even when the existence of humans is considered, models and abstractions tend to be simplistic and lacking in complex human traits (e. g. creativity, sentiment). We analyse the current scientific landscape in the dimensions that overlap in the field of strategic decision making and posit that to provide means to a more informed and robust decision-making, humans should not only be seen as elements that need to accept and adopt decisions, but also as actors that affect their outcomes. Humans should be understood as central pieces and the strategic decision-making process should thus consider their importance both in techniques that foster co-creation, and also in developing dynamic models that demonstrate their influence and impact. In this article, we describe this problem-space and outline an approach integrating Decision Intelligence, Enterprise Architecture, Design Thinking, and architectural principles to achieve a human-centric, adaptive strategic design. We also discuss the influence of information presentation and visuals for meaningful participation in strategic decision-making processes.

Keywords: Strategic decision-making · Decision intelligence ·
Human-in-the-loop · Enterprise architecture · Digital twins · Design thinking

1 Introduction

The nature of enterprises has evolved, and so has our understanding of it. Whereas at some point enterprises were seen just as a vehicle for benefiting shareholders (by means of profits), nowadays they are understood as more complex organisations with an ethical and social role [1, 2]. The centrepieces of these complex organisations are the people that work in them, interact or consume their produce [3]. Consequently, companies evolved from being product-centric, to being customer-centric and are now seen as being human- or stakeholder-centric. These last two concepts are complementary

© IFIP International Federation for Information Processing 2022
Published by Springer Nature Switzerland AG 2022
L. M. Camarinha-Matos (Ed.): DoCEIS 2022, IFIP AICT 649, pp. 35–49, 2022.
https://doi.org/10.1007/978-3-031-07520-9_4

among themselves: a 'stakeholder-centric organisation' focuses its activities on being beneficial to all its stakeholders [1], i.e., "those with whom the business interacts in pursuit of achieving its goals" [4], following an increasing concern with corporate social responsibility, corporate reputation, and responsible governance [5], while a 'human-centric organisation' is one that is designed in face of an understanding of human traits and preferences [6, 7].

This shift is in part the result of changes to the nature of work. In recent history, links between workers and companies have loosened and even physical connections are less obvious, as the emergence of temporary contracts, offshoring, co-working spaces, and remote work [8], among other characteristics, have shown [9]. In consequence, the assumption of workers as stable resources with static links to the companies was replaced by concerns about knowledge retention [10] and competition for the most sought-after expertise in the market at a given moment [11]. Companies themselves have also become geographically distributed [12], automated [13], and cater to wider areas in result of globalisation [14, 15], adding to the dispersion and challenging the fabric of organisational culture [16–18]. Even if at first sight seemingly paradoxical, these changes result in a different nature of work, that, in its efforts to retain knowledge and expertise, emphasises knowledge [19], innovation [20], team-based work [21, 22], and even project-based [23] work as a paradigm for operation, thus centring itself on human workers and on their relationship with the other blocks in the organisation [24]. A growing trend in the last decade is to extend interactions to stakeholders and experts outside of the organisation, e.g., for innovation purposes [24, 25]. Project-orientation is one of the latest iterations in stakeholder-centric organisations, basing activities on coordinated and time-limited projects (mostly for innovation) and fluid teams of collaborating elements for specific objectives [23, 26].

The study of enterprises reflected this evolution, emphasising human elements in strategy, and in strategic decision-making (SDM) in particular. Scientific studies in collaboration and aspects related to team-based decisions, digital support of worker decisions to alleviate stress or managing communication in distributed teams are emerging, with trust being an important facet of decision-making. In collaborative teams, multiple levels of trust emerge – interpersonal, at team level, and outwards trust, affecting the effectiveness of knowledge sharing and cooperation [27].

In another perspective, technology is also shaping strategy. In [24], the impact of digital technologies is classified in three-orders: *convergent change*, or change that does not alter the main processes of the company; *transforming work*, where processes and perspectives suffer significant change, but still within the existing business operating model; and *transforming the organisation*, where the structure, business and values of the company are changed, typically in reaction to second-order changes.

The common denominator in all these research lines is the need to have a clearer understanding of how humans impact and are impacted by organisations' operations and strategies, and by the decision-making process, in particular.

In the next section of this document a brief description of SDM is provided and the concepts of enterprise architecture (EA), decision intelligence (DI) and design thinking (DT) in the context of SDM are introduced. In the third section, approaches to address human elements in SDM are analysed and conclusions are drawn.

This paper lays out the problem-space of the influence of humans in SDM by providing a broad review of the current landscape and approaches to the various domains that intersect in the area of strategic decision-making, while laying down the foundations to further research on the subject. A research question is thus drawn from here. The presented position is that, to make better strategic decisions, a more comprehensive model of human actors, both as stakeholders involved in the decision process and as affected parties of the decisions, is required.

2 Background

Strategic decision is typically a high-level, long-term management decision that is infrequent, may result in significant change, and may need to be translated in applicable processes inside the organisation [28]. It is unstructured and complex, requiring significant resources, affecting activities, long-term, involving different functions and elements, which can be both internal or external [29]. Strategic decisions comprise a goal, obstacles and constraints, and estimated path [30]. On a general level, the process that culminates in the strategic decision starts with gathering of information and evidence, which is analysed and processed into inputs for the decision process. These steps are in fact preceded by the identification of a need, complexity or environmental change [31, 32]. James March, in his foundational work *"The technology of foolishness"* [33] argues for the frequent pre-existence of decisions before goals (also referred in [34]). More than that, goals are many times achieved indirectly and evidence is an *ex-post* rational construct to support a vision. Strategic decision can be seen as a mediation between competing views or weighing capabilities and potentials [35].

In fact, the process of decision-making itself is not as straightforward or sequential as classical approaches suggest [36]. Over the years, two conflicting lines of thought were developed: a *rational* (or formal or rational) approach, indicating a well-defined process with clear phases and an *incremental* (or informal, or unstructured) approach, with an adaptive nature comprising emerging, instead of planned steps [37, 38]. Organisations employ both approaches, sometimes in the same process [36, 37, 39].

Considering human stakeholders in the SDM process does not imply that strategic decision should not be supported by facts and evidence, but only that the complexity of strategic decision is not yet completely matched by current algorithms and technologies and there is an interesting topic for research on how to improve utility. In fact, the utility of artificial intelligence (AI) can be maximised through the combination of human intelligence and AI in a team that combines human stakeholders and machines [40].

The early stages of industry 4.0 that we are now witnessing, with Cyber-Physical & Human Systems (CPHS) where humans and robots work together, highlight the importance of addressing the questions related to human actors in the context of production. Ethical issues, in particular, are of key importance, since automation and autonomy rely on machines capabilities to operate within realms that until now were exclusive to humans (e.g. production planning, operative safety) [41]. Technologies used to achieve the goals of Industry 4.0 can be distributed in three main group: *cognition-enhancing technologies* (cognitive computing, computer vision, AI, Big Data, cloud computing); *interaction technologies* (physical human-machine interfaces, exoskeletons, augmented reality); and *sensorial technologies* (Internet of Things, activity trackers, wearables). Decision-making in this context needs to take into consideration the acceptance of human actors towards this work environment and the defined objectives [42]. From these characteristics, four core design principles can be drawn: Interconnection, Information transparency, Assisted technical support; and Decentralised decisions [43].

2.1 Supporting Methods for Strategic Decision-Making

Enterprise Architecture (EA) *"provides a long-term view of a company's processes, systems, and technologies so that individual projects can build capabilities-not just fulfil immediate needs"* [44]. It aims to manage complexity and promote alignment of strategy with processes and resources [45]. Although earlier incarnations were focused on the perspective of information technologies (IT) to realize the strategy, posterior developments in research and practice consider it from a wider viewpoint, covering the enterprise as a whole [46–48]. It can thus be said that EA is a tool for strategic decision, providing meaningful information and advice through models and roadmaps regarding current and future states of the organisation [48–50].

Decision Intelligence (DI) results from the realisation that decision-making and context-filtering techniques have not been brought up to the level of the latest developments in information technologies, big data, machine learning or AI in general. It also comes from the understanding that in the current context, purpose and value system are still provided by humans. The aim of DI is to integrate existing technologies by unifying them on a single framework. DI sees technology as tool that must be used according to the intended objectives of the decision-making process under penalty of being a distraction instead of an enabler [51]. Technology by itself has much less value then when used in collaboration with humans on a problem-focused environment, to understand how the building blocks of the problem work together [51, 52].

In face of the current societal environment characterised by *volatility, uncertainty, complexity* and *ambiguity* (VUCA), organisations are bombarded with fast-paced demands and at the same time are gathering copious amounts of information that goes largely unused [52, 53] or counterproductively result in increased decision bias, costs or delays. To combat this, decision proficiency is required to be able to filter the insights that matter and discard those that do not. Having the adequate level of information for a decision does not mean having all the information available: market requirements and VUCA mean that there may be a limited time for information acquisition and processing and the amount of uncertainty therefore increases. To minimise this, information processing capabilities should be tuned to fit intelligence requirements, including time-to-decision. For this, it is paramount that decision-makers are able to identify context of the decision (intelligence requirements in light of the problem frame), while having adequate processing power (by developing decision-making models that provide relevant answers to the problem) and accessing the necessary information to provide answers to the raised questions [52] These must then be translated in decisions, according not only to the input data, but also to the proficiency of the decision-maker. It is important to note that strategic decision and innovation, while relying on intelligence, are also change agents and implicate risk and uncertainty in results. Repeating exactly the same approach as always will hardly result in change or innovation. This is one of the main challenges of following formulaic methods for SDM or using a similar approach to the rest of the ecosystem (e.g., the same algorithm for information gathering or decision-making across a whole sector). And this is the crucial point for the need for Human-AI collaboration in DI.

As previously seen, strategizing involves a great deal of uncertainty, particularly in contexts of innovation where there are knowledge gaps in both technologies and markets [54]. Tapping into copious amounts of data or resort to managers' intuition poses challenges to the effectiveness of the decision-making and its outcomes. **Design Thinking** (DT) to support SDM was abundantly researched as a tool to overcome those challenges [54–57]. DT has been shown to minimises cognitive bias [31, 54, 55] in the decision-making process, such as confirmation bias, over optimism or oversight of barriers, by using co-creation, building empathy and challenging assumptions [54, 56, 57]. It is also a practice that enables to reduce the existing divide between top management and operations and provides valuable insights into the market while filtering the required information volume and cognitive load, by introducing visual and material representations. The main procedural benefit from DT in this context is the combinations of analytical and intuitive thinking, surfacing tacit knowledge through the means of images and materialisation.

Four distinct activities can be identified in DT as a practice for SDM:

reviewing – an individual analysis of materials and design contents, to support subsequent discussions;

simulating – a group interaction with different materials to produce better insights into users;

conversing – an open discussion on the subject of decision to create alignments and shared understandings about the strategic issues; and

collaborating – to organise and create materials, generating complex solutions and shared understandings [54].

But design practices go beyond simple ideation for decision-making. They can contribute and improve strategy development in different steps of the strategy: *human-centred design* for a new perspective on opportunities; *prototype* and test models and required capabilities for future practices; identify and *deal with uncertainties and dynamics* in managing the portfolio of existing and future offerings; *storytelling and engagement* when increasing scale from prototype to market; and apply *design practices to support the whole strategical development* of organisations and create incremental or disruptive innovation [57].

3 Looking for the Human in the Loop

There is no doubt that AI is a very valuable tool for decision-making. It provides a plethora of tools and capabilities to gain insights into existing data to understand current contexts and future trends. But processing copious amounts of information without criteria is not an efficient way to operate on a strategic level. More than that, resorting to AI without reviewing capacities raises questions of transparency and accountability

[58]. Finally, humans are still the agents and receptors of the activities and strategies of organisations. If their influence on the process and the impact that decisions have on their lives and actions are not accounted for, the decision-making process will always be impaired. This means that human stakeholders must be modelled as more than just units of work, comparable to other physical resources in the organisation. Cognitive aspects, creativity, sentiment, interplay, all of them come into play in this context.

In the field of SDM, a significant trend is to analyse and steer the use of AI in decision-making, either complementing, expanding, or emulating human intelligence. Studies also address human biases as cautionary constraints to develop better AI [58, 59]. On the other hand, explainability, transparency and unpredictability present obstacles to the autonomous use AI in critical subjects. Yet, there is nowadays a prevailing feeling that technology provides better decisions than humans (called 'automation bias') [58]. Ultimately, the use of the same tools and techniques for SDM, which is an eminently creative process, may lead to a lack of diversity that impairs innovation and loss of the richness of human and social heterogeneities in favour of a monolithic, uniformised society managed by algorithms and scripted procedures [1].

3.1 Towards Industry 5.0 – The Ethics of the New Human-Centricity

This centrality of the human aspect is emphasised by the emergence of a new wave of industrial development, sometimes coined as Industry 5.0, centred on intelligent manufacturing, with a focus on human intelligence in collaboration with robotics and artificial features that complement and extend human capabilities. The main differentiating characteristic is that technologies (e.g. big data, AI, etc.) adapt to the need of human actors instead of the contrary [60]. In this context, robots and humans collaborate or work in synergy, being aware, and able to understand and anticipate each other's actions [61]. For this, new sensorial skills and techniques will be required (eye motion detection, near infrared spectroscopy). Industry will also strive on mass-customisation, requiring a new perspective into productions, integrating elements of industrial production and artisanship [61–63]. The concept of Industry 5.0 goes beyond manufacturing, tapping into cultural, moral and lifestyle issues, integrating elements from Social Sciences and Humanities with a systemic approach to accurately model humans and machines in interplay [64]. This approach to industry and work presents some technological and scientific challenges, both regarding design. Machines and AI will not follow explicit rules but autonomously maximise compliance to goals, raising key ethical issues that must be addressed from the design stages [41]. Use of detailed data and sensorial inputs is also a serious issue – to which point is ethically acceptable to acquire private data and act upon it to minimise failures and hazards?

Machine ethics can be considered from a deontological (rule-, or principle-based according to established social values; or from a consequential perspective (especially utilitarian, where ethical decisions are considered according to their consequences or outcomes). Ethical issues should also be seen in two different scopes: the ethical design of digital systems (which guides the behaviour and actions of authors, researchers and developers designing the system); and the design of ethical digital systems (focused on the behaviour and actions of the systems themselves) [65].

But there is a marked shift in the current approach to ethical issues. These are designed *a priori* as a requirement, as an additional value, instead of being seen as a cost or a constraint to value-adding requirements [42]. When defining or evaluating the performance of future industrial systems, and in order to address the issues raised by the enabling future digital systems, ethical issues should be considered an indicator, together with efficiency, effectiveness and relevance [66]. SDM in the context of this new work environment, where machines and humans work as symbiotic systems also requires consideration for potential ethical risks that arise in these environments (e.g. lack of programmed common sense and bad conscience, decisional ambiguity, limits to mutual interaction, master-slave dependency; emotional dependency) [67].

3.2 Modelling of Cognitive and Behavioural Aspects

To increase the accuracy of decision-making, better models of humans and their inter-actions in this context are needed, including models for human behaviour. Methods for considering humans in models can be classified according to the degree of detail in which they consider human behaviour:

- *simplify* – bypassing human behaviour through simplification, either by omitting, aggregating or substituting it in the model;
- *externalise* – in which behavioural aspects are obtained outside of the model via user input, expert systems or datasets;
- *flow* – by considering group behaviour as flow, using continuous simulation or system dynamics;
- *entity* – where humans are elements equivalent to other resources and have statuses, eventually interact with the model in specific steps of the process;
- *task* – using Discrete-Event Simulation, individual performance attributes are included in the interaction within the model, affecting general rules;
- *individual* – using cognitive architectures (e.g. Visual, Cognitive, Auditory, Psy-chomotor – VCAP; Physis, Emotion, Cognition and Status – PECS; Adaptive Control of Thought-Rational – ACT-R [68]) to model human behaviour [69].

Another approach regards modelling emotions. Most used emotional models are Ekman and Friesen, who consider six plus one main categories: *anger, disgust, fear, happiness, sadness,* and *surprise,* plus *neutral*; and Russell's theory, who states that emotions can be distributed along two axes: the valence-arousal model. Twelve emo-tions distributed along four quadrants: *Pleased, Happy, Excited, Annoying, Angry, Ner-vous, Sad, Bored, Sleepy, Calm, Peaceful,* and *Relaxed.* Research on mood modelling and lower frequency emotion changes is still scarce [68]. Models of personality can be achieved through types of modelling, like the Big Five Personality factors (*openness; conscientiousness; extroversion; pleasantness;* and *neuroticism*) and applying text min-ing tools for linguistics analysis (e.g. Linguistic Inquiry and Word Count – LIWC or Structured Programming for Linguistic Cue Extraction - SPLICE) [70]. *Irrationality* is also a subject of research [71, 72] as are *persuasiveness,* or *superstition* in heuristics [73]. Modelling and simulating knowledge characteristics is also essential for representing humans in SDM. Character models are created for individuals, including context-based perceptible attributes, character saliences (like notable physical attributes); potential belief mutations. Evidence is considered the base to acquire knowledge, like (self-) *reflection, observation, transference, confabulation* or lie (an additional type, called *implant*, is also included for the single purpose of setting base simulation information). This knowledge can be reinforced or deteriorated [74]. Propagation of knowledge and mediation is an adjacent subject of research [75–77]. Other lines of research focus on modelling creativity, by employing natural language processing and ontologies [78]. Domain ontologies are indeed useful to generate better user representations [79]. Most of these models are used in different operational decision-making activities (task-related decisions), gaming (character definition) or in robotics (e.g. to detect or induce human reactions), but human cognitive models for SDM still require further research.

Digital twins started out as real-time simulators running in parallel with industrial processes to estimate and observe internal states and variables, and to predict future outcomes. Over the years, their use widened, and they began being used in various areas beyond manufacturing, like health, security, safety, transport, energy, mobility and communications.

Human Digital Twins (HDT) are psychophysiological virtualisations of human beings, usually applied to specific scenarios [70]. HDT can represent cognitive characteristics, including how humans react, what they do, found obstacles and user feelings. These are translated to an ontology [80]. HDT have a set of characteristics that should include identification, sensors to receive data from the human twin or the environment (they eventually may have actuators, depending on the purpose, information processing capabilities that may include an ontology and machine learning techniques, and they should also have real-time communication capabilities to provide and receive and process critical data [81]. HDT can be used for decision-making purposes like agile planning in manufacturing [82] or co-creation for decision-making [83], albeit with limited strategic focus or concern for humanist modelling.

In the context o Industry 4.0, digital twins are required to model the represented world adequately and accurately, assessing the circumstances and consequences, managing the complexity of infrastructure, process, and interactions, including human individual and collective behaviour, many of them not yest devised in setup or training, which still present significant challenges [41].

3.3 The Human Factor in Supporting Methods for Strategic Decision-Making

Early approaches to EA were mainly static and structure based. Newer approaches and iterations consider the importance of the elements that provide dynamics to EA artifacts and tools now provide dynamic modelling and simulation features. But the human factor still requires more analysis in these frameworks. TOGAF, FEA and others generically consider the relevance of modelling humans but provide no frameworks for that. Zachman and UAF explicitly identify stakeholders, but their links and dynamics to other models in the framework are not detailed. Recent research identifies the gap in human modelling [84] and suggests ways of addressing it, highlighting the importance of trust [27] and sociological, psychological, and emotional issues that, at micro-level, shape the culture of organisations [85]. However, most of the approaches address the same limited number of stakeholders [86]. Additionally, no significant research was found regarding models for emotional and implicit characteristics. Humans are still modelled as simplistic resources, at the same level of equipment and processes.

Decision Intelligence addresses this issue. The underlying theory is that the acritical use of machine learning and AI for prediction and SDM poses an unnecessary burden in companies' resources and wastes strong assets in decision-making and impact analysis, today only available in human beings. The objective of DI is to look to these technologies as tools to provide meaningful support to informed decisions by expert and seasoned decision-makers in the organisation. But work is still required to stabilise this discipline and systematise its integration with other methods and tools for SDM.

Impact of Humans in the Decision Process
Strategic decision does not end in the moment when decisions are made. When considering humans in decision-making, science mostly observes them as stakeholders of the decision process, but there is also a different extent to which they should also be considered as key actors. SDM impacts people working in companies and people consuming the results of that work (be it services or products). And their acceptance rejection or aptitude to adopt the outcomes of decisions constitutes a second-link consequence of the decision-making process that requires further analysis and observation [33]. Thus, the implementation and observation of the effectiveness of change, including multiple-link effects, are essential stages [51]. And it is once more essential to consider the influence of human stakeholders in purveying, enabling, or adopting change. Factors like influence and trust are crucial also here [27, 87]. The excessive focus on rationality not only does omit important repercussions of decisions, but it is also undesirable, as it can become an obstacle to strategy implementation [88]. Capturing tacit knowledge is a possible way to feed future decision-models with meaningful information [89].

The Importance of Visualisation
In this interaction between humans and other elements in the SDM process, a burden in information processing arises. Visualisation is critical here. Presenting information visually has benefits in enabling a faster processing by decision-makers, but also in minimising biases and extracting patterns from complex or unstructured data [51, 57]. Visual analytics are an emergent field centred in extracting meaningful information from large volumes of data, in providing new perspectives on existent data [90] or even in ethical approaches to decision-making [91, 92]. Typically, decision outcomes are first visualised inside the decision-makers' heads and then put into practice. Graphical visualisation allows decision-makers to envisage second-link effects of decisions better than by using words alone [51]. Charts and graphics can be systematised according to the purpose. 3D and augmented reality are potential tools for this [93]. More than that, diagrams may elicit convergence, highlight commonalities and identify boundaries in heterogenous groups of decision-makers [94] But studies show there is also potential for visualisation bias [95] Additional research in this subject is thus required.

4   Summary and Future Discussion

The relevance and the importance given in current research to humans integrated in today's companies, namely as stakeholders in strategic decisions, was analysed in this document. Evidence suggests that while humans are becoming a centrepiece of SDM, they are still modelled in a simplistic way, without emphasis on elements that distinguish them from machines and provide unique features when making and adopting decisions. The adoption of decisions is a field where modelling and simulation could provide further support, to understand potential outcomes. This requires work in modelling but also understanding human traits and their role in social interaction (both with other humans and other elements in the organisation). Simulation of mechanisms of individual decision-making, such as character traits, behaviour, creativity or emotions, and emergence of negotiated decisions and factors that concur to this, like trust, knowledge transfer, power balance, or communication, provide space for better regulation and traceability of the decision-making process.

On another level, modelling influence of human factors in cause-effect chains of decision-making and impact of decisions on stakeholders can provide a better understanding of decision failures and successes in medium- and long-term. These can be anticipated by means of digital twins and simulation. These, combined with AI are potential tools for devising mechanisms of redundancy and alternative paths in SDM.

From this work, a research question arises:

> **RQ:** What is a suitable way to model complex human traits and relations and the way to increase the effectiveness and acceptance rates of SDM in organisations?

From the research in this paper, we can conclude that humans influence and are impacted by SDM, but critical elements of their characterisation are not being addressed in a way that allows their accurate simulating and consequently the effective evaluation of (i) how the decision-making process effectively occurs; and (ii) how the decision-making outcomes influence and are impacted by stakeholders involved or affected by them. The objective is to provide insight into new approaches on how to predict and react to influence or resistance of human actors to strategic change.

This work has multiple limitations and challenges. Complex human traits (e.g. creativity, emotions) are not easy to model or translate into clear and accurate dynamic models. DT and DI have a strong procedural approach but not much is specified regarding how individual and collective complex human characteristics should be transformed into archetypes and artifacts. The knowledge areas presented here are diverse and an exhaustive analysis of all of them by a single research line would not be feasible.

In the end, it is important to highlight that, with all the technological and scientific developments that occurred in the last decades, and in spite of many previsions in contrary, human beings are still the key element in work and production, in the sense that complex decisions, strategies, or responsibilities still rely on them. More than that, proposed new approaches to industry, work and society show a clear understanding of how crucial it is to re-adjust the perspective and centre it on the human aspects. Work represents one of the largest amounts of time spent in life by humans. Tools that support a better understanding of how humans are influenced and influence their work environment, and a contemporary approach to the issues and concerns that arise from emerging business landscapes are needed.

References

1. Kassa, E.A., Mentz, J.C.: Towards a human capabilities conscious enterprise architecture. Information **12**(8), 327 (2021)
2. Tran, T.: Corporate Social Responsibility and Profits: A Tradeoff or a Balance? Stanford University (2015)
3. Yang, A., Uysal, N., Taylor, M.: Unleashing the power of networks: shareholder activism, sustainable development and corporate environmental policy. Bus. Strat. Environ. **27**, 712–727 (2017)
4. Latif, K.F.: The development and validation of stakeholder-based scale for measuring University Social Responsibility (USR). Soc. Indic. Res. **140**(2), 511–547 (2017). https://doi.org/10.1007/s11205-017-1794-y
5. Javed, M., Akhtar, M.W., Husnain, M., Lodhi, R., Emaan, S.: A stakeholder-centric paradigm bids well for the "business case" - an investigation through moderated-mediation model. Corporate Soc. Responsibility Environ. Mgmt. **27**(6), 2563–2577 (2020)
6. Narayanan, J., Puranam, P., Vugt, M.V.: Human Centric Organization Design: A Perspective from Evolutionary Psychology. INSEAD Working Paper No. 2021/63/STR (2021)
7. Shaikha, I., Randhawa, K.: Managing the risks and motivations of technology managers in open innovation: Bringing stakeholder-centric corporate governance into focus. Technovation, vol. 114 (2022)
8. Yang, L., et al.: The effects of remote work on collaboration among information workers. Nature Human Behav. **6**, 43–54 (2021)
9. Aroles, J., Mitev, N., d. Vaujany, F.-X.: Mapping themes in the study of new work practices. New Tech. Work Employm. **34**(3), 285–299 (2019)
10. Singh, D.: Literature review on employee retention with focus on recent trends *Intl.* J. Sci. Res. Sci. Tech. **6**(1), 425–431 (2019)
11. Tarique, I.: Contemporary talent management. Routledge Research Companions in Bus. & Economics (2022)
12. Henry, M.S., Roux, D.B., Parry, D.A.: Working in a post Covid-19 world: Towards a conceptual framework for distributed work. South African J. Bus. Mgmt. **52**(1), 2155 (2021)
13. Coombs, C., Hislop, D., Taneva, S.K., Barnard, S.: The strategic impacts of intelligent automation for knowledge and service work: an interdisciplinary review. J. Strat. Info. Sys. **29**(4), 101600 (2020)
14. Gorynia, M.: Competition and globalisation in economic sciences. Selected aspects. Econ. Bus. Rev. **5**(3), 118–133 (2019)
15. Teer-Tomaselli, R., Tomaselli, K., Dludla, M.: Peripheral capital goes global: naspers, globalisation and global media contraflow. Media Cult. Soc. **41**(8), 1142–1159 (2019)
16. O'Donovan, N.: From knowledge economy to automation anxiety: a growth regime in crisis? New Polit. Econ. **25**(2), 248–266 (2020)
17. Khmelevsky, Y., Li, X., Madnick, S.: Software development using agile and scrum in distributed teams. In: IEEE Intl. Sys. Conf., 1–4 (2017)
18. Stray, V., Moe, N.B.: Understanding coordination in global software engineering: A mixed-methods study on the use of meetings and Slack. J. Sys. Sw. **170**, 110717 (2020)
19. Azeem, M., Ahmed, M., Haider, S., Sajjad, M.: Expanding competitive advantage through organizational culture, knowledge sharing and organizational innovation. Technol. Soc. **66**, 101635 (2021)
20. Na, Y.K., Kang, S., Jeong, H.Y.: The effect of market orientation on performance of sharing economy business: focusing on marketing innovation and sustainable competitive advantage. Sustainability **11**(3), 729 (2019)

21. Hernandez, A.K.L., Fernandez-Mesa, A., Edwards-Schachter, M.: Team collaboration capabilities as a factor in startup success. J. Tech. Mgmt. Innov. **13**(4), 13–23 (2018)
22. Prokop, V., Stejskal, J., Hudec, O.: Collaboration for innovation in small CEE countries (2019)
23. Gemünden, H.G., Lehner, P., Kock, A.: The project-oriented organization and its contribution to innovation. Intl. J. Proj. Mgmt. **36**(1), 147–160 (2018)
24. Baptista, J., Stein, M.-K., Klein, S., Watson-Manheim, M.B., Lee, J.: Digital work and organisational transformation: Emergent Digital/Human work configurations in modern organisations. J. Strategic Info. Sys. **29**(2), 101618 (2020)
25. Lee, K., Yoo, J.: How does open innovation lead competitive advantage? a dynamic capability view perspective. PLoS ONE **14**(11), e0223405 (2019)
26. Alla, B., Sergiy, B., Svitlana, O., Tanaka, H.: Entropy paradigm of project-oriented organizations management. In: CEUR Works. Proceedings (2020)
27. Costa, A.C., Fulmer, C.A., Anderson, N.R.: Trust in work teams: an integrative review, multilevel model, and future directions. J. Organ. Behav. **39**(2), 169–184 (2018)
28. Verboven, S., Berrevoets, J., Wuytens, C., Baesens, B., Verbeke, W.: Autoencoders for strategic decision support. Decision Supp. Sys. vol. 150 (2021)
29. Nooraie, M.: Factors influencing strategic decision-making processes. Int. J. Acad. Res. Bus. Soc. Sci. **2**(7), 405–429 (2012)
30. Yu, X.-B.: What is an organizational strategic decision? In: The Fundamental Elements of Strategy, pp. 45–59. Springer, Singapore (2021). https://doi.org/10.1007/978-981-33-4713-7_4
31. Acciarini, C., Brunetta, F., Boccardelli, P.: Cognitive biases and decision-making strategies in times of change: a systematic review. Manage. Decis. **59**(3), 638–652 (2022)
32. Shrivastava, P., Grant, J.H.: Empirically derived models of strategic decision-making processes. Strategic Mgmt. J. **6**(2), 97–113 (1985)
33. March, J.: The Technology of Foolishness (original text from 1971). In: Shaping Entrepreneurship Research, Routledge (2020)
34. Larsen, B.: Whatever happened to "The Technology of Foolishness"? does it have any potential today? Scandinavian J. Mgmt. **36**(1), 101093 (2020)
35. Kay, J.: Obliquity. Capitalism & Society, vol. 7, no. 1 (2012)
36. Aristodemou, L., Tietze, F.: Technology Strategic Decision Making (SDM): an overview of decision theories, processes and methods. Centre for Tech. Mgmt. working paper series, no. 5 (2019)
37. Ismail, K.M., Zhao, X.: Comprehensiveness in strategic decision making: toward clarifying the construct. Am. J. Mgmt. **17**(4), 133–142 (2017)
38. Alhawamdeh, H.M., Alsmairat, M.A.K.: Strategic decision making and organization performance: a literature review. Int. Rev. Mgmt. Mktg. **9**(4), 95–99 (2019)
39. Intezari, A., Gressel, S.: Information and reformation in KM systems: big data and strategic decision-making. J. Knowl. Mgmt. **21**(1), 71–91 (2017)
40. Dear, K.: Artificial intelligence and decision-making. RUSI J. **164**(5–6), 18–25 (2019)
41. Trentesaux, D., Karnouskos, S.: Engineering ethical behaviors in autonomous industrial cyber-physical human systems. Cogn Tech Work 24, 113–126 (2022)
42. Longo, F., Padovano, A., Umbrello, S.: Value-oriented and ethical technology engineering in industry 5.0: a human-centric perspective for the design of the factory of the future. Appl. Sci. **4182**, 10 (2020)
43. Rahanu, H., Georgiadou, E., Siakas, K., Ross, M., Berki, E.: Ethical issues invoked by industry 4.0. In: Yilmaz, M., Clarke, P., Messnarz, R., Reiner, M. (eds.) EuroSPI 2021. CCIS, vol. 1442, pp. 589–606. Springer, Cham (2021). https://doi.org/10.1007/978-3-030-85521-5_39
44. Ross, J.W., Weill, P., Robertson, D.: Enterprise Architecture As Strategy: Creating a Foundation for Business Execution. Harvard Business Press (2006)

45. Wegmann, A.: On the systemic enterprise architecture methodology (SEAM). In: Proceedings of the 5th International Conference on Enterprise Information Systems (2003)
46. Sánchez, M., Villalobos, J., Paola, L.: OT modeling: the enterprise beyond IT. Bus. Info. Sys. Eng. **61**, 399–411 (2019)
47. Lapalme, J., Gerber, A., d. Merwe, A.V., Zachman, J., Marne De Vries, K.H.: Exploring the future of enterprise architecture: a Zachman perspective. Comput. Ind. **79**, 103–113 (2016)
48. Shanks, G., Gloet, M., Someh, I., Frampton, K., Tamm, T.: Achieving benefits with enterprise architecture. J. Strategic Info. Sys. **27**(2), 139–156 (2018)
49. Jusuf, M.B., Kurnia, S.: Understanding the benefits and success factors of enterprise architecture. In: Proceedings of the 50th Hawaii International Conference on System Sciences (2017)
50. Jayakrishnan, M., Mohamad, A.K., Abdullah, A.: Digitalization approach through an enterprise architecture for malaysia transportation industry. Int. J. Civil Eng. Tech. **9**(13), 834–839 (2018)
51. Pratt, L.: Link: How Decision Intelligence Connects Data, Actions, and Outcomes for a Better World, Emerald Publishing Limited (2019)
52. Moser, R., Rengarajan, S., Narayanamurthy, G.: Decision intelligence: creating a fit between intelligence requirements and intelligence processing capacities. IM Kozhikode Soc. Mgmt Rev. **10**(2), 160–177 (2021)
53. Duan, Y., Edwards, J.S., Dwivedi, Y.K.: Artificial intelligence for decision making in the era of Big Data – evolution, challenges and research agenda. Int. J. Info. Mgmt. **48**, 63–71 (2019)
54. Knight, E., Daymond, J., Paroutis, S.: Design-led strategy: how to bring design thinking into the art of strategic management. California Mgmt Rev. **62**(2), 30–52 (2020)
55. Kotina, E., Koria, M., Prendeville, S.: Using design thinking to improve strategic decisions during collaborative sensemaking. In: Design Mgmt Academy Conf., Hong-Kong, (2017)
56. Graf, S.: Design thinking for strategizing? – a critical literature review. J. Emerging Trends Mktg Mgmt **1**(1), 110–119 (2021)
57. Liedtka, J., Kaplan, S.: How design thinking opens new frontiers for strategy development. Strategy Leadership **47**(2), 3–10 (2019)
58. Johnson, J.: Delegating strategic decision-making to machines: Dr. Strangelove Redux? J. Strat. Stud. **45**, 1–39 (2020)
59. Korteling, J.E., Brouwer, A.-M., Toet, A.: A neural network framework for cognitive bias. Front. Psychol. **9**, 1561 (2018)
60. Fonda, E., Meneghett, A.: The Human-Centric SMED. Sustainability **14**(51), 514 (2022)
61. Nahavandi, S.: Industry 5.0—a human-centric solution. Sustainability **11**(16), 4371 (2019)
62. Østergaard, E.H.: Welcome to industry 5.0. Universal Robots (2018)
63. Maddikunta, P.K.R., et al.: Industry 5.0: a survey on enabling technologies and potential applications. J. Ind. Info. Integration **26**, 100257 (2022)
64. Skobelev, P., Borovik, S.: On the way from industry 4.0 to industry 5.0: from digital manufacturing to digital society. Int. Sci. J. "Industry 4.0" **II**(6), 307–311 (2017)
65. Trentesaux, D., Karnouskos, S.: Engineering ethical behaviors in autonomous industrial cyber-physical human systems. Cogn. Technol. Work **24**(1), 113–126 (2022)
66. Berrah, L., Cliville, V., Trentesaux, D., Chapel, C.: Industrial performance: an evolution incorporating ethics in the context of industry 4.0. Sustainability **13**(9209) (2021)
67. Pacaux-Lemoine, M.-P., Trentesaux, D.: Ethical risks of human-machine symbiosis in industry 4.0: insights from the human-machine cooperation approach. IFAC-PapersOnLine **52**(19), 19–24 (2019)
68. Cavallo, F., Semeraro, F., Fiorini, L., Magyar, G., Sinčák, P., Dario, P.: Emotion modelling for social robotics applications: a review. J. Bionic Eng. **15**(2), 2543–2141 (2018)
69. Greasley, A., Owen, C.: Representing Human Behavior. In: Behavioral Operational Research, Palgrave Macmillan, London, pp. 47–63 (2016)

70. Sun, J., Tian, Z., Fu, Y., Geng, J., Liu, C.: Digital twins in human understanding: a deep learning-based method to recognize personality traits. Intl. J. Comp. Integrated Manuf. **34**(7–8) (2021)
71. Wängberg, T., Böörs, M., Catt, E., Everitt, T., Hutter, M.: A game-theoretic analysis of the off-switch game. In: Everitt, T., Goertzel, B., Potapov, A. (eds.) AGI 2017. LNCS, vol. 10414, pp. 167–177. Springer, Cham (2017). https://doi.org/10.1007/978-3-319-63703-7_16
72. Gatherer, D.: The spread of irrational behaviors by contagion: an agent micro-simulation. In: A Memetics Compendium, p. 727 (2008)
73. Liu, J.: The Superstitious Heuristic in Strategic Decision-making (Dissertation). City Univ. of New York (2019)
74. Ryan, J., Mateas, M.: Simulating character knowledge phenomena in Talk of the Town. In: Game AI Pro 3, AK Peters/CRC Press, pp. 433–448 (2017)
75. Bakanova, N., Bakanov, A., Atanasova, T.: Modelling human-computer interactions based on cognitive styles within collective decision-making. Adv. Sci. Tech. Eng. Sys. J. **6**(1), 631–635 (2021)
76. Xu, B., Liu, R., He, Z.: Individual irrationality, network structure, and collective intelligence: an agent-based simulation approach. Complexity **21**(S1), 44–54 (2016)
77. Tomlin, D.: Consensus decision-making: performance of heuristics and mental models. Evol. Hum. Behav. **42**(4), 316–330 (2021)
78. Jordanous, A., Kelle, B.: Modelling creativity: identifying key components through a corpus-based approach. PLoS ONE, vol. 11, no. 10 (2016)
79. Hale, J., et al.: An ontology-based modelling system (OBMS) for representing behaviour change theories applied to 76 theories. Wellcome Open Research, vol. 5, no. 177 (2020)
80. Saariluoma, P., Cañas, J., Karvonen, A.: Human digital twins and cognitive mimetic. In: International Conference on Human Interaction & Emerging Technologies (2020)
81. Saddik, A.E.: Digital Twins: the convergence of multimedia technologies. IEEE Multimed. **25**(2), 87–92 (2018)
82. d. Santos, C.H., Lima, R.D.C., Leal, F., d. Queiroz, J.A., Balestrassi, P.P., Montevechi, J.A.B.: A decision support tool for operational planning: a Digital Twin using simulation and forecasting methods. Production, vol. 30 (2020)
83. West, S., Stoll, O., Meierhofer, J., Züst, S.: Digital Twin providing new opportunities for value co-creation through supporting decision-making. Applied Sci. **11**(3750) (2021)
84. Oberhauser, R., Sousa, P., Michel, F.: VR-EAT: visualization of enterprise architecture tool diagrams in virtual reality. In: International Symposium on Business Modeling & Sw. Design (2020)
85. Aromaa, E.: Emotion as soft power in organisations. J. Org. Effectiveness: Ppl Perf. **7**(4), 341–357 (2020)
86. Gonzalez-Lopez, F., Bustos, G.: Integration of business process architectures within enterprise architecture approaches: a literature review. Eng. Mgmt. J. **31**(2), 127–140 (2019)
87. Battilana, J., Casciaro, T.: Power, social influence and organizational change: the role of network position in change implementation. In: Academy of Mgmt Proceedings (2010)
88. Healey, M.P., Hodgkinson, G.P.: Making strategy hot. California Mgmt. Rev. **59**(3), 109–134 (2017)
89. Cho, S.Y., Happa, J., Creese, S.: Capturing tacit knowledge in security operation centers. IEEE Access **8**, 42021–42041 (2020)
90. Keivanpour, S., Ait Kadi, D.: Strategic eco-design map of the complex products: toward visualisation of the design for environment. Intl. J. Prod. Res. **65**(24), 7296–731 (2018)
91. Parkavi, A., Jawaid, A., Dev, S., Vinutha, M.S.: THE PATTERNS THAT DON'T EXIST: Study on the effects of psychological human biases in data analysis and decision making. In: 3rd Intl Conf. on Comp. Sys. & Info. Tech. for Sustainable Sols. IEEE (2018)

92. Ahn, Y., Lin, Y.-R.: FairSight: visual analytics for fairness in decision making. IEEE Trans. Visualiz. Comput. Graphs **26**(1), 1086–1095(2019)
93. Hollberg, A., et al.: Review of visualising LCA results in the design process of buildings. Build. Environ. **190**, 107530 (2021)
94. Pluchinotta, I., Salvia, G., Zimmermann, N.: The importance of eliciting stakeholders' system boundary perceptions for problem structuring and decision-making. Eur. J. Op. Res. **1**(1), 280–293 (2021)
95. Ellis, G., Dix, A.: Decision Making Under Uncertainty in Visualisation? In: IEEE VIS2015, Chicago (2015)

Cyber-Physical Systems

Asynchronous Communication Between Modular Cyber-Physical Production Systems and Arduino Based Industrial Controllers

Fábio M. Oliveira[1,2(✉)], André Rocha[1,2], Duarte Alemão[1,2], Nelson Freitas[1,2], and José Barata[1,2]

[1] School of Science and Technology, NOVA University of Lisbon, Campus de Caparica, Lisbon, Portugal
`{fmo,andre.rocha,d.alemao,n.freitas,jab}@uninova.pt`
[2] Uninova-CTS, Campus de Caparica, Caparica, Portugal

Abstract. In a new world where the virtual and physical world is more and more connected, there is a need to project physical devices as digital clones, but the inverse is also true, projecting physical objects from software assets. The proposed work is an approach to connect virtual (software) and the physical (machines) twins using two asynchronous solutions: persistent bi-directional communication and publish subscribe methods on Arduino based controllers. The focus will be in the interaction of virtual and physical reality in order to track the products mainly for academic and investigation proposes but with focus on the applicability on legacy controllers from shop floors, which were not conceived and projected to have these features.

Keywords: Modular cyber-physical production systems · Virtual environment · Industrial agents · Industrial controllers · Asynchronous communication · MQTT · Websockets · FIPA

1 Introduction

The fourth industrial revolution [1] is on its way, gaining more and more enthusiasts in academy and industry. This revolution is characterized by digitalization, focusing on technology and digital transformation, concentrating on adding value to users, integration and gathering of new data and, on developing communication technologies to create sustainable solutions or highly customizable products with agile and flexible approaches [2]. Transferring all the capabilities proposed by this new paradigm is not easy and the industry is trying to adapt in a cost sustainable way.

The legacy controllers used on some assembly lines are not suitable to face this new paradigm and the substitution of those can carry a lot of investment [3]. Also, a holarchy should be present on the shop floor to enable a fast, flexible, agile, and resilient production line that features data creation and consumption [3].

L. M. Camarinha-Matos (Ed.): DoCEIS 2022, IFIP AICT 649, pp. 53–61, 2022.
https://doi.org/10.1007/978-3-031-07520-9_5

A holarchy can be executed on a software platform of agents Multiagent Systems (MAS). Retrofitting some of these legacy controllers with Arduino-based microcontrollers or Raspberry Pi micro-computers seems to be a cost-effective solution with low downtimes.

In this scenario, the question that arrives is: "Is it possible to use a MAS high-level system with a retrofitted robot?".

Our proposal is to use synchronous communication protocols to provide interaction between MAS and legacy controllers through Arduino-based microcontrollers in order to use a holarchy at a high level and keep the retrofitting costs low.

This paper is divided into the following structure: chapter two where the works of integration between MAS and the physical systems are explored, chapter three where we propose a framework, chapter four in which the demonstration scenario is explained, chapter five where our results are shown and a conclusion and future work on chapter six.

2 Related Work

In recent past years, we assisted in the emergence of Cyber-Physical Systems (CPS) applied to several challenges. CPS enables a set of flexible features over data for the final users ranging from processing data acquired by tiny sensors to managing large data collection. It also enables to sharing of data, provides security, and facilitates application support [4]. CPS provides not only access to data but also empowers the connection between different computing devices, namely concurrent processing in distributed environments and supporting information sharing in heterogeneous scenarios guaranteeing responses from the user queries at a suitable time [5, 6]. When CPS is applied to the fields of production and manufacturing sites it is denominated Cyber-Physical Production Systems (CPPS). This new concept of CPS, CCPS, is suitable for the development of the fourth industrial revolution [7, 8].

In industry, the possibility of having a logical representation of a physical asset has many advantages since it reduces the complexity of implementing systems. Nevertheless, linking physical components with logical representations is not an easy task [9]. Some works integrate solutions based on the Internet of Things (IoT) where new sensors are copulated to the PLC to harvest data [10].

Smart factories take the advantage of CPPS to face the product's shorter life cycles and high customization, required by the clients. A smart factory is composed of vertical integration (between management software like MES – Manufacturing Execution System, or ERP – Enterprise Resource Plan, to the shop floor) and horizontal integration (between shop floor machines)[11]. Some authors already detected gap's in the vertical integration, for instance between the management layers and the producing machinery (robots and PLC) at the bottom [12].

A smart factory has, as one of the key factors, the ability to use agile, robust, and dynamic production lines. To couple with this challenge, one of the solutions is to use distributed and reconfigurable control systems [13]. These systems have an holonic approach [14], with a focus on modularity, that can be implemented using a Multi-Agent System (MAS) [15].

When using a MAS as a control system, an architecture must be chosen. The two big groups of architecture are centralized coordination, where one or more Agents are responsible to mediate and coordinate the actions of other Agents (an example can be consulted at [16]) or the decentralized coordination approach where all Agents are responsible for creating and executing a production plan. Focusing on the decentralized approaches, each Agent can communicate with the others through asynchronous messages [17]. One of the most used protocols to communicate between Agents is the Agent Communication Language standardized by Foundation for Intelligent Physical Agents (FIPA) [18]. On the decentralized architecture itself, several approaches were explored like the one depicted in Fig. 1 [19], where every entity communicates with each other using the MAS platform, or the other depict in Fig. 2 [20], where some entities only communicates with the ones chosen, but the most suitable to use on production sites is the Product Agent architecture [21].

Fig. 1. Multi Agent platform prototype

Fig. 2. Team of agents on AGV challenge

When using the Product Agent architecture approach, the Product Agent (PA) is responsible to handle the list of actions to be done to the product and negotiate with the Resource Agents (RAs) to which manufacturing processes the product must be submitted. In order to, it must search for suitable RAs, request and schedule the actions [22].

An approach for the RA is presented in Lepuschitz, et al. [23] but, as stated in Ribeiro and Hochwallner [24] there are still some challenges in the integration between the Cyber-Representation and the production system. The work of Ding, et al. [25] identifies as a challenge the synchronization loop and states as some hypotheses the development of industrial networks, the data protocols, and the interfaces. Even in recent literature such as Hyre, et al. [26] where the DT is clearly defined, the communication between the physical and cyber world is not clearly demonstrated. The work of Samir, et al. [27] uses both persistent bi-directional communication and publish-subscribe methods on a truck company, through its Plant Service Bus (PSB), but does not use the MAS environment.

3 Proposed Framework

The proposed work is a framework with three levels: Multi-Agent System (MAS) environment, an Integration Layer, and the Real/Physical System (as depicted in Fig. 3).

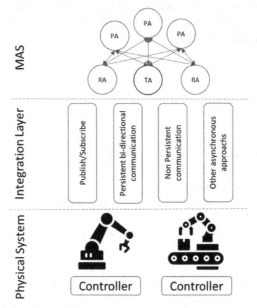

Fig. 3. Proposed framework

On the first layer, the MAS environment, it is applied a Product/Resource architecture as presented in the IDEAS project [28]. The Product Agents (PA) and the Resource Agents (RA) can communicate with each other's using a FIPA compliant protocol to require and make available Skills on the system. The RAs are modular cyber-physical production systems representations. A Transport Agent (TA), also FIPA compliant, can provide transport for the products from the beginning of the line to the exit and between RAs. The RA has the capability of using asynchronous communication mechanisms to provide low-level integration. On the other side, Physical Systems also have the capability to use asynchronous communication mechanisms to exchange messages. The main contribution of this kind of framework is that between the RA and the Physical systems there is no need of using a FIPA compliant protocol since the proposed integration layer requires only the use of an asynchronous protocol chosen by the end-user. This integration layer is not dependent on the asynchronous protocol chosen and more than one protocol can be used at a given time.

The advantage to using this approach is to enable controllers that already have asynchronous protocols made available by the manufacturers (for instance OPC protocol) also complaint to receive messages from a MAS environment, in particular FIPA compliant communications, without the need of instantiating their own Agents on the default hardware which can be a big challenge.

4 Demonstration Scenario

Using JAVA and JADE, a virtual demonstration scenario was created. It consists of several conveyors and three stations. In this scenario, the conveyors are managed by TA and the RAs associated with stations D_7, D_8, and D_9. The RA associated with station D_7 communicates with the corresponding controller through the MQTT protocol. The RA associated with station D_8 communicates with the controller through WebSocket protocol and station D_9 only executes a virtual skill.

The graphical interface, that helps understand how the PAs are running on the production lines is present in Fig. 4. Several RAs offering several skills can be deployed but the ones associated with station D_7 and station D_8 will always use asynchronous communication protocols. RAs associated with station D_9 will always use FIPA protocol to execute the virtual skill.

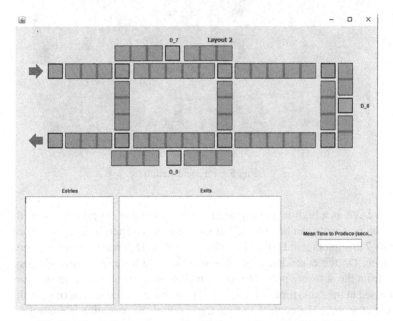

Fig. 4. Simulation environment with three stations: D_7, D_8, D_9

The controllers used are M-Duino since they are compatible with Arduino and can use 24V sensors and actuators.

Although the physical kit also has a conveyor, it is considered that it is part of the station and not part of the transport system.

When the product reaches the position D_7 or D_8, a message is sent through one of the message protocols (MQTT or Websockets, respectively) and the physical station waits for a product to be detected on the sensor from the first conveyor. As soon as the product is detected on the sensor the station executes the skill and when the product is detected on the sensor from the last conveyor a message is sent, through the same communication protocol to the virtual environment. From this point on, the TA resumes its work and conduces the product through the rest of the virtual system.

Depending on the 'skills' required by the product, it can go from one physical station to another. In Fig. 5 the blue arrow indicates the sensor from the position on the first conveyor (initial position) and the green arrow indicates the sensor from the position on the last conveyor (final position).

Fig. 5. Physical station

Since JAVA is a high-level programming language that supports threads, the communication protocols can be executed at the same time. Therefore, a product can be at station D_7 and another at D_8 and another on station D_9 and the entire system is able to continue. On the controller side, although possible to react to several messages in parallel from the software point of view, it makes no sense to force a second *product* to be processed at the same time at the same station, since each station is only available for a *product* at a time. The control and management of the operation is controlled by the MAS and the *TA* knows if the position on the station is free or not to deploy the *product*. The message protocol is only activated when the simulation environment deploys a *product* in the station (the *product* is on the *resource*).

It is out of the scope of this work to handle to multiple requests when the physical system is busy or to make priorities from different *products*.

5 Results

To demonstrate that this is a valid framework a set of tests was made. The first batch of tests conducted on the demonstration scenario was designed to verify that the concept was able to be applied. The second batch of tests was done to evaluate the performance of two asynchronous protocols.

Fifty products were created, and they asked for a skill available on a resource that was associated with station D_7 (usage of MQTT protocol). Afterward, another fifty products were created that asked for a skill available on a resource that was associated with station D_8 (usage of WebSocket protocol).

All *products* were able to be produced in both situations.

In the second batch of tests, it was measured the round trip time (RTT) of the messages between the Resource Agent and the hardware. Fifty products were created to use each protocol, in three different runs.

When a product arrives at the station, a message is sent with the timestamp. The controller that receives the message replies with the same content. Upon the delivery of this message, the MAS is able to calculate the RTT using the "current" timestamp and the message timestamp. The execution time is not within the scope of this work since it can depend on the skill required, so the skill was empty and only the RTT was measured. The resume of RTT is depicted in Table 1.

Table 1. RTT resume table.

Protocol - Run/RTT (ms)	Min	Max	Average	Standard deviation
MQTT – Run1 (50 products)	368	1338	837,10	283,59
MQTT – Run2 (50 products)	365	1329	858,52	286,44
MQTT – Run3 (50 products)	405	1349	879,40	285,92
Websockets – Run1 (50 products)	45	1026	504,66	285,52
Websockets – Run2 (50 products)	28	1009	530,48	306,21
Websockets – Run3 (50 products)	43	1010	528,06	286,34

6 Conclusion

This work proposes a framework with an integration layer using asynchronous communication to connect a holarchy and physical devices. There were conducted tests using JADE (MAS environment), Websockets (persistent bi-directional communication), and MQTT (publish/subscribe communication) as examples of asynchronous protocols to validate this approach in a demonstration scenario where Agents ask for skills on Resources that communicate with the hardware. It was possible to use this approach with both protocols and the time difference between both on the laboratory tests in NOVA University facilities let us infer that the Websockets protocol is slightly faster.

Also, the fact of removing the FIPA protocol represents a decrease in the complexity on the controller's side. In future work, more protocols should be tested such as OPC or Rest Services and a benchmark should be created to understand on which conditions a protocol should be used in place of another. It is also interesting to create a Hub-like system on the integration layer that could accept requests from several asynchronous protocols and transfer them into the hardware-capable protocols. Arduinos seems to be a cost-effective platform to deploy these solutions because of the cost, flexibility, and the easiness to program them but further work should also include other microcontrollers and microcomputers such as Raspberry Pi or Zynq boards.

Acknowledgment. We acknowledge the Portuguese FCT program UIDB/00066/2020 for providing partial financial support for this work.

References

1. Gilchrist, A.: "Industry 4.0. Opportunities and challenges of the new industrial revolution for developing countries and economies in transition. In: 2030 Agenda Sustain. Dev. Goals (2016). https://doi.org/10.1007/978-1-4842-2047-4
2. Li, G., Hou, Y., Wu, A.: Fourth Industrial Revolution: technological drivers, impacts and coping methods. Chin. Geogra. Sci. **27**(4), 626–637 (2017). https://doi.org/10.1007/s11769-017-0890-x
3. Mařík, V., McFarlane, D.: Industrial adoption of agent-based technologies. IEEE Intell. Syst. **20**(1), 27–35 (2005). https://doi.org/10.1109/MIS.2005.11
4. Jirgl, M., Bradac, Z., Fiedler, P.: Human-in-the-loop issue in context of the cyber-physical systems. IFAC-PapersOnLine **51**(6), 225–230 (2018). https://doi.org/10.1016/j.ifacol.2018.07.158
5. Sztipanovits, J., Bapty, T., Koutsoukos, X., Lattmann, Z., Neema, S., Jackson, E.: Model and tool integration platforms for cyber-physical system design. Proc. IEEE **106**(9), 1501–1526 (2018). https://doi.org/10.1109/JPROC.2018.2838530
6. Zeng, D., Gu, L., Yao, H.: Towards energy efficient service composition in green energy powered Cyber-Physical Fog Systems. Futur. Gener. Comput. Syst. **105**, 757–765 (2020). https://doi.org/10.1016/j.future.2018.01.060
7. Ribeiro, L.: Cyber-physical production systems' design challenges. IEEE Int. Symp. Ind. Electron. 1189–1194 (2017). https://doi.org/10.1109/ISIE.2017.8001414
8. Monostori, L.: Cyber-physical production systems: roots, expectations and R&D challenges. Proc. CIRP **17**, 9–13 (2014). https://doi.org/10.1016/j.procir.2014.03.115
9. Hehenberger, P., Vogel-Heuser, B., Bradley, D., Eynard, B., Tomiyama, T., Achiche, S.: Design, modelling, simulation and integration of cyber physical systems: Methods and applications. Comput. Ind. **82**, 273–289 (2016). https://doi.org/10.1016/j.compind.2016.05.006
10. Botta, A., De Donato, W., Persico, V., Pescapé, A.: Integration of Cloud computing and Internet of Things: a survey. Futur. Gener. Comput. Syst. **56**, 684–700 (2016). https://doi.org/10.1016/j.future.2015.09.021
11. Lucke, D.W.E., Constantinescu, C.: Smart factory - a step towards the next generation of manufacturing. In: Manufacturing Systems and Technologies for the New Frontier, London, pp. 115–118. Springer, London (2008). https://doi.org/10.1007/978-1-84800-267-8_23

12. Tamas, L., Murar, M.: Smart CPS: vertical integration overview and user story with a cobot. Int. J. Comput. Integr. Manuf. **32**(4–5), 504–521 (2019). https://doi.org/10.1080/0951192X.2018.1535196
13. Onori, M., Barata, J., Frei, R.: Evolvable assembly systems basic principles. IFIP Int. Fed. Inf. Process. **220**, 317–328 (2006). https://doi.org/10.1007/978-0-387-36594-7_34
14. Van Brüssel, H., Bongaerts, L., Wyns, J., Valckenaers, P., Van Ginderachter, T.: A conceptual framework for kolonic manufacturing: identification of manufacturing holons. J. Manuf. Syst. **18**(1), 35–52 (1999). https://doi.org/10.1016/S0278-6125(99)80011-9
15. Leitão, P.: Agent-based distributed manufacturing control: a state-of-the-art survey. Eng. Appl. Artif. Intell. **22**(7), 979–991 (2009). https://doi.org/10.1016/j.engappai.2008.09.005
16. Leusin, M.E., Kück, M., Frazzon, E.M., Maldonado, M.U., Freitag, M.: Potential of a multi-agent system approach for production control in smart factories. IFAC-PapersOnLine **51**(11), 1459–1464 (2018). https://doi.org/10.1016/j.ifacol.2018.08.309
17. Andreadis, G., Klazoglou, P., Niotaki, K., Bouzakis, K.D.: Classification and review of multi-agents systems in the manufacturing section. Proc. Eng. **69**, 282–290 (2014). https://doi.org/10.1016/j.proeng.2014.02.233
18. Dale, J.: "FIPA Agent Communication Language Specification (2002). http://www.fipa.org/repository/aclspecs.html. Accessed 5 Jan 2022
19. Feng, S.C.: Preliminary design and manufacturing planning integration using web-based intelligent agents. J. Intell. Manuf. **16**(4–5), 423–437 (2005). https://doi.org/10.1007/s10845-005-1655-4
20. Rzevski, G.: A framework for designing intelligent manufacturing systems. Comput. Ind. **34**(2), 211–219 (1997). https://doi.org/10.1016/s0166-3615(97)00056-0
21. Kovalenko, I., Barton, K., Tilbury, D.: Design and implementation of an intelligent product agent architecture in manufacturing systems. IEEE International Conference on Emerging Technologies and Factory Automation ETFA, pp. 1–8 (2017). https://doi.org/10.1109/ETFA.2017.8247652
22. Kovalenko, I., Ryashentseva, D., Vogel-Heuser, B., Tilbury, D., Barton, K.: Dynamic resource task negotiation to enable product agent exploration in multi-agent manufacturing systems. IEEE Robot. Autom. Lett. **4**(3), 2854–2861 (2019). https://doi.org/10.1109/LRA.2019.2921947
23. Lepuschitz, W., Zoitl, A., Vallée, M., Merdan, M.: Toward self-reconfiguration of manufacturing systems using automation agents. IEEE Trans. Syst. Man Cybern. Part C Appl. Rev. **41**(1), 52–69 (2011). https://doi.org/10.1109/TSMCC.2010.2059012
24. Ribeiro, L., Hochwallner, M.: On the design complexity of cyberphysical production systems. Complexity 2018 (2018). https://doi.org/10.1155/2018/4632195
25. Ding, K., Chan, F.T.S., Zhang, X., Zhou, G., Zhang, F.: Defining a Digital Twin-based Cyber-Physical Production System for autonomous manufacturing in smart shop floors. Int. J. Prod. Res. **57**(20), 6315–6334 (2019). https://doi.org/10.1080/00207543.2019.1566661
26. Hyre, A., Harris, G., Osho, J., Pantelidakis, M., Mykoniatis, K., Liu, J.: Digital twins: representation, replication, reality, and relational (4Rs). Manuf. Lett. **31**, 20–23 (2021). https://doi.org/10.1016/j.mfglet.2021.12.004
27. Samir, K., Maffei, A., Onori, M.A.: Real-Time asset tracking; a starting point for digital twin implementation in manufacturing. Procedia CIRP **81**, 719–723 (2019). https://doi.org/10.1016/j.procir.2019.03.182
28. Ribeiro, L., Barata, J., Onori, M., Hanisch, C., Hoos, J., Rosa, R.: Self-organization in automation - the IDEAS pre-demonstrator. In: IECON Proceedings of the (Industrial Electronics Conference, pp. 2752–2757, November 2011. https://doi.org/10.1109/IECON.2011.6119747

Mechanisms for Service Composition in Collaborative Cyber-Physical Systems

Artem A. Nazarenko[✉] and Luis M. Camarinha-Matos

School of Science and Technology and UNINOVA-CTS, Nova University of Lisbon,
2829-516 Monte Caparica, Portugal
{aan,cam}@uninova.pt

Abstract. Recent advances in the IoT and Cyber-Physical Systems (CPS) enabled the possibility to combine capillary services or even services from different domains, such as smart home, smart city, smart infrastructure, etc. Thus, it is possible now to talk about the collaborative IoT or collaborative CPS, where services are not isolated from each other, but collaboratively offer added value and should provide advanced mechanisms for conflict resolution. However, still more efforts are needed to explore the ways of how capillary services might be selected and combined in an automated or semi-automated way forming composed or collaborative services. This process includes various stages, such as identification of selection criteria, discovery, negotiation, etc., that need to be considered from the very beginning of the system's design. For this reason, we propose an ontology that addresses issues related to various collaborative aspects of service composition. Moreover, we discuss the composition of services or coalition formation principles with advanced mechanisms for negotiation and conflict resolution considering, for instance, the access rights and ownership.

Keywords: Collaborative Cyber-Physical Systems · Collaborative services · System design

1 Introduction

With the progress of the Industry 4.0 development, the Cyber-Physical Systems (CPS) have been adopted in many areas of human activities, such as home and industrial process automation, healthcare, smart agriculture, etc. According to [2] the current industrial stage presumes deep integration between the operational systems and information and communication technologies (ICT). It is important to understand the processes and main drivers behind this trend. The drivers can be split into social and economic, as well as technological. Examples of social and economic ones are [1]: (i) short development periods, (ii) individualization of demand, (iii) flexibility, (iv) decentralization, and (v) resource efficiency. The technological drivers include: (i) further automation of various manufacturing processes, (ii) digitalization and networking, (iii) miniaturization, and (iv) increased availability of electronic components. In other words, the new CPS are

L. M. Camarinha-Matos (Ed.): DoCEIS 2022, IFIP AICT 649, pp. 62–73, 2022.
https://doi.org/10.1007/978-3-031-07520-9_6

not isolated and single problem focused, but rather encompassing multiple aspects and addressing complex systems [2].

Thus, a Complex CPS can be represented as an ecosystem that is composed of tens or hundreds of heterogeneous entities collaborating with each other in order to provide composed services. The modeling of IoT/CPS elements is well known and can be advantageous in multi-owners' landscape [14]. These elements or entities can be both of technical nature, such as sensors and actuators, as well as social nature as represented by human users. The human users can be at the same time the service consumers and the service owners, or the owners of several devices involved in the service provision. Effective support to these complex relations raises the need to introduce collaborative mechanisms for the orchestration of the involved CPS entities. In this regard, we can speak now of Collaborative CPSs that are characterized by "jointly acting and sharing information, resources and responsibilities in order to achieve a common goal" [3]. Thus, the CCPSs, contrary to ordinary CPS, lay larger emphasis on increased connectivity, collaboration, and distributiveness, allowing them to enrich their functionality. Moreover, we can differentiate between the internal collaborative entities – coming from within the considered CPS, and external collaborative entities – coming from the outside. Both the internal and external entities are part of a CCPS environment.

In this context, to deliver a composed service, a CCPS has to allocate the needed competencies and thus discover the components that will be able to provide the necessary functionality. The process of service composition can be compared to the process of coalition formation [4]. The collaborative mechanisms are tightly interrelated with service composition aspects. The main purpose of a service is to satisfy the users' needs through allocation of required capabilities. In general, and in addition to interoperability issues, the process of services composition can face significant obstacles that can arise due to possible conflicts. One example could be, if different users with equal access rights attempt at acquiring the same service at the same time and in the same location/using the same resources. The mechanisms for conflict resolution should be introduced right from the design phase of the Collaborative CPS. Another challenge is to define how different constituents of the Collaborative CPS are interrelated.

In this work, we address these two challenges. Thus, the main research question guiding the work is:

What could be a suitable set of models and organizational structures to support the design of increasingly complex and evolving CCPSs?

However, the current work addresses only some aspects of the general question formulated above. Thus, we can formulate the guiding research sub-questions for this particular paper as:

What could be a suitable upper ontology to represent the service-centric model of a CCPS?

What can be a set of reasoning mechanisms to support collaborative service composition in CCPS?

In the proposed solution, conflict resolution mechanisms are introduced as Prolog rules, and to map different Collaborative CPS concepts we provide an ontology covering the identified critical aspects. A prototype development is then discussed.

2 Contribution to Digitalization and Virtualization

Digitalization can be defined as the process of applying digital technologies [7] and is often interlinked with other terms such as digitization and digital transformation. However, the digitization term is more specifically used to describe the process of moving from analogue to digital data representation, while digital transformation is often seen as process of "restructuring economies, institutions and society on a system level" [8]. The notion of digital transformation can be also applied at the technological level addressing the evolution of legacy systems [9], i.e., the effects of digitalization on characteristics and performance of existing systems. In the context of our work, digitalization is considered as a corner stone due to the need to address the integration of the designed system with other important drivers of digitalization, such as Machine Learning and Automated Reasoning in general.

In this regard virtualization can be seen as an important part of the digitalization process. The notion of virtualization refers to a set of technologies enabling abstraction of underlying resources, while providing a logical view of resources [5]. Implementation of virtualization technologies can significantly improve the performance, facilitate system evolution, and improve system management through representing physical resources in more suitable form for processing. This paper addresses some aspects of virtualization, namely logical representation of physical resources. In this case, physical resources are, for instance, sensors and actuators and services are their logical representations. Virtualization of a CPS can be expressed at various complexity levels, from simple approaches where only a small part of the physical world is depicted, to more complex approaches or digital twins, providing a high level of computational and graphical identity of a CPS or a process [6]. This work contributes to this complex perspective.

3 Design Framework for the Proposed Solution

The proposed solution is based on the Collaborative CPS design framework previously described in [13]. The framework includes three pillars: (i) Application Domain, (ii) CCPS Design, (iii) Knowledge Base, as inspired by the design science research paradigm. The application domain delivers all relevant information about the domain, such as spaces, users, roles, physical environment peculiarities, etc., where the designed system is going to be deployed. This information is derived from the domain specific scenario and is used as an input for the Collaborative CPS design phase.

During the design phase, the input information from the Application Domain is formalized to create a virtual abstraction of the physical environment. During this stage a designer can form the future system from the available functional building blocks. The process of formalization is supported through ontologies and taxonomies stored within the Knowledge Base. For instance, taxonomies can represent the details of a specific application domain, so that the designer can select the appropriate one, allowing the design tool to stay domain agnostic. The rules, available from the Knowledge Base, specify many aspects of the system behavior, for instance determining the conflict resolution or service composition principles. Moreover, the formalized models of key concepts to be used in the Collaborative CPS are available in the Knowledge Base. In terms of practical implementation, we adopted the following tools: Python environment for the Collaborative CPS design phase, Neo4j graphical database and Prolog engine for the Knowledge Base implementation. The Collaborative CPS design framework is illustrated below (Fig. 1):

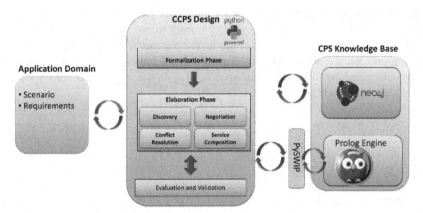

Fig. 1. Collaborative CPS design framework

The aforementioned tools were selected due to a set of reasons. First the Prolog engine provides powerful querying and reasoning capabilities and the PySWIP library allows for querying from within a Python program. Python is a suitable environment for the Collaborative CPS design pillar, enabling simple integration of various functional modules. And finally, the Neo4j, that is a graph-oriented database, is suitable to store different taxonomies, as well as to provide functionalities to track and define the ties between different components of the designed system. In other words, the graph-based approach allows identifying the strength of connections between the different nodes. For instance, during the operation phase, different devices can support a composed service for a limited time, so that they are connected and every time they build a coalition with the same devices the value of connection will change/increase.

4 Ontology

Ontologies are helpful for a wide variety of tasks in the process of CPS design. One example is the task of IoT/CPS system's configuration at the system level [10]. In the mentioned publication, the ontology proposed by the authors represents the structure or main concepts of sensor configuration mechanisms implemented in the CASCoM solution. This ontology, however, is purely focused on the sensor configuration tasks, without tackling the actuators and only slightly touching the high-level abstraction aspects.

Independently of various forms and types, ontologies include a vocabulary of concepts with definitions and the structure on how these concepts are interrelated, limiting the possible interpretations of the concepts in the modeled area [12]. In other words, the general characteristics specific to every ontology are: the vocabulary of concepts that are explicitly defined and the way they are formed into a connected graph. For the specific area of Collaborative CPS design, an ontology addressing the core concepts and relationships among them can be used by a designer to implement the system's layout. This allows for the designer to be focused on the system's functionality and service design, rather than on implementation of basic building blocks supporting the above mentioned process.

In our ontology we intentionally ignore some data processing aspects, such as, for instance, measurement accuracy or quality in order to not overload the ontology, but still be able to demonstrate how the high-level concepts wrap up lower-level details including sensors, actuators, state, etc. Another significant issue with many Ontologies is the problem that they are too domain specific [11]. In the proposed Ontology we tried to stay domain agnostic to some extent (Fig. 2).

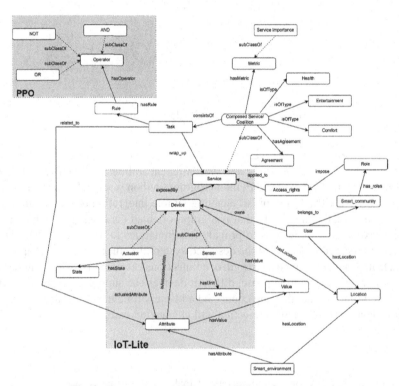

Fig. 2. Excerpt of a collaborative CPS service ontology

The ontology building process is partially based on the approach described in [19]. The first step implies the definition of terminology characterizing the observed domain. During the next step the analysis of available ontologies that, for instance, are developed and provided by W3C, is accomplished. The following step involves definition of the textual description for the terms selected during the first step or the import of the textual descriptions for the terms used from the W3C ontologies. On the next stage the domain terms that have parent-child (subClassOf) relations are organized in a Taxonomy, similarly to the ISA (is-a) hierarchy. Followed by parthood or excretion of meronymy to establish connections of complex terms to their sub-components. Finally, the last step includes ontology composition.

The proposed Ontology – Collaborative CPS Service Ontology (**CCSO**) – is an ontology explicitly identifying the aspects intrinsic to the process of collaborative service establishment in a CPS ecosystem. The high-level concepts of the ontology are the Smart Environment and the Smart Community. The Smart Environment is the abstraction addressing the technical aspects of the designed system that is used to describe the surrounding enriched with sensing, actuating, and computing capabilities with increased contextual awareness and extended interaction capabilities [16]. The Smart Community, on the other hand, is the abstraction defining the group of human users sharing common interests, preferences, and resources that are having a common social bond. The proposed ontology also includes elements of other well-known ontologies, such as Privacy Preference Ontology (PPO) [17] and IoT-lite [15]. The PPO contains the notion of "Operator" [17] that can be used for the rules design of the planned services. Another ontology used is the IoT-lite which offers, for instance, the notions of the sensor, actuator and device [15] – the underlying definitions for the Smart Environment. Thus, the IoT-Lite is the IoT specific ontology for managing data that covers some important low-level aspects of the design process.

The CCSO ontology considers the following aspects:

- Assuming that every "*Device*" provides a "*Service*", thus device and service are related.
- "*Device*" can be of several types (mostly sensors and actuators, however, not only)
- "*Sensor*" measures certain "*Value*" within the environment.
- The "*Value*" is associated to "*Attribute*". According to [15], "*Attribute*" is some property of an object (e.g. temperature, humidity, etc.)
- On the other hand, "*Actuator*" has a "*State*" (e.g., on/off, open/closed, etc.).
- Both "*Value*" and the "*State*" are related to "*Attribute*".
- A particular case of object that has an "*Attribute*" is the "*Smart Environment*".
- "*Smart Environment*" has an associated physical "Location".
- Moreover, every "*User*" has certain "*Location*" within the system (that might be changed).
- Every "*Device*" is owned by a "*User*".
- Every "*User*" belongs to a "Smart *Community*", within which he/she has a "Role".
- Every "*Role*" affects the "*Access right*" in certain way.
- "*Access right*" affects the access to a "*Service*".
- A set of "Services" can be combined into a "*Composed Service/Coalition*"
- "*Composed Service/Coalition*" is of a certain type (e.g., Health, Entertainment, Comfort).
- Moreover, it possesses a set of "*Metrics*" to assess the service.

– It also has a set of *"Tasks"*. The notion of a "Task" has the meaning similar to the one of the business process [18], since the business process defines the way the "Service" is performed. "Task" has also a set of associated "Rules".

For the next stage, we are planning to elaborate in more details the willingness of devices to collaborate. The idea is that devices/assets have two operating modes – the so called "slave" mode, when the user/admin tells them what to do and the "free reasoning" mode when devices with the help of reasoning rules can discover the new assets and negotiate possible coalition formation. For the second case there is a need of ontologies that will define how the device/asset has to proceed to form a coalition. In the design mode, these ontologies can be updated or extended on demand.

5 Rule-Based Reasoning

The reasoning component is the crucial part of the proposed solution. Reasoning mechanisms are responsible for many tasks, such as service discovery, service composition, and conflict resolution. To implement the reasoning part, a decision was made to use the Prolog engine as a powerful reasoning tool. Prolog is used through the PySWIP interface, enabling Prolog querying from within Python programs. Moreover, Python is used as a bridging point between the designer interface, Neo4j graph-oriented database and directly Prolog.

The rules can be used for addressing the reasoning challenges related to various CPS/IoT aspects. One example is the implementation of attribute-based access control (ABAC) model to manage the access in publish-subscribe networks based on MQTT [20]. These authors also consider the conflict resolution policy relying on XACML standard that provides several possibilities for conflict resolution (deny overrides, permit overrides, etc.). The limitation of their approach is that the authors do not consider different user groups having different access rights. In [21] the authors use basic Prolog rules to retrieve the sensor values or acquire data or conditions of the physical devices. The authors mention the conflict resolution module as a part of the future work. Different from the mentioned approaches, we specifically cover the issue of service composition trying to provide a high level technology-agnostic ecosystem for services management with conflict resolution mechanisms.

Concerning service composition, the rule-based approach is addressed in [22] where the authors provide a framework for service composition in assembly systems. The core idea of the framework relies on the notion of microservice implying that a service is represented as a collection of sub-components called microservices. The authors consider that the IoT-compliant assembly workers exposing their properties as microservices. However, the proposed approach is not adapted to the automatic or semi-automatic service discovery and composition. In [23] the authors allocate several stages of the service composition process, namely: (i) encapsulation of all resources as services, (ii) formulation or capture of the user demand, and (iii) bridging the customer demand with existing service or provide the optimal service composition.

The goal of the proposed design framework is to allow the designer not only to define the physical layout or structure of the system, but also to import and embed the corresponding reasoning mechanisms from the Knowledge Base to the design advisory or supervision component of the designed system. These reasoning mechanisms are delivered as functional ready-to-use blocks that will support the operational phase. One of these reasoning mechanisms is the service discovery, which serves the goal of bridging the user's demand and the proposition or suggesting a configuration for the service composition. The main idea here is to find the devices, e.g., sensors and/or actuators, that might satisfy the user needs that are formulated as user preferences. Below is a code snippet illustrating the discovery mechanisms:

```
from pyswip import Prolog
prolog = Prolog()
prolog.assertz("sensor(sens_1, temperature, 20, room_1, john_smith)")
prolog.assertz("sensor(sens_1, temperature, 20, room_1, john_smith)")
prolog.assertz("sensor(sens_2, humidity, 50, room_1, jane_smith)")
prolog.assertz("actuator(act_1,   temperature,   [increase,  decrease,
maintain], room_1, john_smith)")
prolog.assertz("actuator(act_3,    humidity,    [increase,   decrease,
maintain], room_1, john_smith)")
prolog.assertz("actuator(act_2,   temperature,   [increase,  decrease,
maintain], room_2, john_smith)")
prolog.assertz("preference(john_smith, temperature, 20)")
prolog.assertz("preference(john_smith, humidity, 50)")
prolog.assertz("preference(jane_smith, temperature, 25)")
prolog.assertz("user(john_smith, room_1)")
prolog.assertz("user(jane_smith, room_1)")
prolog.assertz("find_service(User, [Sensor, Actuator]) :- user(User,
Smart_Environment),sensor(Sensor,Feature,_,Smart_Environment,_),actua
tor(Actuator,Feature,_,Smart_Environment,_),preference(User,Feature,_
)")
prolog.query("find_service(%s, [X,Y])")
user = 'john_smith'
seen = set()
result = []
for soln in prolog.query("find_service(%s, [X,Y])" % (user)):
    if soln not in result:
        result.append(soln)
```

By combining different reasoning mechanisms the designer can create a kind of a sequence that will be the part of the supervision component of the designed system. For instance, such sequence can have the following structure: firstly, discover devices with required capabilities secondly check the discovered devices for possible conflicts and then accomplish the service composition. In this way, during the system's development stage, the designer defines the structure and the order of capillary reasoning blocks execution through sequences establishment. For instance, the above-mentioned code allows the system to retrieve the sensors and actuators that are coping with the same attribute or parameter, are in the same location, and can satisfy the user need formulated within the Prolog fact "preference". It is worth mentioning, that a set of user's preferences can be activated automatically. For instance, considering a Smart Home scenario, if a user enters a room, the temperature parameter can be automatically adjusted based on the "preference" field. This example serves the goal of demonstration that the system designer gets the discovery mechanism from the knowledge base without the need to additionally implement it. The discovery reasoning mechanism is part of another tool used to launch the negotiation process, if, for instance, the devices have different owners or are used by another user. After devices with required capabilities are discovered, conflict check mechanisms that need to find contradictions in users' needs and preferences that are in the same Smart Environment are launched. For this purpose, we consider the following code as a part of a complex conflict check reasoning mechanism:

```
check_task(Task,                        Bag)                        :-
task(Task,Sensor,_,_,Actuator,_,_,_,Location),        findall(Name,
(task(Name,Sensor,_,_,Actuator,_,_,_,Location), Name \= Task), Bag).

no_conflict(Task,H)   :-   check_task(Task,  Bag),  member(H,  Bag),
task(H,_,_,Tar_Value,_,_,Tar_Action,_,_),task(Task,_,_,Ini_Value,_,_,
Ini_Action,_,_), Ini_Value == Tar_Value, Ini_Action == Tar_Action.
```

The "Task" specifies the flow of actions required to provide a service addressing specific user need. In the case of composed service, the task has also the orchestration functions of different sub-services that are comprised in the composed service. Thus, the Task identifies the parameter/attribute that needs to be changed, as well as the required actuator action. As an example of actuator action – a thermostat example, which can increase the temperature, if it is lower than the one identified in the user preference, decrease if it is higher or maintain it, if it is around the preferred one. Thus, the first part of the code checks if there are tasks manipulating the same parameter and the second one defines the tasks that have no conflict. If the users have the same preferences there is no conflict, even if the users have different access rights and roles.

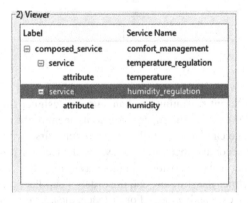

Fig. 3. Composed service viewer

The Fig. 3 demonstrates the part of the prototype, namely the viewer displaying the structure of the composed services. The designer can establish a composed service through combination of different sub-services. The idea is that every composed service consists of a set of capillary services managing various attributes. In this example, the composed service "comfort_management" consists of the "temperature_regulation" and "humidity_regulation" sub-services. Every sub-services will subsequently have an attribute (humidity, temperature, etc.), which later, during the operation phase, will be connected with the real world devices delivering capabilities related to attribute. The proposed framework should assist the CCPS designer in building the system's structure and the logical core of the system. The logical core, in this context, contains a set of reasoning modules composed of reasoning rules. The framework enables the virtualization, i.e., abstraction from the low level, when the physical assets with corresponding functionality are managed as virtual entities (like digital twins). Contrary to some mentioned approaches, the proposed framework is intended to be technology agnostic, possessing some general reasoning modules that can be applied to various application domains. The next steps planned include the enriching of the reasoning core with further reasoning mechanisms and to consider the semi-automatic service composition during the operational phase. However, the focus is on the design phase and the tools that can be helpful for the CCPS designer to provide customized solutions.

6 Conclusion

This work is a logical continuation of previous works addressing some practical aspects of the Collaborative CPS design framework. The rising need to improve the digitalization of the complex systems affecting the digital transformation, forces to take the digitalization related challenges into consideration. In this regards, complex CPS composed of different heterogeneous constituents has to be designed in a certain way, when different mechanisms for services composition, conflict resolution, service discovery, etc., are stipulated. These reasoning mechanisms are the part of the supervision component of the designed system that will be executed during the operation phase. The designer is able to combine these mechanisms to develop a supervision component supporting the designed system. We provide some examples of the reasoning mechanisms devoted to service discovery and conflict check implemented in Prolog. These will be available for the designer from the Knowledge Base of the framework. Moreover, a collaborative service ontology is provided, indicating core concepts and their interrelations. Finally, the part of the CCPS design framework to construct the composed services was provided.

As a part of further work, we are developing rules for service composition that will include coalition formation and dissolution mechanisms, as well as introducing some domain-specific taxonomies that will be stored and available from Neo4j.

Acknowledgments. This work was supported in part by the Portuguese FCT foundation through the program UIDB/00066/2020.

References

1. Lasi, H., Fettke, P., Kemper, H.-G., Feld, T., Hoffmann, M.: Industry 4.0. Bus. Inf. Syst. Eng. **6**(4), 239–242 (2014). https://doi.org/10.1007/s12599-014-0334-4
2. Frank, A.G., Dalenogare, L.S., Ayala, N.F.: Industry 4.0 technologies: implementation patterns in manufacturing companies. Int. J. Prod. Econ. **210**, 15–26 (2019). https://doi.org/10.1016/j.ijpe.2019.01.004

3. Nazarenko, A.A., Camarinha-Matos, L.M.: Towards collaborative cyber-physical systems. In: 2017 International Young Engineers Forum (YEF-ECE), Almada, pp. 12–17 (2017). https://doi.org/10.1109/YEF-ECE.2017.7935633
4. Barata, J., Camarinha-Matos, L.M.: Coalitions of manufacturing components for shop floor agility - the CoBaSA architecture. Int. J. Network. Virtual Org. **2**, 50–77 (2003). https://doi.org/10.1504/IJNVO.2003.003518
5. Yu, F.R., Liu, J., He, Y., Si, P., Zhang, Y.: Virtualization for distributed ledger technology (vDLT). IEEE Access **6**, 25019–25028 (2018). https://doi.org/10.1109/ACCESS.2018.2829141
6. Martins, H.C., Neves, C.: Shop floor virtualization and industry 4.0. In: 2019 IEEE International Conference on Autonomous Robot Systems and Competitions (ICARSC), pp. 1–6 (2019). https://doi.org/10.1109/ICARSC.2019.8733657
7. Ritter, T., Pedersen, C.L.: Digitization capability and the digitalization of business models in business-to-business firms: past, present, and future. Ind. Mark. Manag. **86**, 180–190 (2020). https://doi.org/10.1016/j.indmarman.2019.11.019
8. Rachinger, M., Rauter, R., Müller, C., Vorraber, W., Schirgi, E.: Digitalization and its influence on business model innovation. J. Manuf. Technol. Manag. **30**(8), 1143–1160 (2018). https://doi.org/10.1108/jmtm-01-2018-0020
9. Osório, A.L., Camarinha-Matos, L.M., Dias, T., Gonçalves, C., Tavares, J.: Open and collaborative micro services in digital transformation. In: Camarinha-Matos, L.M., Boucher, X., Afsarmanesh, H. (eds.) PRO-VE 2021. IAICT, vol. 629, pp. 393–402. Springer, Cham (2021). https://doi.org/10.1007/978-3-030-85969-5_36
10. Perera, C., Zaslavsky, A., Compton, M., Christen P., Georgakopoulos, D.: Semantic-driven configuration of internet of things middleware. In: 2013 Ninth International Conference on Semantics, Knowledge and Grids, pp. 66–73 (2013). https://doi.org/10.1109/SKG.2013.9
11. Agarwal, R., et al.: Unified IoT ontology to enable interoperability and federation of testbeds. In: 2016 IEEE 3rd World Forum on Internet of Things (WF-IoT), pp. 70–75 (2016). https://doi.org/10.1109/WF-IoT.2016.7845470
12. Hildebrandt, C., et al.: Ontology building for cyber-physical systems: application in the manufacturing domain. IEEE Trans. Autom. Sci. Eng. **17**(3), 1266–1282 (2020). https://doi.org/10.1109/TASE.2020.2991777
13. Nazarenko, A.A., Camarinha-Matos, L.M.: The role of digital twins in collaborative cyber-physical systems. In: Camarinha-Matos, L.M., Farhadi, N., Lopes, F., Pereira, H. (eds.) DoCEIS 2020. IAICT, vol. 577, pp. 191–205. Springer, Cham (2020). https://doi.org/10.1007/978-3-030-45124-0_18
14. Gonçalves, C., Osório, A.L., Camarinha-Matos, L.M., Dias, T., Tavares, J.: A collaborative cyber-physical microservices platform – the SITL-IoT case. In: Camarinha-Matos, L.M., Boucher, X., Afsarmanesh, H. (eds.) PRO-VE 2021. IAICT, vol. 629, pp. 411–420. Springer, Cham (2021). https://doi.org/10.1007/978-3-030-85969-5_38
15. IoT-Lite Ontology. https://www.w3.org/Submission/iot-lite/#term_Attribute
16. Nazarenko, A.A., Camarinha-Matos, L.M.: Basis for an approach to design collaborative cyber-physical systems. In: Camarinha-Matos, L.M., Almeida, R., Oliveira, J. (eds.) DoCEIS 2019. IAICT, vol. 553, pp. 193–205. Springer, Cham (2019). https://doi.org/10.1007/978-3-030-17771-3_16
17. Sanchez, O.R., Torre, I., Knijnenburg, B.P.: Semantic-based privacy settings negotiation and management. Futur. Gener. Comput. Syst. **111**, 879–898 (2020). https://doi.org/10.1016/j.future.2019.10.024
18. Camarinha-Matos, L.M., Afsarmanesh, H., Oliveira, A.I., Ferrada, F.: Cloud-based collaborative business services provision. In: Hammoudi, S., Cordeiro, J., Maciaszek, L.A., Filipe, J. (eds.) ICEIS 2013. LNBIP, vol. 190, pp. 366–384. Springer, Cham (2014). https://doi.org/10.1007/978-3-319-09492-2_22

19. De Nicola, A., Missikoff, M.: A lightweight methodology for rapid ontology engineering. Commun. ACM **59**(3), 79–86 (2016). https://doi.org/10.1145/2818359
20. Gabillon, A., Gallier, R., Bruno, E.: Access Controls for IoT Networks. SN Computer Science **1**(1), 1–13 (2019). https://doi.org/10.1007/s42979-019-0022-z
21. Bohé, I., Willocx, M., Lapon, J., Naessens, V.: Towards low-effort development of advanced IoT applications. In: Proceedings of the 8th International Workshop on Middleware and Applications for the Internet of Things (M4IoT 2021), pp. 1–7. Association for Computing Machinery, New York (2021). https://doi.org/10.1145/3493369.3493600
22. Thramboulidis, K., Vachtsevanou, D.C., Kontou, I.: CPuS-IoT: a cyber-physical microservice and IoT-based framework for manufacturing assembly systems. Annu. Rev. Control. (2019). https://doi.org/10.1016/j.arcontrol.2019.03.0
23. Xue, X., Wang, S., Lu, B.: Manufacturing service composition method based on networked collaboration mode. J. Netw. Comput. Appl. **59**, 28–38 (2016). https://doi.org/10.1016/j.jnca.2015.05.003

Hippo-CPS: Verification of Boundedness, Safeness and Liveness of Petri Net-Based Cyber-Physical Systems

Marcin Wojnakowski[✉], Mateusz Popławski, Remigiusz Wiśniewski,
and Grzegorz Bazydło

Institute of Control and Computation Engineering, University of Zielona Góra,
65-516 Zielona Góra, Poland
{m.wojnakowski,m.poplawski,r.wisniewski,
g.bazydlo}@issi.uz.zgora.pl

Abstract. The paper describes the Hippo-CPS tool in the verification of Petri net-based cyber-physical systems. In particular, verification of the key properties such as boundedness, safeness and liveness is presented and discussed. Hippo-CPS allows for analysis of the control part of the CPS with the set of various algorithms (such as reachability tree exploration or place invariants computation) giving the designer an opportunity to select the most suitable technique. Each method is based on the theoretical background (with adequate algorithms, theorems, and proofs, described in other Authors' works). Moreover, the efficiency and effectiveness of the presented methods were verified experimentally.

Keywords: Petri nets · Boundedness · Safeness · Liveness · Verification · Analysis · Cyber-physical systems

1 Introduction

Petri net is a fruitful modelling technique used for the graphical specification of broadly defined control systems [1, 2]. It is supported by methods toward verification, validation, and analysis that enable checking the correctness and reliability of the prototyped system [3–6]. The broad possibilities of formal verification of Petri net-based systems [7] have formed them popular in numerous areas of life, including embedded systems [8], manufacturing systems [9, 10], management systems [11], logic controllers [12], smart homes [13], transport management [14] and cyber-physical system (CPS) [15]. The latter consolidates computational and physical components [16]. Industry 4.0 could benefit from CPS concept [17]. CPS emphasizes the interactions between control (cyber) and physical parts of the system. The Petri net-based approach focuses on the modelling of the control part of the CPS [18]. Moreover, this approach applies the system analysis methods at the earlier specification stage, which permits to reduce the time and cost of prototyping the entire control system [19]. The main properties of CPS described by

© IFIP International Federation for Information Processing 2022
Published by Springer Nature Switzerland AG 2022
L. M. Camarinha-Matos (Ed.): DoCEIS 2022, IFIP AICT 649, pp. 74–82, 2022.
https://doi.org/10.1007/978-3-031-07520-9_7

Petri nets are boundedness, safeness, and liveness [2, 4–6, 18, 19]. A bounded Petri net ensures that the model has a finite number of reachable states in the system [20]. A safe model establishes the behaviour of the control part [21, 22]. The liveness is responsible for the absence of deadlocks in the system [23]. In addition, several design techniques are dependent on algorithms that require bounded, safe, or live Petri nets as their input, e.g., [18, 24, 25].

There are two wide-known analysis approaches that allow examining the boundedness, safeness, and liveness of Petri nets. The first one is based on the reachability tree exploration [26], while the second one applies the methodology of linear algebra for instance by calculating place invariants [27]. However, both techniques have serious limitations, since the number of reachable states in the reachability tree or invariants can be exponential [7], which in practice means that results may not be found within the assumed time [5, 6]. It is claimed that the method is not efficient in that case.

This paper describes the modules of the Hippo-CPS tool for efficient and effective analysis of boundedness, safeness, and liveness properties. The main contributions can be summarized as follows:

- proposition and description the module of the Hippo-CPS tool aimed at the liveness verification of the Petri net-based CPS;
- proposition and description two (alternate) modules of the Hippo-CPS tool aimed at the safeness verification the Petri net-based CPS;
- proposition and description two (alternate) modules of the Hippo-CPS tool aimed at the boundedness verification of the Petri net-based CPS;
- the presented modules are based on the authors' algorithms;
- the efficiency and effectiveness of the presented modules were verified experimentally with the set of 242 test-modules (benchmarks).

2   Technological Innovation for Digitalization and Virtualization

The ongoing industrial revolution 4.0 is dominated by smart and intelligent devices. This is the effect of the processes currently taking places like an intense digitalization and digital transformation of all sectors of society. This transformation and digitalization are supported by the development of efficient, flexible, agile, and sustainable solutions. The cyber-physical systems also will play a big role in these processes of the 4th industrial revolution [17], because they are designed in terms of efficiency, flexibility, and low energy consumption. On the other hand, the modern CPSs are very often complex, concurrent, and hierarchical (modular), and designing their control parts without efficient and effective methods and tools is nowadays rather impossible.

The Hippo-CPS tool presented in the paper attempts to fulfil these requirements. It offers the modules for the analysis of boundedness, safeness, and liveness of Petri net (used for describing the control part of the CPS). The implemented innovative analysis methods are efficient (in some cases even sixty times faster than the classic method) and effective (i.e., could obtain results for the benchmarks, where the popular methods were not able to complete the task within one hour).

3 Related Tools

There are many tools that permit for analysis of the boundedness, safeness, and liveness properties of the Petri net-based system. Let us present selected ones from 25 tools examined by us, that can be applied to the verification of the Petri net properties.

IOPT-Tools [28, 29] is one of the most functional and well-developed software for creating, editing, and analysing Petri nets. The simulator component allows for performing advanced manual analysis of the model. IOPT-Tools can also automatically analyse typical Petri net properties such as boundness, safeness, and occurrence of deadlocks, but the verification of the net properties is based only on the state-space exploration. The limitation of the tool is that the broader analytical research of the model is impossible like place invariants coverage. Hence, the checking properties of some Petri net models cannot be accomplished efficiently.

PIPE2 is an open-source Petri net editor and analysis software. An advantage of the tool is open access to the source code and the possibility to develop own analysis modules or edit existing ones. The tool enables, among others, verification of boundedness, safeness, deadlocks occurrence, determination of the Petri net class, computation of place and transitions invariants, and determination of siphons. Furthermore, PIPE generates a graphical representation of the reachability graph. On the other hand, the limitations of the functionalities are the lack of the strict liveness analysis, and problems with the state-space analysis module. Using the latter feature causes the exponential computation, which for relatively small models (about twenty places and transitions) can end with application error or suspension of the program.

CPN Tools is a common system for creating, editing, and analysing Petri net models. It is not only limited to coloured Petri nets but also applicable to other classes of Petri nets. The latest version (4.0.1) of the tool was released 7 years ago. Using the program could be quite complicated for a new user, and probably without studying extensive documentation, performing the simulation or analysis of the modelled Petri net is impossible. However, the documentation and user guide are available on the official website of the tool.

Yasper is a simple graphical tool with a Petri net simulation module. The graphical user interface (GUI) appears to be friendly and accessible. However, the tool has not been developed since 2005. Moreover, a major limitation of the program is the lack of Petri net analysis methods apart from the manual simulator feature.

JSARP is an interesting tool for the analysis and simulation of Petri net models. The program has a very intuitive and friendly GUI. The simulator allows for a graphical indication of the fired transitions. The analysis module based on the reachability graph provides information about the boundness and liveness of a designed Petri net. Unfortunately, the tool has a very limited ability to analyse the Petri net properties, limited only to the boundness and liveness.

There are more Petri net tools, but unfortunately, many of them have not been developed for years, e.g., PAPETRI, PROD, PETRUCHIO. Some tools were only an academic application of novel methods and were abandoned after the projects ended. However, it is pleasing that new tools are constantly being developed and that modelling using Petri nets and their analysis is a popular topic in the literature.

4 Hippo-CPS

Hippo-CPS consists of several separate modules supporting designers in the designing process of concurrent systems specified by Petri nets. The tool was launched in 2005 and since that it has been constantly developed. Now, it is mainly aimed at cyber-physical systems (especially at design and verification of their control part), but not only limited to them. This paper is focused on the proprietary algorithms that are included within Hippo-CPS. In particular, verification of boundedness, safeness, and liveness are the main objectives of the work. The main bottlenecks of the existing techniques refer to the computational complexity of algorithms. Exact methods guarantee optimal results, but they require examining all the possible cases. Therefore, in the worst case, the solution may be not found in the assumed time. On the other hand, approximate algorithms are able to find results, but the solution may not be optimal. It means that analysis methods balance between efficiency (run-time of algorithms) and effectiveness (remaining results). Hippo-CPS permits for verification of the main properties with the application of alternative methods (exact, approximate). Let us describe them in more detail.

4.1 Boundedness Analysis

The boundedness of a Petri net can be verified within Hippo-CPS by two algorithms. The first one is based on the construction of a tree of reachable states in the system. The method searches for an unbounded place to oppose that the tested model is bounded. The idea is strictly based on the definition of boundedness, that is, if there exists one unbounded place (in any marking), the whole Petri net is unbounded by the definition [6]. Therefore, the state space generation process is interrupted once the unbounded place is found. This is done by acquiring places marked by ω according to Murata's tree generation algorithm. Furthermore, the size of the tree is reduced and hence the whole computational time is reduced. Nevertheless, the method is exponential in the general case. However, applied reductions may heavily influence the run-time of the algorithm. Results of experiments showed that the technique is effective for 223 benchmarks (out of 242). This means that for 92% of all tested cases the method was able to find a solution. For the remaining benchmarks, the run-time of the algorithm exceeded the assumed time (which was set to 1 h).

The second method for the boundedness analysis utilizes the linear algebra technique. The applied technique computes the reduced set of place invariants (p-invariants) in the analysed Petri net-based system, according to the algorithm shown in [20]. In opposite to the technique based on the reachability tree, computation of the reduced set of p-invariants is an approximate method. Therefore, the algorithm is oriented mainly on the efficiency (run-time), but it has a strict limitation. According to the theorem shown in [26], a Petri net-based system is bounded if it is covered by place invariants. However, the lack of coverage of a Petri net by place invariants does not imply unboundedness. It should be noted that obtaining all p-invariants is exponential in the general case. Therefore, the utilized method allows computation of a reduced set (just required for the coverage) of place invariants [20]. Performed experiments confirmed the efficiency of the method. The results were achieved for all examined benchmarks. However, in the case of 28 benchmarks (which states 11.6% of all examined tests), the algorithm indicated that the system is not covered by p-invariants, and thus we do not know if the system is bounded or not. In such cases, additional verification is required (for example with the application of reachability tree). Nevertheless, let us clearly underline that this particular method is oriented on the preliminary analysis of the system, and the results are obtained much faster than in the other, similar techniques.

4.2 Safeness Analysis

Examination of the safeness property can be performed with the Hippo-CPS in two ways. The first technique is based on the reachability tree. The algorithm consecutively searches for the unsafe places in the Petri net. Once such a place is found, the method terminates with the information that the system is not safe. The applied technique is based on the theoretical algorithm, shown in [21]. The experimental verification indicated that the method was able to find the solution for 218 tested cases. This means that it is effective for 90% of all examined benchmarks.

The second approach applies place invariants and further computation of the state machine components (SMCs) cover in the analysed system. In particular, the method firstly searches for the subsequent place invariants and examines whether they form proper SMCs (according to the algorithm shown in [22]). Since the technique is approximate, it is aimed at efficiency. Indeed, the experimental results confirmed that the method was able to compute results for all tested cases. However, similarly to the technique presented in the previous subsection, the method is not effective in the case of systems that are not covered by SMCs [22]. There were 31 (18.8%) such benchmarks in the performed experiments.

4.3 Liveness Analysis

Liveness is the third main property (along with boundedness and safeness) that is very often verified in the Petri net-based system. Hippo-CPS offers a technique that is based on the reachability tree analysis. However, let us underline that in opposite to the boundedness and safeness verification of the system, examination of liveness is much more complicated. First of all, a full state space of the system ought to be generated. Next, according to the guidelines shown in [30], verification of liveness is determined by the boundedness of the Petri net. In the other words, the method is effective for bounded systems. In particular, the analysis procedure consists of the exploration of the generated reachability tree, starting from the final state and finishing at the initial state with simultaneous checking, whether all the transitions are present on that path [23]. The number of states increases exponentially, and this is the main bottleneck of the method. Experimental results showed that the method is effective for 223 benchmarks (out of 242). This means that the algorithm was able to find the result (indicate whether the system is live or not) for 92% of all tested cases.

4.4 Case-Study Example

Let us show the functionality of the presented Hippo-CPS tool by an example. Figure 1 shows a cyber-physical system describing a coffee machine for independent making a caffeinated and decaffeinated drink with four shared resources. Two kinds of coffee can be made in one big machine (started by pressing button *b1* or *b2*, respectively). There are four shared resources: (1) a grinder that grinds the coffee beans, (2) a nozzle that prepares hot water and pushes it with high pressure into one of the directions, (3) a milk nozzle to troth the milk (make a milk foam), and (4) a chocolate dispenser that sprinkles the chocolate on top of the drink. The prepared drink is taken by the customer before starting a new one.

That real-life example was analysed by all the algorithms shown in Sect. 4. The reachability tree analysis showed that the system is bounded and safe. The results were achieved within 35.780 ms and 36.216 ms (for boundedness and safeness verification, respectively). Moreover, the same CPS was examined with the use of linear algebra. Hippo-CPS confirmed previous results, by finding six p-invariants that cover the Petri net. Moreover, six SMCs cover the system. This means that the system is bounded and safe. However, in opposition to the reachability tree analysis, the run-time of algorithms was much quicker. In particular, the solutions were found after 0.313 ms (boundedness), and 0.338 ms (safeness). Let us underline that such results confirm theoretical assumptions since approximate algorithms were faster than exact ones. Nevertheless, both types of methods reached the same results: the system is bounded and safe. Finally, the liveness of the modelled coffee machine was checked. The applied Hippo-CPS technique finished in 38.906 ms with the information that the system is live. Concluding, the verification of the system was completed successfully. The modelled cyber-physical system is live, bounded, and safe.

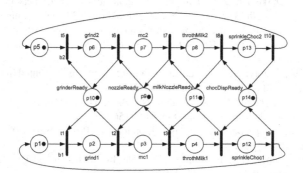

Fig. 1. A cyber-physical system Petri net-based specification real-life example.

5 Conclusions

Verification of the main properties of the Petri net-based systems (especially control parts of the CPSs) with the application of the Hippo-CPS tool was presented in the paper. In particular, verification of boundedness, safeness, and liveness was described and discussed in detail. It should be exposed that Hippo-CPS offers an alternative analysis of particular properties (boundedness, safeness), giving the designer an opportunity to choose the most suitable algorithm. Results of experiments confirmed the efficiency and effectiveness of the presented methods. The exact algorithms were effective, but due to the exponential complexity were not able to compute results for all tested cases. On the other hand, approximate techniques were efficient and always founded solutions. However, in the case of systems not covered by p-invariants (or SMCs), the result is insufficient, and additional analysis is required.

The main limitation refers to the verification of liveness. Although there are alternative techniques for boundedness and safeness examination, Hippo-CPS currently offers only one method for liveness analysis. Therefore, the future work includes enhancement of the tool by other mechanisms oriented on the liveness verification of the Petri net-based CPS. Moreover, it is planned to perform researchers oriented on the particular classes of the Petri net.

Acknowledgements. This work is supported by the National Science Centre, Poland, under Grant number 2019/35/B/ST6/01683.

References

1. Zhu, Q., Zhou, M., Qiao, Y., Wu, N.: Petri net modeling and scheduling of a close-down process for time-constrained single-arm cluster tools. IEEE Trans. Syst. Man Cybern. Syst. **48**(3), 389–400 (2018). https://doi.org/10.1109/TSMC.2016.2598303
2. Girault, C., Valk, R.: Petri Nets for Systems Engineering: A Guide to Modeling, Verification, and Applications. Springer, Heidelberg (2003). https://doi.org/10.1007/978-3-662-05324-9.
3. Grobelna, I., Karatkevich, A.: Challenges in application of Petri nets in manufacturing systems. Electronics **10**(18), 2305 (2021). https://doi.org/10.3390/electronics10182305
4. Li, Z.: System modeling and control with resource-oriented Petri nets by NaiQi Wu and MengChu Zhou. Int. J. Prod. Res. **49**(21), 6585–6586 (2011). https://doi.org/10.1080/002 07543.2010.515415
5. Wiśniewski, R.: Prototyping of Concurrent Control Systems Implemented in FPGA Devices. Springer, Cham (2017). https://doi.org/10.1007/978-3-319-45811-3
6. Karatkevich, A.: Dynamic Analysis of Petri Net-Based Discrete Systems. Springer, Heidelberg (2007). https://doi.org/10.1007/978-3-540-71560-3
7. Murata, T.: Petri nets: properties, analysis and applications. Proc. IEEE **77**(4), 541–580 (1989). https://doi.org/10.1109/5.24143
8. Yakovlev, A., Gomes, L., Lavagno, L. (eds.): Hardware Design and Petri Nets. Springer, Cham (2000). https://doi.org/10.1007/978-1-4757-3143-9
9. Koh, I., DiCesare, F.: Transformation methods for generalized Petri nets and their applications to flexible manufacturing systems. In: [1990] Proceedings. Rensselaer's Second International Conference on Computer Integrated Manufacturing, pp. 364–371, May 1990. https://doi.org/ 10.1109/CIM.1990.128126
10. Kaid, H., Al-Ahmari, A., Li, Z., Davidrajuh, R.: Automatic supervisory controller for deadlock control in reconfigurable manufacturing systems with dynamic changes. Appl. Sci. **10**(15), 5270 (2020). https://doi.org/10.3390/app10155270
11. Aalst, W.M.P.: Workflow verification: finding control-flow errors using Petri-net-based techniques. In: van der Aalst, W., Desel, J., Oberweis, A. (eds.) Business Process Management. LNCS, vol. 1806, pp. 161–183. Springer, Heidelberg (2000). https://doi.org/10.1007/3-540-45594-9_11
12. Barkalov, A., Titarenko, L., Mielcarek, K.: Improving characteristics of LUT-based Mealy FSMs. AMCS **30**(4), 745–759 (2020). https://doi.org/10.34768/amcs-2020-0055

13. Shih, C.-S., Chou, J.-J., Reijers, N., Kuo, T.-W.: Designing CPS/IoT applications for smart buildings and cities. IET Cyber-Phys. Syst. Theory Appl. **1**(1), 3–12 (2016). https://doi.org/10.1049/iet-cps.2016.0025

14. Guo, Y., Hu, X., Hu, B., Cheng, J., Zhou, M., Kwok, R.Y.K.: Mobile cyber physical systems: current challenges and future networking applications. IEEE Access **6**, 12360–12368 (2018). https://doi.org/10.1109/ACCESS.2017.2782881

15. Wiśniewski, R., Bazydło, G., Szcześniak, P., Wojnakowski, M.: Petri net-based specification of cyber-physical systems oriented to control direct matrix converters with space vector modulation. IEEE Access **7**, 23407–23420 (2019). https://doi.org/10.1109/ACCESS.2019.2899316

16. Lee, E.A., Seshia, S.A.: Introduction to Embedded Systems: A Cyber-Physical Systems Approach, 2nd edn. The MIT Press, Cambridge (2016)

17. Lee, J., Bagheri, B., Kao, H.-A.: A cyber-physical systems architecture for Industry 4.0-based manufacturing systems. Manuf. Lett. **3**, 18–23 (2015). https://doi.org/10.1016/j.mfglet.2014.12.001

18. Grobelna, I., Wiśniewski, R., Wojnakowski, M.: Specification of cyber-physical systems with the application of interpreted nets. In: Proceedings of the IECON'19 - 45th Annual Conference of the IEEE Industrial Electronics Society, Lisbon, Portugal, pp. 5887–5891 (2019)

19. Li, B., Khlif-Bouassida, M., Toguyéni, A.: On–the–fly diagnosability analysis of bounded and unbounded labeled petri nets using verifier nets. Int. J. Appl. Math. Comput. Sci. **28**(2), 269–281 (2018). https://doi.org/10.2478/amcs-2018-0019

20. Wojnakowski, M., Wiśniewski, R.: Verification of the boundedness property in a Petri net-based specification of the control part of cyber-physical systems. In: Camarinha-Matos, L.M., Ferreira, P., Brito, G. (eds.) DoCEIS 2021. IAICT, vol. 626, pp. 83–91. Springer, Cham (2021). https://doi.org/10.1007/978-3-030-78288-7_8

21. Wojnakowski, M., Popławski, M., Wiśniewski, R., Bazydło, G.: Safeness analysis of petri net-based cyber-physical systems based on the linear algebra and parallel reductions. Presented at the 17th international conference of computational methods in sciences and engineering, Heraklion, Greece, September 2021

22. Wojnakowski, M., Wiśniewski, R., Bazydło, G., Popławski, M.: Analysis of safeness in a Petri net-based specification of the control part of cyber-physical systems. AMCS **31**(4), 647–657 (2021). https://doi.org/10.34768/amcs-2021-0045

23. Popławski, M., Wojnakowski, M., Bazydło, G., Wiśniewski, R.: Reachability tree in liveness analysis of petri net-based cyber-physical systems. Presented at the 17th international conference of computational methods in sciences and engineering, Heraklion, Greece, September 2021

24. Badouel, E., Bernardinello, L., Darondeau, P.: Polynomial algorithms for the synthesis of bounded nets. In: Mosses, P.D., Nielsen, M., Schwartzbach, M.I. (eds.) CAAP 1995. LNCS, vol. 915, pp. 364–378. Springer, Heidelberg (1995). https://doi.org/10.1007/3-540-59293-8_207

25. Esparza, J., Silva, M.: A polynomial-time algorithm to decide liveness of bounded free choice nets. Theoret. Comput. Sci. **102**(1), 185–205 (1992). https://doi.org/10.1016/0304-3975(92)90299-U

26. Reisig, W.: Nets consisting of places and transitions. In: Reisig, W. (ed.) Petri Nets: An Introduction, pp. 62–76. Springer, Heidelberg (1985). https://doi.org/10.1007/978-3-642-69968-9_6

27. Martínez, J., Silva, M.: A simple and fast algorithm to obtain all invariants of a generalised Petri net. In: Application and Theory of Petri Nets, pp. 301–310. Springer, Heidelberg (1982). https://doi.org/10.1007/978-3-642-68353-4_47

28. Wisniewski, R., Bazydło, G., Gomes, L., Costa, A., Wojnakowski, M.: Analysis and design automation of cyber-physical system with hippo and IOPT-tools. In: IECON 2019 - 45th Annual Conference of the IEEE Industrial Electronics Society, vol. 1, pp. 5843–5848, October 2019. https://doi.org/10.1109/IECON.2019.8926692
29. Gomes, L., Moutinho, F., Pereira, F.: IOPT-tools — a Web based tool framework for embedded systems controller development using Petri nets. In: 2013 23rd International Conference on Field programmable Logic and Applications, p. 1, September 2013. https://doi.org/10.1109/FPL.2013.6645633
30. Wang, S., Zhou, M., Li, Z., Wang, C.: A new modified reachability tree approach and its applications to unbounded Petri nets. IEEE Trans. Syst. Man Cybern. Syst. 43(4), 932–940 (2013). https://doi.org/10.1109/TSMCA.2012.2226878

Estimation of the End-to-End Delay in 5G Networks Through Gaussian Mixture Models

Diyar Fadhil[1,2]([envelope]) and Rodolfo Oliveira[1,2]([envelope])

[1] Departamento de Engenharia Electrótecnica e de Computadores, FCT, Universidade Nova de Lisboa, 2829-516 Caparica, Portugal
d.fadhil@campus.fct.unl.pt, rado@fct.unl.pt
[2] Instituto de Telecomunicações, Aveiro, Portugal

Abstract. Network analytics provide a comprehensive picture of the network's Quality of Service (QoS), including the End-to-End (E2E) delay. In this paper, we characterize the E2E delay of heterogeneous networks when a single known probabilistic density function (PDF) is not adequate to model its distribution. To this end, multiple PDFs, denominated as components, are assumed in a Gaussian Mixture Model (GMM) to represent the distribution of the E2E delay. The accuracy and computation time of the GMM is evaluated for a different number of components. The results presented in the paper consider a dataset containing E2E delay traces sampled from a 5G network, showing that the GMM's accuracy allows addressing the rich diversity of probabilistic patterns found in 5G networks and its computation time is adequate for real-time applications.

Keywords: End-to-End delay · Quality of service · Gaussian mixture model

1 Introduction

Network analytics was introduced to analyze network problems caused by the enormous increase of connected devices [1]. The Quality-of-Service (QoS) metrics are performance indicators of the network status. One of the most tangible QoS metrics is the End-to-End (E2E) delay. Due to the different requirements of each service in terms of throughput, reliability, and time sensitivity, it is crucial to know the E2E delay probabilistic features. For instance, in 5G networks, Ultra-Reliable Low Latency Communication (URLLC) applications demand low latency networks [2], while other applications such as opportunistic sensing do not have such requirements.

The E2E delay is defined as the time needed to transfer a packet from one endpoint to another, i.e., the time between the instant the transmission starts at the source node and the instant the packet is completely received at the destination node. From a network management viewpoint, it is essential to identify the network E2E delay profile, so that its suitability to support different delay-constrained services can be assessed over time. Using probabilistic models to determine the E2E delay distribution is also crucial to support different delay management strategies [3].

© IFIP International Federation for Information Processing 2022
Published by Springer Nature Switzerland AG 2022
L. M. Camarinha-Matos (Ed.): DoCEIS 2022, IFIP AICT 649, pp. 83–91, 2022.
https://doi.org/10.1007/978-3-031-07520-9_8

In this section, we motivate the paper, its contributions, and the related work in the field. Section 2 introduces the scope of the paper. The proposed methodology and its performance evaluation are presented in Sect. 3 and Sect. 4, respectively. Finally, Sect. 5 concludes the paper.

Research Question and Motivation. The critical challenge in characterizing the E2E delay is determining which mixed distributions represent the set of experimental data collected over time. Due to the network's heterogeneous nature, especially due to the difference radio access and communication technologies available in 5G networks [4], the characterization of the E2E delay is a complex task due to different delay patterns imposed by the multiple technologies set up in the network. Consequently, the E2E delay often does not follow a single and known probability density function (PDF) but a mixture of them. This motivates a modeling approach based on probabilistic mixture models that combine two or more distributions to increase the model's accuracy. To this end, the hypothesis explored in this work is the evaluation of modeling the E2E through a Gaussian Mixture Model (GMM) [5]. The research questions addressed in this work are threefold:

(1) What is the impact of the number of GMM components on the model's accuracy error?
(2) How to estimate the parameters of each distribution adopted in the GMM?
(3) How much time does it take to compute the GMM model, and whether it is adequate for real-time applications?

Related Work. A GMM is defined as a parametric probability density function that consists of a linear combination of multiple Gaussian distributions [6]. Different approaches to estimate the distributions' parameters and weights values based on observed data include the Maximum Likelihood Estimation (MLE), Expectation-Maximization (EM), Minimum Message Length (MML), Moment Matching (MM), and Penalized Maximum Likelihood Expectation-Maximization (PML-EM) [5]. The MLE approach maximizes the likelihood function between a known distribution and the observed data. The MML method is an information measure for statistical comparison. The MM method finds the unknown parameters by obtaining the expected values of the random variable's powers of population distribution model equal to the sample moments. MM can be employed as an alternative approach for MLE in most complex problems due to its simple, easy, and quick computation. The PML-EM is an approach to estimate the parameters in cases when the likelihood is relatively flat, which makes the ML estimation determination difficult. The EM is an iterative algorithm that maximizes the likelihood expectation between data and a mixture of distributions. However, EM's convergence rate is influenced by the initialization random values, and it is hard to define the number of mixture model distributions and how they affect the accuracy of the approximation. EM's dependency on the initialized values is one of the main causes of slow convergence, as mentioned in [7].

The GMM adopts Gaussian distributions and every local population optimum for the MLE problem is globally optimal. The GMM has received significant attention in the literature, particularly to support the estimation of QoS network parameters. The work in [8] investigates how to estimate the link-delay distributions based on end-to-end multicast measurements and adopts an MLE-based GMM model. In [9], it is proposed a known conditional distribution and an unknown finite Gaussian mixture to approximate the weighting of the GMM components. The work in [10] proposed an improved EM algorithm to select the number of components of GMM and simultaneously estimate the weight of these components and unknown parameters. The work in [11] suggests a new clutter elimination method based on GMM and EM estimation, which attempts to estimate and perform fast clutter with a small amount of data. The work in [12] provides a comprehensive analysis of actual latency values collected among various data center locations and a GMM approximation is proposed to simulate and emulate the deployment of applications and services in the cloud.

Contributions. The main contribution of this paper is the characterization of the influence of the number of GMM components and the number of data samples on the accuracy of the E2E delay model of a 5G network. By doing so, the GMM's error and its computing time can be drawn as a function of the number of samples and GMM components, which is of high importance to assess the accuracy of the model and its applicability in terms of computing time to be used in practical 5G networks scenarios.

2 Technological Innovation for Digitalization and Virtualization

Digitalization and virtualization are being adopted in non-real-time scenarios, such as offline data analytics adopted in several trading platforms, but also demanding real-time applications, such as autonomous driving. A common need in all these scenarios is the support of efficient communication systems and networks, capable of exchanging huge amounts of data in a short period of time. In critical real-time applications very low latency and E2E delay are required. The work reported in the paper advances the knowledge about the E2E delay of complex networks, by characterizing the E2E delay of 5G networks through mixture distributions. This knowledge is crucial to select the networks according to the requirements of the specific virtualization systems, being a piece of high importance in the implementation of virtualization systems.

3 Methodology

Although Gaussian distributions can model an impressive number of probabilistic scenarios, certain phenomena follow unknown distributions demanding more complex modeling approaches. The mixture models can be a possible solution for these cases. Given that any natural process may depend on several independent factors that form several subpopulations, the GMM models the subpopulations that can then be mixed to describe the whole distribution of the population.

A GMM is defined as a parametric PDF consisting of a linear combination of multiple Gaussian PDFs. The mixture models are usually used for multimodal or multi-peak PDF data. Fitting the multimodal data with a single distribution is not proper and accurate. The mixture models are used to combine different distributions that better match the data density. The Gaussian distribution is adopted in the mixture models due to its theoretical and computational benefits to represent massive datasets [6]. Each Gaussian component is used to represent the subpopulations within an overall population. Three primary parameters define each component of a GMM: the mean, the standard deviation, and a weight. The Gaussian mixture model can be represented as follows

$$p(x) = \sum_{i=1}^{K} w_i \, \mathcal{N}(x|\mu_i \sigma_i) \tag{1}$$

where x is the data measurement, w_i, is the mixture weight for the i-th component, $i = 1, \ldots, K$, and K is the number of mixed Gaussian distributions, aka GMM components. Each component of the GMM is defined as

$$\mathcal{N}(x|\mu_i, \sigma_i) = \frac{1}{\sigma_i\sqrt{2\pi}} \exp\left(-\frac{(x-\mu_i)^2}{2\sigma_i^2}\right) \tag{2}$$

with mean μ_i and standard deviation σ_i. The mixture weights satisfy the constraint

$$\sum_{i=1}^{K} w_i = 1. \tag{3}$$

Therefore, the GMM parameters vector is represented by λ as follows

$$\lambda = \{w_i, \mu_i, \sigma_i\} \quad i = 1, \ldots, K. \tag{4}$$

The parameters λ are estimated based on training or measurement data. The maximum likelihood (ML) estimation is a well-known method that aims to find the mixture model parameters and maximize the GMM likelihood function with given training data. We assume that the vector of the training data samples is represented by $X = x_1, \ldots, x_T$, where the samples $x_1, \ldots, x_T$, are independent. Therefore, the likelihood function is written as

$$p(X|\lambda) = \prod_{t=1}^{T} p(x_t|\lambda), \tag{5}$$

where T represents the number of samples. It is impracticable to maximize the non-linear function of parameters λ that is expressed on the ML function [11]. A practical solution for the ML estimation of the parameters λ can be determined by a numerical approach such as iterative Expectation-Maximization (EM) or similar ones [9]. In EM, initial random values are assigned to λ, which are used to determine the subsequent estimation of parameters λ. In the first step, the initial values of all parameters are determined and employed as an input of the iterative Expectation and Maximization algorithm to reach the convergent values of the different parameters. The initial values of the parameters, λ_0, are computed as follows

$$\mu_i = \frac{T * rand(i)}{2} \sum_{t=1}^{T} x_t, \tag{6}$$

$$\sigma_i = \left(\frac{1}{T} \sum_{t=1}^{T} (x_t - \mu_i)^2 \right)^{\frac{1}{2}}, \tag{7}$$

$$w_i = \frac{1}{K}, \tag{8}$$

where $rand(i)$ represents a random number sampled from a uniform distribution between zero and one. An iterative cycle is then started until the estimated parameters λ reach a specific convergence threshold. The EM algorithm relies on an iterative approach divided in two steps:

E-step: In the Expectation step, the expectation of the likelihood function is calculated based on observed data X and the current model parameters λ_m.

M-step: In the Maximization step, the expectation of the likelihood function is used to compute new model parameters λ_{m+1} that maximize the conditional distribution given by the parameters λ_m and the observed data X. The symbols m, and $m + 1$ indicate consecutive iterations. In the E-step, λ_m is used to indicate the current model parameters. In the M-step, λ_m is used to determine the subsequent model parameter λ_{m+1}. Expanding the E-step and taking separate derivatives concerning the different parameters (M-step), we get the equations as follows

$$\widehat{w}_i = \frac{1}{T} \sum_{t=1}^{T} P(i|\mathbf{x}_t, \lambda_m), \tag{9}$$

$$\widehat{\mu}_i = \frac{\sum_{t=1}^{T} P(i|\mathbf{x}_t, \lambda_m) \mathbf{x}_t}{\sum_{t=1}^{T} P(i|\mathbf{x}_t, \lambda_m)}, \tag{10}$$

$$\widehat{\sigma}_i^2 = \frac{\sum_{t=1}^{T} P(i|\mathbf{x}_t, \lambda_m) x_t^2}{\sum_{t=1}^{T} P(i|\mathbf{x}_t, \lambda_m)} - \widehat{\mu}_i^2, \tag{11}$$

and the subsequent GMM estimation parameters vector is given by

$$\lambda_{m+1} = \{\widehat{w}_i, \widehat{\mu}_i, \widehat{\sigma}_i\} i = 1, \dots, K. \tag{12}$$

The GMM parameters can be estimated by employing the iterative Expectation-Maximization (EM) algorithm and Maximum a Posteriori (MAP) estimation [12]. Although different approaches to parametrize the GMM parameters may provide closed-form expressions [9], its computation complexity is severely increased by the number of distributions used in the mixture model. For instance, if we assume that the GMM consists of $K = 7$ components, the MM estimation needs to calculate and solve 21 equations of the moments to determine the estimations of the parameters. Therefore, the EM algorithm is a well-known approach often adopted to estimate the GMM parameters due to its iterative behavior and improved computational performance.

4   Performance Evaluation

In this section we present the simulation results and evaluate the performance of the method described in Sect. 3. In the EM algorithm a policy was adopted to avoid exceeding the iteration cycle when the level of convergence described by a difference parameter D_m is lower than the convergence threshold γ. D_m is given by

$$D_m = \sum_{k=1}^{K} \left(\left| \mu_{m+1_k} - \mu_{m_k} \right| + \left| \sigma_{m+1_k} - \sigma_{m_k} \right| + \left| w_{m+1_k} - w_{m_k} \right| \right). \qquad (13)$$

The maximum number of iterations was limited to 25000. The MSE is used to find out how the estimated PDF is close to the observed one, and is defined as follows

$$MSE = \frac{1}{T} \sum_{t=1}^{T} (x_t - \hat{x}_t)^2. \qquad (14)$$

The 5Gophers dataset [13] was used as observation data. The dataset contains experimental data simultaneously obtained from three different 5G carriers. Two carriers run mmWave networks while the third one runs a mid-band network. The E2E delay dataset was gathered in three cities in the US with different urban environments. In the further analysis, we have used 2054 data records to determine the accuracy of the model as a function of the number of GMM components $K = 2, 3, 5, 8, 10$, and 12, and the number of samples $T = 10, 25, 50, 100, 200, 500$, and 1000. The threshold γ was set to 0.00001.

Table 1 summarizes the number of iterations of the EM algorithm and the MSE achieved for the different number of components. The EM algorithm was computed using the 2054 data records. Based on the numerical results, when the number of components increases, the number of iterations required to reach the convergence threshold increases because more parameters need to be estimated. On the other hand, the MSE decreases with the number of components because a higher number of components leads to a higher number of degrees of freedom to model the data.

Table 1.   Number of iterations and MSE to compute the GMM.

Components	Number of iterations	MSE
2	24	1.37E−04
3	33	1.00E−04
5	332	6.06E−05
8	2076	3.79E−05
10	2858	2.94E−05
12	4042	2.29E−05

The PDFs obtained with the GMM for 3 and 8 components are represented in Fig. 1. As can be seen in both Table 1 and Fig. 1, the adoption of 8 components increases the model's accuracy when compared to 3 components.

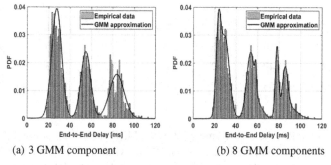

(a) 3 GMM component   (b) 8 GMM components

Fig. 1. GMM approximation for different number of components.

Next, we characterize the impact of the number of E2E delay samples on the GMM's accuracy. The MSE values for a different number of GMM components and samples are summarized in Table 2. For a specific number of GMM components, the MSE decreases as the number of samples increases, which means that the increase of the number of samples leads to a lower error due to the best approximation of the likelihood expectation. In addition, for a fixed number of samples, the MSE decreases with the number of components because the GMM uses more PDFs to represent the experimental data. The computation time of the GMM is presented in Table 3. As a general trend, the computation time increases with the number of samples for a specific number of components. This is due to the longer vector of data samples. In addition, for each number of samples the computation time increases with the number of components due to the increase of GMM complexity.

Table 2. MSE as a function of the number of GMM components and samples.

	$T = 10$	$T = 25$	$T = 50$	$T = 100$	$T = 200$	$T = 500$	$T = 1000$
$K = 2$	3.78E−02	1.25E−02	5.91E−03	2.86E−03	1.41E−03	5.62E−04	2.80E−04
$K = 3$	1.85E−02	9.51E−03	4.47E−03	2.14E−03	1.05E−03	4.14E−04	2.06E−04
$K = 5$	2.83E−03	1.72E−03	1.45E−03	9.25E−04	5.21E−04	2.52E−04	1.25E−04
$K = 8$	5.64E−04	3.80E−04	3.13E−04	2.66E−04	2.20E−04	1.25E−04	6.92E−05
$K = 10$	1.32E−04	1.21E−04	1.07E−04	9.32E−05	8.52E−05	7.69E−05	5.15E−05
$K = 12$	1.13E−04	9.97E−05	8.91E−05	7.09E−05	6.03E−05	4.70E−05	3.50E−05

Table 3. GMM computation time [*ms*] varying the number of GMM components and samples.

	$T = 10$	$T = 25$	$T = 50$	$T = 100$	$T = 200$	$T = 500$	$T = 1000$
$K = 2$	0.68	0.78	0.87	0.91	1.18	1.84	2.53
$K = 3$	0.70	1.23	1.60	2.09	2.94	5.09	9.96
$K = 5$	0.75	1.42	3.47	7.68	19.98	67.1	153.4
$K = 8$	0.77	1.46	4.85	12.04	33.28	190.9	963.3
$K = 10$	0.83	1.49	5.42	12.65	39.87	253.9	1699.3
$K = 12$	0.89	1.53	5.72	16.65	46.76	541.8	1772.2

Figure 2 illustrates the logarithmic plot of the MSE and computation time as a function of the number of components. Each curve represents a specific number of samples. As can be seen in the results, to obtain MSE errors below 1E−04 it is advantageous to decrease the number of samples (T) and increase the number of GMM components (K), as the computational time is more affected by the number of samples than by the number of GMM components. This can be observed for T = 25 and K = 12, where the MSE is below 1E−04 and the computation time is 1.53 ms, which compares for instance with T = 50 and K = 10 where the MSE increases (slightly above 1E−04) and the computation time also increases to 5.42 ms.

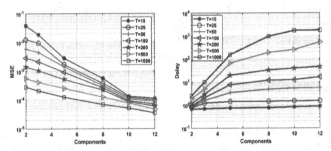

Fig. 2. MSE and computation time (Delay in milliseconds) for different number of GMM components and samples.

The tradeoff between the MSE and the computation time is of great importance because the results show that lower errors can be achieved with the cost of increased computation time. Selecting the best GMM configuration for each network depends on the network operator's requirement, their policies, and the kind of required application. However, the number of GMM components can be varied in such a way that coarser or more accurate E2E delay distributions can be computed.

5 Conclusions

This paper characterized the accuracy and the computation time of the GMM to approximate 5G networks' E2E delay. The results indicate that higher accuracy is achieved as the number of samples and the number of components increases. However, the computation time also increases with the number of samples and components, as identified by the trade-off between the model's error and its computational time presented in Sect. 4. Future work includes the adoption of machine learning approaches to identify the GMM model parameters through unsupervised deep learning neural networks.

References

1. Hung, M.: Leading the IoT, gartner insights on how to lead in a connected world. Gart. Res., 1–29 (2017)
2. Afolabi, I., Taleb, T., Samdanis, K., Ksentini, A., Flinck, H.: Network slicing and softwarization: a survey on principles, enabling technologies, and solutions. IEEE Commun. Surv. Tutor. **20**(3), 2429–2453 (2018)
3. Banavalikar, B.G.: Quality of service (QoS) for multi-tenant aware overlay virtual networks, January 2019. US Patent 10,177,936
4. Ye, Q., Zhuang, W., Li, X., Rao, J.: End-to-end delay modeling for embedded VNF chains in 5G core networks. IEEE Internet Things J. **6**(1), 692–704 (2019)
5. McLachlan, G.J., Lee, S.X., Rathnayake, S.I.: Finite mixture models. Annu. Rev. Stat. Appl. **6**, 355–378 (2019)
6. Reynolds, D.A.: Gaussian mixture models. In: Encyclopedia of Biometrics, vol. 741, pp. 659–663 (2009)
7. Yang, M., Lai, C., Lin, C.: A robust EM clustering algorithm for Gaussian mixture models. Pattern Recogn. **45**(11), 3950–3961 (2012)
8. Lawrence, E., Michailidis, G., Nair, V.: Maximum likelihood estimation of internal network link delay distributions using multicast measurements. In: Proceedings of the 37th Conference on Information Sciences and Systems. Citeseer (2003)
9. Orellana, R., Carvajal, R., Aguero, J.C.: Maximum likelihood infinite mixture distribution estimation utilizing finite Gaussian mixtures. IFAC-PapersOnLine **51**(15), 706–711 (2018)
10. Huang, T., Peng, H., Zhang, K.: Model selection for Gaussian mixture models. Statistica Sinica, 147–169 (2017)
11. Rahman, L., Zhang, J.A., Huang, X., Jay Guo, Y., Lu, Z.: Gaussian-mixture-model based clutter suppression in perceptive mobile networks. IEEE Commun. Lett. **25**(1), 152–156 (2021)
12. Cerroni, W., Foschini, L., Grabarnik, G.Y., Shwartz, L., Tortonesi, M.: Estimating delay times between cloud datacenters: a pragmatic modeling approach. IEEE Commun. Lett. **22**(3), 526–529 (2018)
13. Narayanan, A., et al.: A first look at commercial 5G performance on smartphones. In: Proceedings of the Web Conference 2020, pp. 894–905 (2020)

Health-Related Digitalization

Towards Digital Twin in the Context of Power Wheelchairs Provision and Support

Carolina Lagartinho-Oliveira[1,2](✉), Filipe Moutinho[1,2], and Luís Gomes[1,2]

[1] NOVA School of Science and Technology, NOVA University Lisbon, Caparica, Portugal
ci.oliveira@campus.fct.unl.pt, {fcm,lugo}@fct.unl.pt
[2] Center for Technology and Systems, UNINOVA, Caparica, Portugal

Abstract. Recent advances in digital technologies have been triggered by Industry 4.0, deeply focused on connectivity, real-time data and digitization, with Digital Twin (DT) at the forefront of this. A DT is a virtual counterpart seamlessly linked to a physical entity, both sharing the same properties, characteristics and behavior, using data and information. Applications of DT include real-time monitoring, design/planning, optimization, maintenance, prediction, remote access, etc. This paper gives an overview of the Digital Twin concept and seeks to synthesize the technologies frequently used to enable it. It is also proposed the creation and use of a Digital Twin of a Power Wheelchair to promote the health and wellness of wheelchair users and facilitate services by healthcare professionals in the provision and support of wheelchairs.

Keywords: Digital Twin · Monitoring · Power Wheelchair · Remote control

1 Introduction

The World Health Organization estimates that about 15% of the world's population has a disability [1]. In Portugal, it corresponds to almost 1 million people with the highest prevalence related to mobility [2]. For these people, operating a wheelchair can be a way to be able to live with freedom and independence. To accommodate those who are unable to use a Manual Wheelchair, one can opt for a Power Wheelchair (PWC), which generally offers a wider range of features to meet different needs and user capabilities. The main obstacles are that the industry is currently limited to high-income markets, and those with lower economic resources end up relying on charity services, which in most scenarios only provide low-quality or used products, unsuitable for the user in the context, with lack of repair and follow-up mechanisms. In addition, in many low- and middle-income countries, access to trained healthcare professionals (HCPs) is limited, but they are essential for the proper provision and support of PWCs [3]. Even now, with the COVID-19 pandemic situation, the scenario got worse, with a significant impact on budgets that concern access to PWCs; and by restricting in-person clinic or home visits. Given this, the idea of performing some parts of the provision of wheelchairs remotely, via telehealth and videoconferencing, has been encouraged [4]. Nowadays, the concept

© IFIP International Federation for Information Processing 2022
Published by Springer Nature Switzerland AG 2022
L. M. Camarinha-Matos (Ed.): DoCEIS 2022, IFIP AICT 649, pp. 95–102, 2022.
https://doi.org/10.1007/978-3-031-07520-9_9

of Digital Twin [5] is emerging applied to different areas as a promising approach to gather insightful data shared between the physical and virtual worlds, and facilitate the means to design, monitor, analyze, optimize, predict, control, etc. physical entities [6]. In this way, the following research questions aroused: "How to use Digital Twin in the context of Power Wheelchairs provision and support?" and "To what extent does the Digital Twin represent a real Power Wheelchair?". In view of this, the objective of this paper is to propose the creation and use of a Digital Twin of a PWC to promote the health and wellness of people who use wheelchairs, as well as to facilitate and improve the comprehensive delivery of remote services by HCPs.

2 Relation and Contribution to Digitalization and Virtualization

The use of Digital Twin (DT) in the current days had its boom around 2016, a few years after the proposal of Industry 4.0 in 2013 [7]. Since then, the concept has expanded to different areas, in which new DT applications have emerged to support digitalization as a way of innovation, detecting problems, anticipating challenges and increasing efficiency [8]. Digital Twin allows the virtualization of anything in the real world to be represented in the virtual world, with physical and virtual entities connected sharing the same properties, characteristics and behavior by means of data and information; changes that occur at the physical entity (PE) or at the virtual entity (VE) lead directly to changes in the other. Some of the DT advantages are [9]: (1) it considers large amounts of data derived from different sources, providing a reliable way to model VE and mirror the PE for the duration of its lifecycle; (2) VE synchronizes with the counterpart, which allows DT to monitor and analyze PE in real-time, supporting design, maintenance, control, etc.; (3) it can help optimize the PE, using simulations and predictions, assessing the impact of different scenarios, that can be verified and validated before they occur; (4) it is able of performing diagnostics and intelligent control over the PE, with VE sending instruction when necessary; (5) it allows remote access for human interaction with the PE; just to mention the most relevant advantages. Indeed, due to its advantages, DT can be used in different contexts. This paper proposes the use of DT to promote digitalization and virtualization in the Power Wheelchair sector, in the context of provision and support.

3 Digital Twin Overview

Three common elements to represent a Digital Twin are [10]: a real space, corresponding to the physical world where PEs exist; a virtual space, where VE mirrors PE; and a bidirectional connection for data synchronization between spaces. In [11], a particular proposal highlights the presence of PE and VE interacting with services (Ss) and data (DD) using connections (CN) that link elements. In short, DT supports the representation of PE through VE if: (1) it guarantees the entanglement of entities; (2) PE values are timely mapped to VE; and (3) VE reproduces the relevant PE attributes in the context. These are the properties of entanglement, reflection and representativeness. Optional properties (e.g. replication, composability, memorization or augmentation) [12] will depend on the application and DT type. A DT can be classified according to its position in the lifecycle [13]: Digital Twin Prototype (DTP) or Digital Twin Instance (DTI); or based on individual values [14]: Supervisory Digital Twin (SDT), Interactive Digital Twin (IDT) or Predictive Digital Twin (PDT); etc. In the first case, DTP is the DT of a physical prototype to be used early in the lifecycle to support tests that are difficult to perform during traditional prototyping. In the realization of PE, DTP becomes a DTI, corresponding to the DT already defined; it lasts beyond PE life. In the second group, SDT monitors PE and collects data to support the perception of PE attributes and their relationship to its performance. IDT leads to a more reliable PE by diagnosing and controlling processes. PDT can help drive PE by simulating or predicting the impact of planned or potential scenarios.

Mapping a PE in the digital world starts with cognition of the physical world and data acquisition: measurement technologies capture PE characteristics; sensory technologies and Internet of Things (IoT) technologies collect PE data in real-time; other data is collected through application programming interfaces or web crawlers; etc. [15]. Thus, different data can be used to build and maintain VE, for it to operate faithfully and control PE via power technologies, drive systems, control technologies, among others. To support the data flow and connectivity of all DT elements, transmission technologies are used together with appropriate network architectures, communication and security protocols, middleware platforms, etc. [16]. In addition, all data are made available for further processing, analysis and visualization using storage technologies [15] and ontologies for knowledge representation and management [16]. Data processing helps to eliminate redundant and inconsistent data using data cleaning and transformation technologies [17], to later extract useful information using statistical methods, artificial intelligence (AI) methods [15] and Big Data technologies, such as cloud, fog and edge computing [18]. Data fusion is also suggested to help filter and correlate the processed data [15], which can then be used in functions provided by the DT (e.g. prediction, optimization and validation), encapsulated in services to facilitate their use [17]. Services are based on: virtualization, verification, validation, and simulation technologies [16]; platform-related technologies used to manage resource services, knowledge services, or application services; and application interface technologies to enable user interaction with the services. Even so, mirroring a PE is a long process where it is also up to the VE to reproduce its characteristics, properties and behaviors through different models. Section 5 builds on the aforementioned aspects, focusing on how to enable VE.

4 Digital Twin for Power Wheelchairs Provision and Support

The provision of wheelchairs is a process for users to obtain and maintain their wheelchairs. Since the outbreak of COVID-19, the option to remotely carry out some parts of wheelchair provision is being valued; users can stay at home, reducing the risk of exposure and helping professionals determine day-to-day challenges; and it may be possible for users who do not live near a clinic to have access to HCPs. Still, telehealth do not cover important phases of wheelchair provision, such as when additional modifications and adjustments are required, or HCPs are asked to provide maintenance and repair of technical issues. To deal with this, the use of Digital Twin is proposed in the context of Power Wheelchairs provision and support. Figure 1 presents each step of the provision process, where a DT of a PWC can support the digitalization and virtualization of the product preparation, fitting, training, and follow-up, maintenance and repair steps; 3 groups of participants are also highlighted.

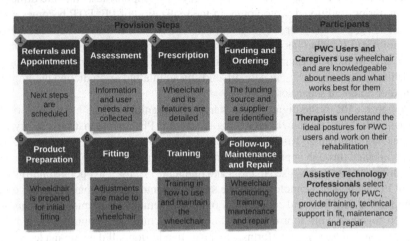

Fig. 1. Steps and participants in the wheelchair provision process.

First, a DT of a PWC can be used during product preparation and fitting to help understand the functioning of the wheelchair and improve the planning and testing of various scenarios for its use. Concretely, assistive technology professionals (ATPs) can use DT to justify, design, and validate new or existing features and parts of the PWC; and simulate PWC's health conditions, to determine and eliminate the cause of problems and undesired situations. ATPs can also use DT to predict the performance of PWC, including the occurrence of unforeseen scenarios. Its predictive capability can also be used during training to anticipate future risks, with PWC users being advised on how to avoid accidents based on PWCs usage data and the computation of patterns of usage and misuse situations. The DT can also guide PWC users with personalized training services, based on the users' health data, therapists' assessments, etc. In the last step, the DT can acquire real-time operational data from PWC and increase user engagement by showing PWC users and caregivers what is happening inside their PWCs, and giving insight on possible consequences of their use. It can also help therapists monitor users' rehabilitation activities, tracing usage patterns and reporting which PWC configurations and functionalities are used. This can influence the planning of the rehabilitation process, and help PWC users to follow it. Also during follow-up, maintenance and repair, a DT of a PWC can trigger alerts to help diagnose problems, as well as identify actions to improve PWC performance. In case of a wheelchair repair, DT facilitates PWC analysis and remote intervention with real-time control over the PWC. Here are some ways to use a DT of a PWC, as a possible answer to the question "How to use Digital Twin in the context of Power Wheelchairs provision and support?".

5   Digital Twin of a Power Wheelchair

In Fig. 2 a conceptual model for a Digital Twin of a Power Wheelchair is shown; the model is based on [11] and has been extended to consider the user element and its interactions. While DT abstracts the complexity of a PWC, offering specific services, users continue to interact with the PWC and contribute with different knowledge.

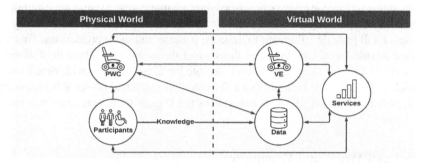

Fig. 2. Proposed conceptual model for a Power Wheelchair DT.

To implement the model, PDT is the type of DT considered; as well as a DTI to adapt PWCs that come with predefined functionalities, or a DTP to add them to those that don't [6]. Properties that characterize the proposed model are: augmentation and servitization for the PWC to be modified, updated and improved by VE augmentation as new services are offered; persistency so if the PWC malfunctions, VE continues reporting to services, and restores it to a known acceptable state; and composability for when a VE represents only a subpart of a PWC, and an aggregation of VEs represents the PWC itself [12]. In fact, the PWC can be seen as an aggregation of the parts that make it up (e.g. joystick module, power module or seating module) and each one can have its VE; the VE in Fig. 2 corresponds to a series of sub-models integrated to mimic specific parts of PWC. To deal with this modularity, the proposal considers a Model-Driven Development (MDD) approach that supports all stages of systems development using models as the primary artifact [19].

MDD ensures a high level of specification abstraction while attaining the level of detail required for a DT; it has the ability to [20]: (1) enable hardware and software design; (2) eliminate errors early in development; (3) facilitate testing with automated verification and validation techniques; and (4) support automatic code generation for target platforms. Besides, MDD supports various modeling formalisms, enabling the use of technologies and tools that are essential for VE. The VE has to represent the PWC (or part of it) in a way that users can analyze and manage it through the services, based on the data; so, the DT model in Fig. 2 represents a real PWC through VE, considering three types of models: geometric, behavioral and rule model.

The geometric model will represent the global solid appearance of the PWC based on data structures of topological and geometric information, used to feed software for three-dimensional modeling, computer-aided design, or virtual reality. The behavioral model will describe the PWC's behaviors according to its state model, dynamic model and kinematic model. The state model will be specified using the Petri net formalism, suitable for the development of complex and concurrent systems. A new class of non-autonomous high-level Petri nets will be created based on IOPT nets [21], colored Petri nets [22], and DS-Pnets [23], which have the potential to reduce the complexity of data modeling and data processing; also, the use of Petri nets will provide evidence on the representation of requirements for the VE state models through their verification and validation, using automation tools supported by MDD. Regarding to the dynamic model and kinematic model, they will be described through mathematical equations; initially, it will be considered a unicycle model to deal with the motion of the PWC. Additionally, the rule model will provide VE means to describe patterns and make predictions. This will be based on rule-based learning algorithms under the unsupervised branch of machine learning [24]. The rule model will allow associate PWC users actions with virtual model of PWC. In this way, it is believed that a DT can represent a real Power Wheelchair and may answer the question "To what extent does the Digital Twin represent a real Power Wheelchair?".

6 Related Work and Discussion

Many users find it difficult to use a wheelchair, even for daily activities. They need to have continue access to HCPs for proper provision, training and follow-up; and that's sometimes limited. Additionally, many users suffer injuries from tips or falls near stairs, ramps or curb [25]; other injuries occur in the scenario of wheelchair breakdown. So, although a PWC is designed to promote the well-being of many users, it often ends up being abandoned, or it does not bring any benefit. In this sense, innovations and proposals for wheelchair revolve around technological advances; examples are: alternative control devices, assessment and prescribing tools, simulators and training applications, or mobility aids. Some examples of recent technology include: LUCI, which is a smart technology accessory that is mounted on a PWC to allow the user to navigate with greater safety and independence [26]; blind spot sensor systems used to easily provide obstacle detection and avoidance [27]; and a fleet management system to provide access to valuable data and analysis of customers' wheelchairs and improve diagnostic [28]. None of these proposals use Digital Twin which can offer multiple benefits: (1) promote the well-being and safety of PWC users; (2) increase their engagement; (3) support PWCs adaptation and repair, increasing their safety and reliability, while reducing maintenance costs; and (4) offer new mechanisms for HCPs to remotely assist more people.

7 Conclusions and Future Work

This paper presents a proposal for the creation of a Digital Twin of a Power Wheelchair, enabling new services for wheelchairs users, as well as their HCPs. So far, there is no evidence of its application in this sector. Several ways of using DT in the context of provision and support of PWCs were pointed out. The proposal of a conceptual model identifies the Model-Driven Development approach to combine different sub-models and allow specification, verification, simulation and implementation of the virtual entity in the DT. In particular, a new extended Petri net formalism will aim to model VE state model. As future work, it is intended to analyze different descriptions of VE dynamic and kinematic models while associating them to a geometric model; in parallel, the new formalism of Petri net will begin to be defined; and it is intended to call participation of users, therapists, and ATPs to assess their opinions, comments and recommendations on the values of the proposed DT.

Acknowledgements. This work was partially financed by Portuguese Agency "Fundação para a Ciência e a Tecnologia" (FCT), in the framework of project UIDB/00066/2020, and under the PhD scholarship with the reference 2020.08462.BD, through national funds from the MCTES ("Ministério da Ciência, Tecnologia e Ensino Superior").

References

1. World Health Organization & World Bank, World report on disability (2011). https://apps. who.int/iris/handle/10665/44575. Accessed 8 Mar 2021
2. Instituto Nacional de Estatística, "Censos 2011" (2011). https://censos.ine.pt/xportal/xmain? xpid=CENSOS&xpgid=censos2011_apresentacao. Accessed 6 Apr 2021
3. World Health Organization, Assistive technology (2018). https://www.who.int/news-room/ fact-sheets/detail/assistive-technology. Accessed 9 Mar 2021
4. Watanabe, L.: H.R. 2168 Includes Telehealth Options for CRT Clinicians, Mobility Management, March 2021. https://mobilitymgmt.com/articles/2021/03/29/hr-2168-telehealth-clinic ians.aspx. Accessed 19 Feb 2022
5. Grieves, M., Vickers, J.: Digital twin: mitigating unpredictable, undesirable emergent behavior in complex systems. In: Kahlen, F.-J., Flumerfelt, S., Alves, A. (eds.) Transdisciplinary Perspectives on Complex Systems, pp. 85–113. Springer, Cham (2017). https://doi.org/10. 1007/978-3-319-38756-7_4
6. Singh, M., Fuenmayor, E., Hinchy, E.P., Qiao, Y., Murray, N., Devine, D.: Digital twin: origin to future. Appl. Syst. Innov. **4**(2), 36 (2021). https://doi.org/10.3390/asi4020036
7. Kagermann, H., Wahlster, W., Helbig, J.: Recommendations for implementing the strategic initiative INDUSTRIE 4.0, Forschungsunion, acatech (2013). https://www.din.de/blob/ 76902/e8cac883f42bf28536e7e8165993f1fd/recommendations-for-implementing-industry-4-0-data.pdf. Accessed 2 Mar 2022
8. Hinduja, H., Kekkar, S., Chourasia, S., Chakrapani, H.B.: Industry 4.0: digital twin and its industrial applications. Int. J. Sci. Eng. Technol. **8**(4) (2020). https://www.ijset.in/wp-content/ uploads/IJSET_V8_issue4_241.pdf. Paper number 241
9. Liu, M., Fang, S., Dong, H., Xu, C.: Review of digital twin about concepts, technologies, and industrial applications. J. Manuf. Syst. **58**(Part B), 346–361 (2021). https://doi.org/10.1016/ j.jmsy.2020.06.017
10. Grieves, M.W.: Product lifecycle management: the new paradigm for enterprises. Int. J. Prod. Dev. **2**(1/2), 71–84 (2005). https://doi.org/10.1504/IJPD.2005.006669
11. Tao, F., Zhang, M., Nee, A.Y.C.: Five-dimension digital twin modeling and its key technologies. In: Tao, F., Zhang, M., Nee, A.Y.C. (eds.) Digital Twin Driven Smart Manufacturing, pp. 63–81. Elsevier (2019)
12. Minerva, R., Lee, G.M., Crespi, N.: Digital Twin in the IoT context: a survey on technical features, scenarios, and architectural models. Proc. IEEE **108**(10), 1785–1824 (2020). https:// doi.org/10.1109/JPROC.2020.2998530
13. Jones, D., Snider, C., Nassehi, A., Yon, J., Hicks, B.: Characterising the Digital Twin: a systematic literature review. CIRP J. Manuf. Sci. Technol. **29**(Part A), 36–52 (2020). https:// doi.org/10.1016/j.cirpj.2020.02.002

14. High Value Manufacturing Catapult Visualization, Feasibility of an immersive digital twin (2018). https://www.amrc.co.uk/files/document/219/1536919984_HVM_CATAPULT_DIG ITAL_TWIN_DL.pdf. Accessed 2 March 2022
15. Qi, Q., et al.: Enabling technologies and tools for digital twin. J. Manuf. Syst. **58**(Part B), 3–21 (2021). https://doi.org/10.1016/j.jmsy.2019.10.001
16. Lim, K.Y.H., Zheng, P., Chen, C.-H.: A state-of-the-art survey of Digital Twin: techniques, engineering product lifecycle management and business innovation perspectives. J. Intell. Manuf. **31**(6), 1313–1337 (2019). https://doi.org/10.1007/s10845-019-01512-w
17. Tao, F., Zhang, M., Nee, A.Y.C.: Background and concept of Digital Twin. In: Tao, F., Zhang, M., Nee, A.Y.C. (eds.) Digital Twin Driven Smart Manufacturing, pp. 3–28. Elsevier (2019)
18. Pires, F., Cachada, A., Barbosa, J., Moreira, A.P., Leitão, P.: Digital twin in industry 4.0: technologies, applications and challenges. In: 2019 IEEE 17th International Conference on Industrial Informatics (INDIN), vol. 2019, pp. 721–726 (2019). https://doi.org/10.1109/IND IN41052.2019.8972134
19. Meyers, B., Gadeyne, K., Oakes, B.J., Bernaerts, M., Vangheluwe, H., Denil, J.: A model-driven engineering framework to support the functional safety process. In: 2019 ACM/IEEE 22nd International Conference on Model Driven Engineering Languages and Systems Companion (MODELS-C), pp. 619–623 (2019). https://doi.org/10.1109/MODELS-C.2019. 00094
20. Kleidermacher, D., Kleidermacher, M.: Secure embedded software development. In: Kleidermacher, D., Kleidermacher, M. (eds.) Embedded Systems Security, pp. 93–208. Elsevier (2012)
21. Gomes, L., Barros, J.P.: Refining IOPT Petri Nets class for embedded system controller modeling. In: IECON 2018 - 44th Annual Conference of the IEEE Industrial Electronics Society, pp. 4720–4725 (2018). https://doi.org/10.1109/IECON.2018.8592921
22. Jensen, K., Kristensen, L.M.: Colored Petri nets: a graphical language for formal modeling and validation of concurrent systems. Commun. ACM **58**(6), 61–70 (2015). https://doi.org/ 10.1145/2663340
23. Pereira, F., Gomes, L.: The IOPT-Flow modeling framework applied to Power Electronics controllers. IEEE Trans. Ind. Electron. **64**(3), 2363–2372 (2017). https://doi.org/10.1109/TIE. 2016.2620101
24. Fürnkranz, J., Kliegr, T.: A brief overview of rule learning. In: Bassiliades, N., Gottlob, G., Sadri, F., Paschke, A., Roman, D. (eds.) RuleML 2015. LNCS, vol. 9202, pp. 54–69. Springer, Cham (2015). https://doi.org/10.1007/978-3-319-21542-6_4
25. Sung, J., Trace, Y., Peterson, E.W., Sosnoff, J.J., Rice, L.A.: Falls among full-time wheelchair users with spinal cord injury and multiple sclerosis: a comparison of characteristics of fallers and circumstances of falls. Disabil. Rehabil. **41**(4), 389–395 (2017). https://doi.org/10.1080/ 09638288.2017.1393111
26. LUCI, LUCI | Mobility. https://luci.com. Accessed 17 Mar 2022
27. Braze Mobility, Braze Mobility - Blind Spot Sensors for Wheelchairs. https://brazemobility. com. Accessed 17 Mar 2022
28. Permobil, Permobil Connect Fleet Management. https://www.permobil.com/en-us/products/ power-wheelchairs/functions/fleet-management. Accessed 18 Mar 2022

Real-Time PPG-Based HRV Implementation Using Deep Learning and Simulink

Filipa Esgalhado[1,2(✉)], Arnaldo Batista[3], Valentina Vassilenko[1,2], and Manuel Ortigueira[3]

[1] Laboratory of Instrumentation, Biomedical Engineering and Radiation Physics (LIBPHYS), NOVA School of Science and Technology, NOVA University Lisbon, 2829-516 Caparica, Portugal
feo.cardoso@campus.fct.unl.pt

[2] NMT, S.A., Parque Tecnológico de Cantanhede, Núcleo 04, Lote 3, 3060-197 Cantanhede, Portugal

[3] UNINOVA CTS, NOVA School of Science and Technology, NOVA University Lisbon, 2829-516 Caparica, Portugal

Abstract. The Heart Rate Variability (HRV) signal computation relies on fiducial points typically obtained from the electrocardiogram (ECG) or the photoplethysmogram (PPG). Generally, these fiducial points correspond to the peaks of the ECG or PPG. Consequently, the HRV quality depends on the fiducial points detection accuracy. In a previous work, this subject has been addressed using Long Short-Term Memory (LSTM) Deep Learning algorithms for PPG segmentation, from which peak detection can be achieved. In the herein presented work, a *Simulink*® implementation of the LSTM algorithm is obtained for real-time PPG peak detection. HRV and outlier removal blocks are also implemented. The obtained code can be used to be embedded in hardware systems for real-time PPG acquisition and HRV visualization. A Root Mean Square Error (RMSE) mean of 0.0439 ± 0.0175 s was obtained, and no significant differences (p-value < 0.05) were found between the ground truth and the real-time implementation.

Keywords: PPG · HRV · Real-Time · *Simulink*®

1 Introduction

Cardiovascular diseases (CVD) are the leading cause of death worldwide and are a major public health issue [1]. Therefore, it is essential to adopt preventive strategies for CVD's early detection.

The Heart Rate Variability (HRV) represents the time interval between successive heart beats and can be used to assess the status of the autonomic nervous system [2]. This marker reflects the balance between the parasympathetic and sympathetic systems and has been used in the prediction of cardiovascular outcomes [3]. Several time, frequency and non-linear features can be extracted from the HRV, such as the Standard Deviation of Normal-Normal intervals (SDNN), low frequency peak and sample entropy [4]. Some

L. M. Camarinha-Matos (Ed.): DoCEIS 2022, IFIP AICT 649, pp. 103–111, 2022.
https://doi.org/10.1007/978-3-031-07520-9_10

HRV features, such as the SDNN, have been deemed as useful to predict adverse cardiac outcomes [5]. The HRV can be calculated by determining the systolic peak of the photoplethysmogram (PPG) or the R peak of the electrocardiogram (ECG). The PPG signal measures blood volume variations in the microvascular system through an infrared light sensor placed on the skin surface, thus making this a non-invasive technique. Peak detection is an essential step in the determination of the HRV, since erroneously detected or unaccounted peaks lead to errors in the inter-beat time intervals, which affects the features accuracy [6]. The state-of-the-art accounts herein presented refer only to real time systems implementation. The commonly used platforms include Simulink® and LabView.

Real time systems have been developed to process ECG and PPG signals. Tanji et al. [7] developed an ECG noise rejection system in Simulink® for the attenuation of the electromagnetic interference. Tejaswi et al. [8] implemented an Recursive Least Square (RLS) filter in Simulink®, to reduce noise in the ECG signal. Bhogeshwar et al. [9] implemented different filters to denoise the ECG. Mukherjea et al. [11] created a model to generate synthetic PPG waveforms. The developing platform was the Simulink® in both cases. Shiraishi et al. [10] analysed, in real time, the HRV variations during exercise, based on a 12-lead ECG. Bagha et al. [12] developed in LabView, a real time analysis of blood-oxygen saturation levels (SpO$_2$).

The goal of this work was to obtain an HRV estimation from the PPG signal by developing a Simulink® based real-time system with a machine learning module. The innovative aspect of the herein presented work consists on the use of a machine learning algorithm working on PPG signals under the general framework of a real time prototyping platform. Despite the offline nature of the PPG data used in this work, the implementations will be referred as being real time.

2 Methods

A real time peak detection and HRV estimation system was developed in Simulink®. To test and debug the developed system, previously recorded PPG signals with a sampling rate of 50 Hz were used as the input. Figure 1 represents an overview of the developed Simulink® model which is comprised by three main blocks: *Deep Learning, Find Peaks* and *HRV Computation*. A detailed explanation of each block is presented in the respective sub-section.

Fig. 1. Real-time HRV estimation system developed in Simulink®. This system is comprised by three main blocks: *Deep Learning, Find Peaks and HRV Computation.*

2.1 Deep Learning Block

The first block of the prototype is based on a Deep Learning (DL) model that was implemented and tested in the authors' previous work [13], where all the system implementation is detailed and explained. This model was optimized and tested for PPG signals. Figure 2 outlines the implementation steps of the DL model.

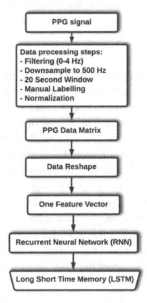

Fig. 2. Flowchart of the implementation steps of the LSTM model as described in [13].

The single layer Long Short-Term Memory (LSTM) model with 200 neurons that was trained in MATLAB and saved in a *mat* format file was subsequently uploaded to the Simulink® based system using the native *Predict* block. The goal of the LSTM network was to classify each data point in two categories: noise or signal. The output of the model is a probability value. Therefore, it was necessary to establish a threshold level for the categories' separation. The LSTM model architecture and the threshold of 0.515 used in the herein presented work were based on the results in [13]. The output of this block is a logic array, where the zero and one correspond to the noise and signal categories, respectively. Figure 3 shows the outline of the *Deep Learning* block.

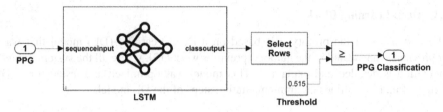

Fig. 3. *Deep Learning* block, with a PPG input, LSTM model and PPG classification.

2.2 Find Peaks Block

After the data classification performed by the Deep Learning block, each data point was classed into two categories: noise and signal. The first step of the *Find Peaks* block is a multiplication of the inputs. As shown in Fig. 4, input 1 is the PPG signal, and input 2 is the output of the Deep Learning block. The format of this output is a logic array where each datapoint is defined by its category. This method ensures that the signal points classified as noise by the deep learning model will not be wrongly identified as peaks. Noise samples will be categorized with zero value in the PPG signal. This step enhances system robustness to noise artifacts. After this step, the peak detection algorithm is implemented. Since a buffer block with three samples using a two-sample overlap was applied for peak detection, it is necessary to have at least three signal samples. The buffer block creates a signal frame which is the input for the native Simulink® *Find Maxima* block, used to obtain the signal peaks. The output of the *Find Peaks* block is the peak vector index. Figure 4 presents in detail the *Find Peaks* block.

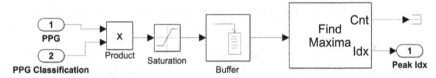

Fig. 4. *Find Peaks* block with two inputs: the PPG signal and its deep learning classification

This block output was the peak index location.
The blocks depicted in Fig. 4 reads as follows:

- A product block implements the multiplication between the PPG signal and the categorical variable that is the output of the LSTM classifier.
- A saturation block ensures that the excursion of the product signal stands from a value close to zero to the PPG peak.
- The buffer block produces a frame of 3 samples, which will be a requirement of the next block, the *Find Peaks*.

2.3 HRV Computation Block

The upper line of the HRV block shown in Fig. 5 was methodological implemented as in [14]. An outlier detector was included, represented in the *If* blocks of the lower line of the Fig. 5, to increase HRV estimation accuracy. The output of the *Find Peaks* block, the peak index, is the input of this block. The blocks in Fig. 5 are described as follows:

- A native *Unbuffer* block was applied to return the signal to its original sample-by-sample format.
- The unbuffered signal is input to an integrator and accumulator processor based on the backward Euler method, with one zero and one pole. This cumulative sum operation is an essential part of the HRV estimation.
- The signal is then integrated and delayed. A native *Sample and Hold* block was implemented in order to find the sample distance between consecutive peaks [14]. This block is triggered by the signal transitions in the *Peak Idx* input.
- After determining, in number of samples, the distance between peaks it is necessary to convert this value to seconds, in order to obtain the HRV. To achieve this, the distance is divided by the 50 Hz sampling frequency.
- To minimize the possibility of peak detection errors and increase the robustness of the developed system, an *IF cycle* based on the HRV values was introduced. A threshold of 0.3 s is applied. The *IF cycle* evaluated if a difference above 0.3 s is present in the HRV vector. If this difference is detected the HRV maintained its previous value. The *Merge* block combines the result of the *If* and *Else* blocks on a single output. The outputs of the *HRV Computation* block are the PPG peak location, output 1, and the HRV estimation, output 2.

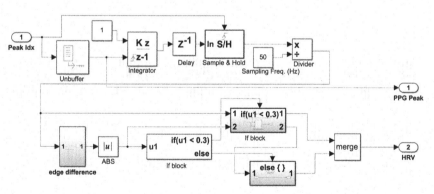

Fig. 5. *HRV Computation* block. From the peak index input, a sample distance between peaks is determined from which the HRV can be obtained. More details can be found in the text.

3 Results

Figure 6 shows the output of the developed system for a 10 s PPG input. This is depicted in the upper plot. The second plot shows the PPG peak location determined with the *Find Peaks* block. The third plot presents the real time HRV estimation, obtained from the time interval between successive peaks. In Fig. 7 a PPG signal with 160 s is represented, where it is possible to observe the natural signal oscillations as a result of the sympathetic and parasympathetic system intervention.

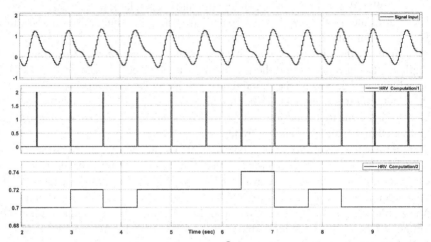

Fig. 6. Ten seconds display output of the Simulink® system. The PPG input signal, peak detection and HRV estimation are represented in the first, second and third plot, respectively.

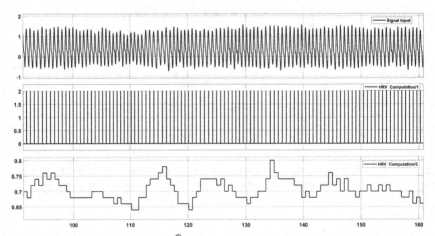

Fig. 7. Display output of the Simulink® system of a PPG signal of 160 s. The PPG input signal, peak detection and HRV estimation are represented in the first, second and third plot, respectively.

To evaluate the robustness of the designed system, a comparison of HRV vectors was performed. Twenty 10 s length PPG signals were analysed. To establish the ground truth, the PPG peaks were marked by expert observation and the HRV was calculated. This HRV ground truth was compared to the HRV extracted from the Simulink®. To compare the performance of system, the Root Mean Square Error (RMSE) and a T-test were performed. A 0.05 significance value was selected for the T-test. The results presented in Table 1 show that the real time HRV estimation adequately represents the ground truth with 0.0439 s and 0.0175 s of RMSE mean and standard deviation, respectively. The T-test results revealed no significant differences between the evaluated HRV vectors.

Table 1. RMSE and T-test results from comparison of HRV vector of gold standard vs. Simulink®.

PPG signal	RMSE (s)	p-value
1	0.040	8.900e−12
2	0.040	1.419e−12
3	0.040	3.742e−12
4	0.041	4.996e−05
5	0.040	4.139e−12
6	0.041	4.995e−05
7	0.040	4.139e−12
8	0.040	1.211e−12
9	0.040	2.358e−13
10	0.047	2.428e−04
11	0.024	1.609e−06
12	0.040	1.171e−12
13	0.040	1.765e−12
14	0.040	6.449e−12
15	0.040	4.522e−12
16	0.040	4.427e−12
17	0.116	9.093e−04
18	0.048	8.488e−06
19	0.040	3.244e−12
20	0.040	1.199e−12

4   Discussion and Conclusion

Nowadays, wearable devices with incorporated PPG sensors are widely available. Smart-watches are an example of such devices that can be used to record biomedical signals, increasing the need for robust real-time algorithms that can compute different features. It is expected that real time deep learning implementation will become popular in wearable devices due to its robustness and increased accuracy. The herein developed system represents an innovation in this respect since it incorporates a LSTM machine learning module.

The results of the herein presented work are a follow up of the authors' theoretical and practical previous implementation in offline platforms. It is often challenging to implement offline algorithms in real time systems due to non-casual processing issues or latency problems. In future work, different deep learning models previously studied will be implemented and tested in the Simulink® system. The produced code could be embedded in hardware platforms such as Android based systems. A simple evaluation of the processing speed of the herein presented model shows that the code can be implemented in the average current Android system without speed or overload issues. Regarding the PPG signal acquisition system on the patient side, it is within the authors' future work to use an Arduino acquisition system with a wi-fi link to the Android system. The herein used 50 Hz PPG sampling frequency is well within the Arduino capabilities.

Acknowledgments. This work was funded and supported by the Fundação para a Ciência e Tecnologia (FCT, Portugal) and NMT, S.A in the scope of the PhD grant PD/BDE/150312/2019.

References

1. Ahmad, F.B., Anderson, R.N.: The leading causes of death in the US for 2020. JAMA **325**(18), 1829 (2021). https://doi.org/10.1001/jama.2021.5469
2. Guidelines, T.N.: American, guidelines, and task force of the European Society of Cardiology the North American Society of Pacing Electrophysiology, "guidelines heart rate variability." Eur. Heart J. **17**, 354–381 (1996). https://doi.org/10.1161/01.CIR.93.5.1043
3. Singh, N., Moneghetti, K.J., Christle, J.W., Hadley, D., Plews, D., Froelicher, V.: Heart rate variability: an old metric with new meaning in the era of using mHealth technologies for health and exercise training guidance. Part one: physiology and methods. Arrhythmia. Electrophysiol. Rev. **7**(3), 193 (2018). https://doi.org/10.15420/aer.2018.27.2
4. Shaffer, F., Ginsberg, J.P.: An Overview of Heart Rate Variability Metrics and Norms. Front. Pub. Heal. **5**, 1–17 (2017). https://doi.org/10.3389/fpubh.2017.00258
5. Buccelletti, F., et al.: Heart rate variability and myocardial infarction: systematic literature review and metanalysis. Eur. Rev. Med. Pharmacol. Sci. **13**(4), 299–307 (2009). https://www.researchgate.net/publication/26754890
6. Sheridan, D.C., Dehart, R., Lin, A., Sabbaj, M., Baker, S.D.: Heart rate variability analysis: how much artifact can we remove? Psychiatry Investig. **17**(9), 960–965 (2020). https://doi.org/10.30773/pi.2020.0168
7. Tanji, A.K., de Brito, M.A.G., Alves, M.G., Garcia, R.C., Chen, G.-L., Ama, N.R.N.: Improved noise cancelling algorithm for electrocardiogram based on moving average adaptive filter. Electronics **10**(19), 2366 (2021). https://doi.org/10.3390/electronics10192366
8. Tejaswi, V., Surendar, A., Srikanta, N.: Simulink implementation of RLS algorithm for resilient artefacts removal in ECG signal. Int. J. Adv. Intell. Paradig. **16**(3/4), 324 (2020). https://doi.org/10.1504/IJAIP.2020.107529

9. Bhogeshwar, S.S., Soni, M.K., Bansal, D.: Design of Simulink model to denoise ECG signal using various IIR & FIR filters. In: 2014 International Conference on Reliability Optimization and Information Technology (ICROIT), February 2014, pp. 477–483 (2014). https://doi.org/10.1109/ICROIT.2014.6798370

10. Shiraishi, Y., et al.: Real-time analysis of the heart rate variability during incremental exercise for the detection of the ventilatory threshold. J. Am. Heart Assoc. 7(1), e006612 (2018). https://doi.org/10.1161/JAHA.117.006612

11. Mukherjea, A., Chaudhury, P., Karkun, A., Ghosh, S., Bhowmick, S.: Synthesis of PPG waveform using PSPICE and Simulink model. In: 2019 Devices for Integrated Circuit (DevIC), March 2019, pp. 428–432 (2019). https://doi.org/10.1109/DEVIC.2019.8783684

12. Bagha, S., Shaw, L.: A real time analysis of PPG signal for measurement of SpO2 and pulse rate. Int. J. Comput. Appl. 36, 45–50 (2011). https://doi.org/10.5120/4537-6461

13. Esgalhado, F., Fernandes, B., Vassilenko, V., Batista, A., Russo, S.: The application of deep learning algorithms for PPG signal processing and classification. Computers 10(12), 158 (2021). https://doi.org/10.3390/computers10120158

14. Lukáč, T., Ondráček, O.: Using Simulink and Matlab for real-time ECG signal processing. In: Conference on MATLAB (2012)

Neuromotor Evaluation of the Upper Limb During Activities of Daily Living: A Pilot Study

Patrícia Santos[1,2,3(✉)], Cláudia Quaresma[1,2], Inês Garcia[2], and Carla Quintão[1,2]

[1] Physics Department, NOVA School of Science and NOVA University of Lisbon, 2829-516 Caparica, Portugal
patricia.santos@campus.fct.unl.pt
[2] Laboratory for Instrumentation, Biomedical Engineering and Radiation Physics (LIBPhys-UNL), Physics Department, NOVA School of Science and Technology, NOVA University of Lisbon, 2829-516 Caparica, Portugal
[3] Health Department, Superior School of Health, Polytechnic Institute of Beja, 7800-111 Beja, Portugal

Abstract. Upper limb function impairment is one of the most common sequelae in stroke. Conventional evaluation methods, based on scales, do not provide an objective assessment of patient's performance. A pilot study was conducted to characterize neuromotor biosignals of the upper limb, during activities of daily living (ADLs). We use BiosignalsPlux® device to monitor the contraction pattern of the shoulder muscles in five ADLs with different motor patterns, through electromyography. Thus, the main purpose of this article is to describe the results of the application of these sensors in the characterization of the contraction pattern of the shoulder muscles during ADLs performed by healthy subjects. The results shows that the pattern of contraction of the shoulder muscles differs between ADLs directed at the midline and directed at the contralateral side; presents different behaviors in distinct ADLs directed at the midline; as well as in ADLs directed to the contralateral side.

Keywords: Neuromotor evaluation · Upper limb · Technology · Activities of daily living · Biomechanics

1 Introduction

Functional deficits associated with the upper limb are one of the most frequent sequelae caused by cerebrovascular diseases, such as stroke [1, 2]. About 50% of the subjects with this diagnosis are not completely independent after 6 months of the stroke episode [3]. The upper limb paresis is the most frequent and severe neuromotor deficit associated to stroke, being characterized by a decrease in muscle strength [4], and loss of autonomy in ADLs [5]. It is estimated that 37%–55% of subjects with stroke have deficits in the performance of these activities [6], related to the omission of small actions, changes in the sequence and in the quality of their performance, as demonstrated in studies related to the preparation of meals [7] and hygiene [8].

© IFIP International Federation for Information Processing 2022
Published by Springer Nature Switzerland AG 2022
L. M. Camarinha-Matos (Ed.): DoCEIS 2022, IFIP AICT 649, pp. 112–121, 2022.
https://doi.org/10.1007/978-3-031-07520-9_11

The methods used in clinical practice to assess upper limb neuromotor deficits in stroke patients continue to be based on qualitative assessment scales, which generates subjective trends [9] and does not allow an objective assessment of the performance or effectiveness of therapies [10].

1.1 Technologies for Studying the Human Movement in Stroke Patients

Many studies have been realized on human movement [11, 12], both in terms of kinematics, kinetics, and biosignal analysis [13–15], however these studies in stroke patients have been performed essentially on the lower limb. Other studies, focusing on upper limb functionality in stroke patients, study kinetic and kinematic parameters, using only optoelectronic motion analysis systems, during simulated tasks of transporting cylindrical objects and not during ADLs [16]. In other studies, full-body suits with inertial measurement unit sensors (3D accelerometer, 3D magnetometer, and 3D gyroscope) are used to measure kinematic parameters in ADLs [17]. There are still studies that analyze the motor pattern of the upper limb in stroke patients, while performing tasks such as drinking water from a glass, but the evaluation is again directed to the analysis of kinematic parameters [18, 19].

Although the cited studies used technology during the assessment, none of them analyzed the contraction pattern of the upper limb muscles in the real context of ADLs. For this, it is essential to analyze the amplitude of muscle activation through EMG.

EMG is the measurement of the electrical signal associated with muscle activity. Muscle excitation is then analyzed through the amplitude of the EMG signals, which means that the more motor units are recruited and the higher the firing rates, the greater the contraction by the muscle [20].

Through the EMG signal, muscle contraction and relaxation data are obtained, indicating whether the muscle is actively participating in the execution of the movement. The quality and precision of the generated signals also depend on the correct positioning of the electrodes in the muscles that we intend to analyze [21].

2   Technological Innovation for Digitalization and Virtualization in Life Improvement

The analysis of muscle contraction through EMG has a fundamental role in stroke patients, as these patients present significant changes in their movements [22] that can limit the range of motion of the shoulder and elbow during ADLs.

Stroke patients develop compensatory movements, based on altered movement patterns through the contraction of other muscles, which will compensate for the decrease in strength, alteration of tone, among others [23]. Prolonged use of altered movement patterns has a negative impact on joint alignment [24], limiting range of motion and contributing to muscle contractures and weaknesses [25], impairing the rehabilitation process.

To verify the existence of inadequate pattern of muscle activation during ADLs, it is necessary to know the normal pattern of muscle activation in these activities through EMG, in healthy individuals, however, in the literature, there is no data on this.

It is essential that the data related to the muscle activation amplitude can be submitted to a digitalization and virtualization process, to be presented and visualized in graphs representing the muscle activation pattern, both in healthy subjects and later in stroke patients.

It is only possible to interpret the increase and decrease in muscle activation amplitude, that is, muscle contraction and relaxation, as well as the sequence of muscle amplitude activation peaks during the activities itself, in the different ADLs, through the visualization of the data.

This pilot study aims to develop a protocol to analyze the activation pattern of the EMG activity of the shoulder muscles during ADLs, as well as to explore the characteristics of this same pattern (amplitude and sequence of muscle activation peaks). To this end, the main shoulder muscles were identified [26] and the ADLs most prone to compensatory movements (eating, drinking, dressing or personal care) [27].

The question of this investigation focuses on exploring the applicability of this protocol in identifying the normal pattern of muscle activation in different ADLs. Subsequently, this protocol will be validated in a larger sample, to answer a research question related to the doctoral project, that is, to explore and know the normal pattern of activation amplitude of the main shoulder muscles in ADLs.

3   Materials and Methods

3.1   Participants in Clinical Investigation

This protocol was applied to a female participant, right-handed, aged 38 years, selected by convenience, who met the established criteria. As exclusion criteria, diagnosis of neuromotor, cognitive or language deficits, left hand dominance and changes in visual acuity not compensated by glasses or contact lenses were defined. Ethical and confidentiality principles were guaranteed, the volunteer joined the study after reading and signing the informed consent.

3.2   Measurement System

A device for collecting EMG signals, the Biosignalsplux®, was used. This device was connected by wireless with the OpenSignals (r)evolution Software®, this software was used for data acquisition, visualization, and processing, being a specific software for PLUX® biosignal hardware platforms [29]. In this study, 6 channels were used to record bipolar EMG related to 6 different muscles. Each bipolar signal was recorded from electrodes placed 2 cm apart [30].

The electrodes were placed according to the agonist muscles of the main shoulder movements (Table 1), namely the Pectoralis Major, Anterior Deltoid, Middle Deltoid, Posterior Deltoid, Upper Trapezius and Lower Trapezius responsible for flexion, extension, abduction, adduction, elevation, and depression of the scapula [26]. Signal was collected at a sample frequency of 1000 Hz [31].

Table 1. Agonist muscles of the main shoulder movements.

Muscle	PM	AD	MD	PD	UT	LT
Shoulder movements	ADD	F	ABD	E	SE	SD
Electrode's position						

Abbreviation: PM, Pectoralis Major; AD, Anterior Deltoid; MD, Middle Deltoid; PD, Posterior Deltoid; UT, Upper Trapezius; LT, Lower Trapezius; ADD; Adduction; ABD, Abduction; F, Flexion; E, Extension; SE, Scapular elevation; SD, Scapular depression.

3.3 Experimental Procedure

The volunteer was instructed to perform two types of activities: directed to the midline (drinking from a cup, eating soup and brushing teeth) and directed to the contralateral side (brushing the hair on the left side of the head and washing the left upper limb). The materials chosen consisted of a cup, a tablespoon, a bowl, a toothbrush, and a hairbrush.

In all activities directed at the midline, the objects were placed 20 cm from the edge of the table and aligned with the midline of the subject's body. The subject was seated in a chair (40 cm high), next to a table (75 cm high), with knees and hips flexed at 90°, with the upper limbs resting on the table, shoulder in neutral position, elbow flexed at 90°, forearm in pronation, wrist in neutral position and fingers in extension.

In all the activities directed to the contralateral side, the subject was only seated in a chair (40 cm high), with knees and hips flexed at 90°, with the upper limbs supported on the thighs, shoulder in a neutral position, elbow flexed at 45°, forearm and wrist in neutral position and fingers semi-flexed. Within these activities, only brushing the hair contemplated an object (the brush), which was already in the subject's hand, when the activities began.

As these activities consist of complex movements of the joints of the upper limbs, it is important to distinguish their phases [32, 33]. These phases are represented in Table 2, as well as the respective movements performed by the shoulder [26].

Regarding the signal processing of the EMG activity, the MATLAB® software was used. The signal was then imported into this software, and the channels related to the EM activity signal were selected for each of the activities. After selecting a module of 5700 points (part of the signal to be analyzed), the frequency was transformed into units of time(s), the average of the signal was subtracted, the signal was placed in absolute values, the moving average was applied. at the same. To know the peaks of the activation amplitude of each of the analyzed muscles and the moment in time that they occur in the activity, the maximum values were requested.

Table 2. Activity phases in ADLs.

ADL´s directed at the midline

Phases	1.Starting position to Reaching	2.Grasping	3.transporting to the mouth
Drinking from a cup	ADD, F	ADD, F, SE	F, ABD, SE
Eating soup	ADD, F, SE	ADD, F, SE	F, ABD, SE
Brushing teeth	ADD, F, SE	ADD, SE, F	F, ABD, SE

Phases	4.Introduced in the mouth	5.Return to pick up point	6.Return initial position
Drinking from a cup	F, ABD, SE	ADD, E, SD	E, SE, ABD
Eating soup	F, ABD, SE	ADD, E, SD	E, SE, ABD
Brushing teeth	F, ABD, SE	ADD, E, SD	E, SE, ABD

ADL`s directed at the contralateral side

Phases	Starting position to Reaching	1.Grasping	2.Transporting to the contralateral side
	Does not occur, starts with the upper limb on top of the thigh with the object in hand		
Hair brushing		ADD	F, ADD, SE
Washing upper limb		ADD	F, ADD, SE

Phases	3. Reaching the contralateral side	4. Return to the thigh	5. Return initial position
Hair brushing	F, ADD, SE	ABD, E, SD	ABD, E, SD
Washing upper limb	F, ADD, SE	ABD, E, SD	ABD, E, SD

Abbreviation: ADD, Adduction; ABD, Abduction; F, Flexion; E, Extension; SE, Scapular elevation; SD, Scapular depression.

4   Results

The results of this study are summarized in Tables 3 and 4. It is verified that the ADLs of drinking from the cup and eating the soup show similar amplitude activation patterns (Table 3). However, soup eating activity (Fig. 1) presents a second amplitude peak relative to the upper trapezius.

In the activity of brushing teeth, the activation pattern differs from previous activities.

Table 3. Results of peak muscle activation amplitude in ADLs directed to the midline

Drinking from the cup		Eating soup		Brushing the teeth	
Amplitude of contraction (mV)	Time of amplitude peak (s)	Amplitude of contraction (mV)	Time of amplitude peak (s)	Amplitude of contraction (mV)	Time of amplitude peak (s)
AD 1881	PM 2,22	AD 1695	UT 2,12	UT 1017	AD 2,55
UT 1515	UT 2,35	UT 1124	LT 2,17	AD 828	MD 2,56
MD 1079	MD 2,45	MD 974	PD 2,24	MD 679	UT 2,56
LT 654	PD 2,50	LT 602	MD 2,24	LT 428	PD 2,67
PD 427	AD 2,55	PD 439	AD 2,27	PD 297	PM 2,76
PM 314	LT 2,92	PM 356	PM 2,28	PM 276	LT 2,85

Abbreviation: PM, Pectoralis Major; AD, Anterior Deltoid; MD, Middle Deltoid; PD, Posterior Deltoid; UT, Upper Trapezius; LT, Lower Trapezius.

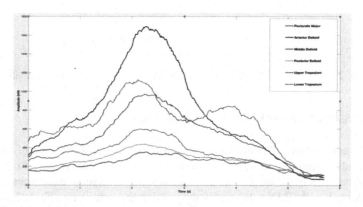

Fig. 1. Amplitude pattern of muscle activation over time of eating soup activity.

It is verified that the activities of washing the arms and brushing the hair have similar activation amplitude patterns (Table 4), but in the arm washing activity, there is also a second activation peak (Fig. 2).

Table 4. Results of peak muscle activation amplitude in ADLs directed to the contralateral side.

Arm washing		Brushing the hair	
Amplitude of contraction (mV)	Time of amplitude peak (s)	Amplitude of contraction (mV)	Time of amplitude peak (s)
AD 2139	LT 1,24	AD 2553	UT 1,31
MD 984	UT 1,39	MD 1365	LT 1,51
UT 894	PM 1,63	UT 1294	PD 1,52
PM 732	AD 1,72	PD 579	PM 1,60
PD 571	PD 1,77	PM 489	AD 1,63
LT 238	MD 1,77	LT 409	MD 1,63

Abbreviation: PM, Pectoralis Major; AD, Anterior Deltoid; MD, Middle Deltoid; PD, Posterior Deltoid; UT, Upper Trapezius; LT, Lower Trapezius.

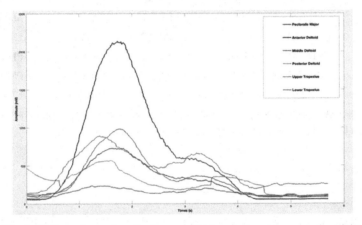

Fig. 2. Pattern of muscle activation amplitude over time of arm wash activity.

5   Discussion of Results and Critical View

The results are indicative that in all activities, are two marked phases: one of increasing the amplitude of muscle activation, corresponding to an increase in contraction and another of decreasing the amplitude, corresponding to a decrease in contraction of the muscle. Regarding the ADLs directed to the midline and considering Table 2, and other studies that mention these same phases of activity [32, 33], it can be inferred that the phase of contraction corresponds to the first four phases of the activity. The phase of decreased contraction corresponds to the remaining phases.

Regarding the ADLs directed to the contralateral side and considering Table 2, it can be inferred that the phase of contraction corresponds to the first three phases of the activity. The phase of decreased contraction corresponds to the remaining phases.

For midline-directed ADLs, the amplitude of muscle activation is similar between the drinking-by-a-glass and soup-eating activities, except for the Upper Trapezius muscle, which, in the relaxation phase, once again, shows an increase in the activation amplitude. According to the analysis of the movements performed in Table 2, this peak may be associated with the demands of the activity itself, namely the last phase of the activity, the phase of returning to the initial position.

The activity of brushing the teeth differs from the previous ones, since there is a more prolonged amplitude of muscle activation in the time in which the activity takes place. being This difference is more evident in the Upper Trapezius, Anterior Deltoid and Middle Deltoid. These muscles, in the final phase of activity, also express an increase in the contraction.

For ADLs directed to the contralateral side, the amplitude of muscle activation is similar between washing the arm and brushing the hair, in most muscles involved in the phase of increased muscle activation. The largest difference is seen in the relaxation phase of the arm washing activity. As in previous activities, the Upper Trapezius, Anterior Deltoid and Middle Deltoid muscles again demonstrate an increase in the amplitude of activation.

Regarding the analysis of the time (s), in which the peaks of maximum amplitude occur during the 5.7 s of the course of activities. It is verified that all muscles in all ADLs directed to the midline, reach their peak of maximum activation amplitude between 2 and 3 s and ADLs directed to the contralateral side between 1 and 2 s.

6 Conclusion and Further Work

This study assumed a central importance in the testing of the experimental protocol, because although the related muscle groups of the shoulder involved in the ADL's are the same, the specificities of the activity point to the existence of different patterns of muscle contraction between the ADL's analyzed. Thus, the results are indicative of differences in the pattern of activation amplitude between ADLs directed to the midline, between ADLs directed to the contralateral side, as well as between these two groups of activities. They are also indicative of similarities between both ADLs directed to the midline and between ADLs directed to the contralateral side, about the time interval in which peaks of muscle activation occur during activities.

These results lead to the need for future work to understand whether these indications are valid in a larger sample, since the application to only one subject constitutes a limitation of the study. The use of EMG together with other technologies, such as accelerometry, for example, to complement the analysis of the shoulder muscle contraction pattern in ADLs is another suggestion for future investigations.

References

1. Parker, V.M., Wade, D.T., Langton Hewer, R.: Loss of an arm function after stroke: measurement, frequency and recovery. Int. Rehabil. Med. **8**, 69–73 (1986)
2. Nakayama, H., Jorgensen, H.S., Raaschou, H.O., Olsen, T.S.: Compensation in recovery of upper extremity function after stroke: the Copenhagen Stroke Study. Arch. Phys. Med. Rehabil. **75**, 852–857 (1994)

3. Meijer, R., Ihnenfeldt, D.S., de Groot, I.J.M., van Limbeek, J., Vermeulen, M., de Haan, R.J.: Prognostic factors for ambulation and activities of daily living in the subacute phase after stroke: a systematic review of the literature. Clin. Rehabil. **17**(2), 119–129 (2003)
4. Beebe, J.A., Lang, C.E.: Absence of a proximal to distal gradient of motor deficits in the upper extremity early after stroke. Clin. Neurophysiol. **119**, 2074–2085 (2008)
5. Wisneski, K., Johnson, M.: Quantifying kinematics of purposeful movements to real, imagined, or absent functional objects: implications for modelling trajectories for robot-assisted ADL tasks. J. Neuroeng. Rehabil. 4–7 (2007)
6. Foundas, A.L., et al.: Ecological implications of limb apraxia: evidence from mealtime behavior. J. Int. Neuropsychol. Soc. **1**, 62–66 (1995)
7. Bieńkiewicz, M., Brandi, M.L., Goldenberg, G., Hughes, C., Hermsdörfer, J.: The tool in the brain: apraxia in ADL. Behavioral and neurological correlates of apraxia in daily living. Front. Psychol. **5**, 353 (2014)
8. Humphreys, G.W., Forde, E.M.E.: Disordered action schema and action disorganisation syndrome. Cogn. Neuropsychol. **15**, 771–811 (1998)
9. Catz, A., Itzkovich, M., Agranov, E., et al.: SCIM-spinal cord independence measure: a new disability scale for patients with spinal cord lesions. Spinal Cord **35**, 850–856 (1997)
10. Zhou, H., Huosheng, H., Tao, Y.: Inertial measurements of upper limb motion. Med. Biol. Eng. Comput. **44**, 479–487 (2006)
11. Harezlak, K., Kasprowski, P.: Application of eye tracking in medicine: a survey, research issues and challenges. Comput. Med. Imag. Graph. **65**, 176–190 (2018)
12. Schenk, P., Colombo, G., Maier, I.: New technology in rehabilitation: possibilities and limitations. In: Pons, J.L., Torricelli, D., Pajaro, M. (eds.) Converging Clinical and Engineering Research on Neurorehabilitation. BB, vol. 1, pp. 963–967. Springer, Heidelberg (2013). https://doi.org/10.1007/978-3-642-34546-3_157
13. Biryukova, E.V., Roby-Brami, A., Frolov, A.A., Mokhtari, M.: Kinematics of human arm reconstructed from spatial tracking system recordings. J. Biomech. **33**, 985–995 (2000)
14. de los Reyes-Guzmán, A., Gil-Agudo, A., Peñasco-Martín, B., Solís-Mozos, M., del Ama-Espinosa, A., Pérez-Rizo, E.: Kinematic analysis of the daily activity of drinking from a glass in a population with cervical spinal cord injury. J. Neuroeng. Rehabil. **20**, 7–41 (2010)
15. Luinge, H.J., Veltink, P.H.: Measuring orientation of human body segments using miniature gyroscopes and accelerometers. Med. Biol. Eng. Comput. **43**, 273–282 (2005)
16. Blaszczyszyn, M., Szczesna, A., Opara, J., Konieczny, M., Pakosz, P., Balko, S.: Functional differences in upper limb movement after early and chronic stroke based on kinematic motion indicators. Biomed Pap Med Fac Univ Palacky Olomouc Czech Repub (2018)
17. Held, J., et al.: Inertial sensor measurements of upper-limb kinematics in stroke patients in clinic and home environment. Front. Bioeng. Biotechnol. **12**, 6–27 (2018)
18. Kim, K., et al.: Kinematic analysis of upper extremity movement during drinking in hemiplegic subjects. Clin. Biomech. **29**, 248–256 (2014)
19. Murphy, M., Murphy, S., Persson, H., Bergström, U., Sunnerhagen, K.: Kinematic analysis using 3D motion capture of drinking task in people with and without upper-extremity impairments. J. Vis. Exp. **133**, 57228 (2018)
20. Abas, N., Bukhari, W.M., Abas, M.A., Tokhi, M.O.: Electromyography assessment of forearm muscles: towards the control of exoskeleton hand. In: 5th International Conference on Control, Decision and Information Technologies, pp. 2–6. IEEE (2018)
21. Moore, K.L., Dalley, A.F.: Clinically Oriented Anatomy. Lippincott Williams & Wilkins, Philadelphia (1999)
22. Dipietro, L., et al.: Changing motor synergies in chronic stroke. J. Neurophysiol. **98**(2), 757–768 (2007)

23. Ellis, M.D., Holubar, B.G., Acosta, A.M., Beer, R.F., Dewald, J.P.: Modifiability of abnormal isometric elbow and shoulder joint torque coupling after stroke. Muscle Nerve. **32**(2), 170–178 (2005)

24. Ludewig, P.M., Cook, T.M.: Alterations in shoulder kinematics and associated muscle activity in people with symptoms of shoulder impingement. Phys. Ther. **80**(3), 276–291 (2005)

25. Kerr, A.L., Cheng, S.Y., Jones, T.A.: Experience-dependent neural plasticity in the adult damaged brain. J. Commun. Disord. **44**(5), 538–548 (2011)

26. Esperança Pina, J.: Anatomia da Locomoção (5ª edição). Lidel, Lisboa (2017)

27. Oosterwijk, A.M., Nieuwenhuis, M.K., van der Schans, C.P., Mouton, L.J.: Shoulder and elbow range of motion for the performance of activities of daily living: a systematic review. Physiother. Theory Pract. (2018)

28. Van Meulen, F., Reenalda, J., Buurke, J., Veltink, P.: Assessment of daily-life reaching performance after stroke. Ann. Biomed. Eng. **43**, 478–486 (2015)

29. Plux Wireless Biosignals S.A. http://plux.info

30. Hermens, H., Freriks, B., Disselhorst-Klug, C., Rau, G.: Development of recommendations for SEMG sensors and sensor placement procedures. J. Electromyogr. Kinesiol. **10**(5), 361–374 (2000)

31. Molina Rueda, F., Rivas Montero, F., Pérez de Heredia Torres, M., Alguacil Diego, I., Molero Sánchez, A., Miangolarra Page, J.: Movement analysis of upper extremity hemiparesis in patients with cerebrovascular disease: a pilot study. Neurologia **27**(6), 343–347 (2012)

32. Kim, K., et al.: Kinematic analysis of upper extremity movement during drinking in hemiplegic subjects. Clin. Biomech. **29**(3), 248–256 (2014)

33. Alt Murphy, M., Murphy, S., Persson, H., Bergström, U., Sunnerhagen, K.: Kinematic analysis using 3D motion capture of drinking task in people with and without upper-extremity impairments. J. Vis. Exp. **28**(133), 57228 (2018)

Gesture-Based Feedback in Human-Robot Interaction for Object Manipulation

Leandro Filipe[1,2](✉), Ricardo Silva Peres[1,2], Francisco Marques[1,2], and Jose Barata[1,2]

[1] Centre of Technology and Systems (CTS), UNINOVA, Caparica, Portugal
{leandro.filipe,ricardo.peres,fam,jab}@uninova.pt
[2] School of Science and Technology, NOVA University of Lisbon, Caparica, Portugal

Abstract. Human-Robot Interaction is a currently highly active research area with many advances in interfaces that allow humans and robots to have bi-directional feedback of their intentions. However, in an industrial setting, current robot feedback methods struggle to successfully deliver messages since the environment makes it difficult and inconvenient for the user to perceive them. This paper proposes a novel method for robot feedback, leveraging the addition of social cues to robot movement to notify the human of its intentions. Through the use of robotic gestures, we believe it is possible to successfully convey the robots' goals in interactions with humans. To verify this hypothesis, a proof of concept was developed in a simulated environment using a robotic arm manipulator that notifies the user using gestures when it needs to correct the pose of an object.

Keywords: Robotics · Human-Robot Interaction · Simulation · Object manipulation · Machine Learning

1 Introduction

With the emergence of Industry 4.0, the role of robotics in the industry has shifted from big unmovable scary machinery to socially accepted anthropomorphic robots with the goal of improving productivity and producing higher quality products at reduced costs [1]. There is also an increased effort in having both humans and robots in the same workspace, since both have their one strengths and limitations, creating a collaborative and safe working environment will result in higher productivity and decreased production times [2].

To better achieve this collaboration, some sort of communication is needed. This should be an intuitive method without the need for expert knowledge. Although existing interfaces meet these requirements, it is believed that in an industrial setting these would not be enough as they would struggle to deliver the intended message [3]. The need then arises for a better interface for Human Robot Interaction (HRI).

When talking about this subject it is difficult to leave out the existing social component. According to Erel et al. [4], there are implicit social cues in robot movement automatically interpreted by the human being, and these need to be taken into account

© IFIP International Federation for Information Processing 2022
Published by Springer Nature Switzerland AG 2022
L. M. Camarinha-Matos (Ed.): DoCEIS 2022, IFIP AICT 649, pp. 122–132, 2022.
https://doi.org/10.1007/978-3-031-07520-9_12

and leveraged by the programmer. Taking this and the previously described challenges into account, the following research question comes naturally.

RQ: *How can social cues be leveraged in robotic movement to improve communication in Human-Robot interaction in a more natural way?*

As a hypothetical solution to this problem, it is proposed the use of robotic gestures to feedback the user of the robot's goals, problems, and intentions, thus improving communication in HRI. Additionally, given the social component of this type of interaction, it is expected that the use of robotic gestures will allow for a more natural and comfortable interaction for the user. Furthermore, it will also allow a greater and easier adoption by users without a more technical background. To validate our hypothesis, a simple proof of concept was developed where a robotic arm is in charge of a pick-and-place task after notifying the user of an incorrect object pose.

With the fourth industrial revolution, many new possibilities came along. More specifically, the recent technological advances in the computational area made possible the use of virtualization as an easier, cheaper, faster way of development. Recent simulation software focuses on the development of life-like scenarios to increase the generability of a solution to the real world.

Moreover, recent changes triggered a shift in development methods, proving the efficiency and usefulness of digitalization and remote work. Teams are now able to develop and collaborate without the pricey overhangs associated with logistics.

Our work takes advantage of simulation as a virtualization method to more easily test and validate our solution. Not only that, the use of life-like scenarios enables the generation of synthetic data to train the used Machine Learning modules, both speeding up the process and reducing costs. Additionally, given the novelty of this subject, the discussion of ideas and possible collaboration will greatly favor this project.

The rest of the document is structured as follows: In Sect. 2 previous work related to this project is presented. Section 3 describes the materials and methods involved in the implementation of this project, containing the system design process (Sect. 3.1), the implementation (Sect. 3.2), and the tests and validation methods used (Sect. 3.3). Section 4 is where the results are analyzed and discussed. Some limitations of this proof of concept are exposed in Sect. 5. Finally, Sect. 6 presents the drawn conclusions and some additional future work is proposed.

2   Related Work

The idea of collaboration between humans and robots it's not unheard of, HRI has been a highly active research topic with the emergence of the Industry 4.0 paradigm [1], and rightly so. There are many reasons for choosing collaborative systems like economic motivations, efficiency in the use of space, and flexibility [2]. Collaborative cells can also adapt well to situations where a constant change in production layout is required since a rigid safety system is not necessary and can more easily be repurposed [5].

Recent research has pointed several different approaches for HRI that pass through speech [6], gestures [7], Augmented Reality (AR) [8], or multimodal systems [9]. Solutions like these are well researched but most of them focus on robot control which we believe covers only half of the problem. For successful collaboration, there needs to be communication from both sides.

On this note, previous work was done regarding situations where the robot needs to notify the user. Berg et al. [10] feedback the user about robot information using a projector to display it. A verbal approach was developed by St. Clair et al. [11] where three types of situated verbalizations aimed at providing useful information are dynamically generated by the robot. However, in many cases like the ones previously listed, the approaches are not tested in a real manufacturing environment, and so there is a lack of assurance that these methods would play well in an industrial setting. This assumption comes from the existence of obstacles such as loud noises that would pose a problem for audio-based solutions, and the additional equipment required for other solutions would be frowned upon by the robot operators.

A new idea then emerges of using robotic gestures to notify the user with information, guide it through difficult tasks, and help to complete objectives. Robot gestures have been previously shown to be socially interpreted by humans and that this phenomenon should be leveraged [4]. Lohse et al. [12] take advantage of this behavior in an experiment where a Nao robot attempts to give route directions with and without robot gestures. The obtained results show that the use of robotic gestures increases user performance and indicates a promising means to improve HRI tasks.

Taking this into account the authors of this paper believe that the use of robotic gestures can be beneficial in HRI tasks in a manufacturing setting. This method is believed to not have to face as many obstacles as different solutions and would improve social acceptance of robots and both assurance and comfortability while collaborating with one. It is then proposed the implementation of a proof of concept that would help validate this hypothesis. Although not tested and validated in a real environment, the goal of this project is to verify the usefulness of an HRI framework of said nature before it is tested in a real industrial setting.

3   Materials and Methods

In this section, the overall planning and execution of the project will be discussed. This includes the architecture design (Sect. 3.1), implementation of the desired features and behaviors (Sect. 3.2), and the methods used to test and validate our solution (Sect. 3.3).

3.1   System Design

For this case study, a simple proof of concept was envisioned to confirm our hypothesis that a robot can give feedback to its human user using only gestures. The scenario that was chosen consists of a pick-and-place example using a robotic arm and a cube. The manipulator's objective is to pick up the cube and place it in a goal position. There is, however, a constraint, the arm can only pick up the cube at a specific orientation. To surpass this challenge the robot needs to ask the user to rotate the cube, using only gestures, until the desired orientation is achieved, after that the cube can be placed in the goal position.

To ensure correct behavior, the robot needs to be able to estimate the cube's position and orientation and plan its movement accordingly. To meet this requirement, the architecture of this project (Fig. 1) will require a pose (position and orientation) estimation model that will receive an RGB image and output the desired information. This information is then passed to a motion planner that is responsible for planning the movement of the robot depending on the position and orientation of the cube. This module is also responsible for deciding whether the cube can be picked up or if the robot needs to inform the user that some adjustments to the cube's orientation are necessary.

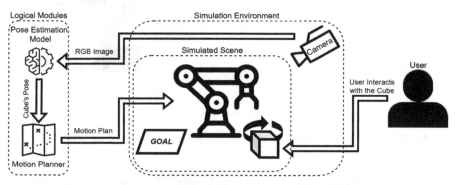

Fig. 1. Proposed architecture for this project.

As can be seen in Fig. 1, the required components are split between logic and interaction modules. The modules responsible for logic operations are not inserted in the simulation environment, since many existing frameworks do not support the necessary tools for robot control. This also serves the purpose of encapsulating similar modules together and isolating the simulation environment, offering greater generalization of our solution and enabling the use of differently implemented modules in conjunction with existing ones.

3.2 Implementation

To implement this project the Unity platform was used since it meets all the requirements imposed for the simulation environment and offers great community support and documentation. Unity also has native support for robotics projects with Unity Robotics Hub which enables the integration with Robotic Operating System (ROS)[1]. Conveniently, Unity Robotics Hub offers an Object Pose Estimation demonstration [13] that already meets most of the requirements for this project. Taking this into account, it was decided to take advantage of the given opportunities and use the aforementioned solution as a starting point for our project.

---

[1] https://www.ros.org/.

As can be seen in Fig. 2, the overall architecture of the Object Pose Estimation tutorial is very similar to the proposed architecture for this project. In both architectures, there is a separation of the logic and interaction modules, wherein Fig. 2 both the pose estimation model and the motion planner modules are implemented within ROS, designed specifically for robotics projects.

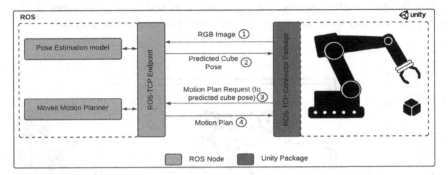

Fig. 2. Unity's architecture for the Object Pose Estimation tutorial. Taken from [13].

Overall, three packages are used for implementing this project, the Unified Robot Description Format (URDF) Importer package[2] to import the robot model into the simulation scene, the TCP Connector package (see footnote 2) so that Unity can communicate with ROS and vice-versa via a TCP endpoint, and the Perception package (see footnote 2) that provides a toolkit for generating large-scale datasets for computer vision training and validation. The ROS workspace comes already configured inside a Docker container with all the necessary dependencies and uses the Moveit [14] motion planner and a custom Convolutional Neural Network (CNN) for pose estimation (CNNs are frequently used in the literature for object pose estimation [15–17]). Figure 3 shows a representation of this model's architecture.

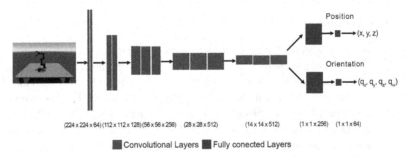

Fig. 3. The pose estimation model. Taken from [13].

---

[2] These packages and the version used are referenced in [13].

This model is a modified implementation of the one presented by Tobin et al. [18] that given an RGB image of the scene, outputs the position and orientation of the cube. To make the model more robust and generalizable to the real world, domain randomization was added by randomizing the pose of the cube, the pose of the target goal, and the lighting of the scene, using the Perception package. The same package is also responsible for labeling each image with a bounding box containing the pose of the cube. The model was trained with a dataset containing 30000 training images and 3000 validation images.

The motion planner that was used is Moveit, one of the most widely used software for robotic manipulation. This module receives the information containing the pose of the cube and the target goal from Unity and plans the motion of the robot accordingly so it can pick up the cube and place it in the goal position. It is in this module that the necessary features to achieve the behavior explained in the previous section were implemented in the Python programming language.

Firstly, an improvement to the overall motion planner was necessary. Although the accuracy regarding the pick-and-place behavior was sufficiently high, the movements produced by the robot were somewhat awkward, resulting in the robot having to do a lot of unnecessary movements. The example utilizes the Open Motion Planning Library (OMPL)[3] with its default RRTConnect [19] algorithm. The replacement of this algorithm for RRT* [20], the additional planning time, and the increased number of concurrent planning jobs were sufficient to achieve a much better result with cleaner motion.

Secondly, to integrate robot feedback through gestures, a verification of the incoming message containing the cube's pose from Unity is needed. The objective here is to check whether the cube has the correct orientation for the manipulator arm to pick it up. For simplification, the desired orientation chosen was $0°$ with a tolerance of $10°$ in both directions, for the z-axis. If the cube's orientation does not meet this requirement the robot is instructed to perform a gesture above the cube. For this purpose, the Pilz Industrial Motion Planner was used in place of the OMPL planner, which enables the generation of circular paths around a center point. The direction of the rotation of the robotic arm depends on the orientation of the cube, the arm always rotates in the direction of the least necessary adjustment, making the user's life a little bit easier. Otherwise, if the cube is in the correct orientation (or inside the allowed interval) the robot can pick it up and place it in the target position.

Finally, a C# script was developed so the user can rotate the cube using a keyboard. The desired plan of action is after being notified by the robot that the cube needs to be rotated, the user will adjust the cube's orientation (preferably rotating it in the optimal direction, as alerted by the robot) and inform the robot that the cube is ready to be placed inside the goal. A shot from the implemented simulation can be seen in Fig. 4 where the robot just finished the circular motion above the cube.

---

[3] https://ompl.kavrakilab.org/.

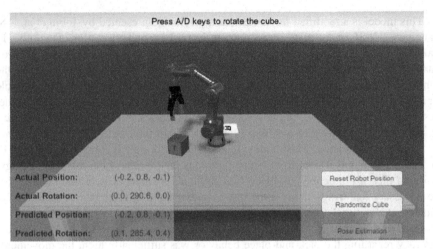

Fig. 4. A shot of the robot after finishing giving feedback and waiting for the user to interact with the cube.

3.3 Tests and Validation

Since the implementation of the starting point for this project has been previously validated, it was decided that the main focus of validation for this work should be the social interpretation of the robot's gestures. With this in mind, an experiment involving 12 participants with higher education on the field (from ages 20–40; 10 male, 2 female) was designed. The experiment aims to provide some feedback on how users perceive and feel about this solution.

The participants were placed in front of the simulation and asked to interact with the robot. It was explained that the objective of the robot is to pick up the cube and place it inside the goal, however, the robot needs the user's help to do so. After interacting with the simulation, the participants were asked to anonymously answer a survey regarding what they just experienced. The survey consists of the nine following questions:

1. **How old are you?**;
2. **What is your gender?**;
3. **What is your level of education?**;
4. **How satisfied are you with the look and feel of the robot's movements?** (weight of 1);
5. **How intuitive is it to understand the robot's feedback?** (weight of 3);
6. **How satisfied are you with the reliability of the solution?** (weight of 2);
7. **How useful do you think this solution would be in a manufacturing setting?** (weight of 2);
8. **Would you recommend this solution to a colleague/friend?**;
9. **How many corrections were made to the cube?**

Additionally, some weight was added to the questions that require a score between one and five so that an overall score can be attributed to this solution and to provide a point of reference for future work. The weights were given from a range of one to three according to the perceived importance of each question.

4 Results Analysis

Questions 4 to 7, inclusive, are the most significant ones in the survey presented to the participants, and as such, special attention was given to them. Looking at the graphs in Fig. 5, the results obtained from these four questions can be seen. In these pictures, the vertical axis corresponds to the number of responses and the horizontal axis represents to the score given in that question.

While the results may not appear as good as expected, this is aligned with the early stage of development of the solution. The usefulness of such validation stems from the possibility to collect valuable feedback for future iterations of the HRI. According to the participants, the look and feel of the robot's movements are mostly pleasant. The robot proves to be reliable for the most part, obtaining an average rating of 3.5 on the reliability scale. While sufficient, perhaps this is an aspect for improvement in future work.

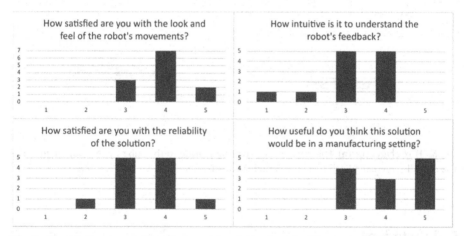

Fig. 5. Graphical representation of some of the obtained results. The vertical axis corresponds to the number of responses and the horizontal axis corresponds to the score given in that question.

Another aspect for improvement is how intuitive the gestures produced by the robot are. Despite getting an average rating overall, there are instances where the solution was rated as not intuitive at all. In addition, some participants reported having difficulty understanding the direction of the circular gesture and how much they had to rotate the cube. This is an important point and will be considered in future implementations.

Lastly, based on what was presented to them, the participants consider this to be a useful solution in a manufacturing setting. Question 7 obtained a significant score with an average of approximately four on a scale of usefulness from 1 to 5. This is an important result because it is a big step in the validation of our solution. Additionally,

10 out of the 12 participants said that they would recommend this solution to a friend or colleague, showing an overall appreciation of this solution.

In addition to these results, an evaluation was also made regarding how many attempts it would take the user to get the cube to the correct position, i.e., how many times the robot had to signal the user to rotate the cube. Figure 6a shows a box chart of the corrections needed to complete the simulation by the participants. Although there was one outlier case where it took the user six attempts to reach the correct orientation of the cube, it took participants on average less than three attempts to correct the orientation of the cube. Ideally, this number would be lower, however, it will serve as an evaluation metric for future solutions.

Finally, the overall score was calculated according to each participant's answers. This result is calculated by multiplying the rating of each of the four questions ranked from 1 to 5 by its respective assigned weight and then adding it all up. Attending to the box plot in Fig. 6b we can see that an average result of $\mu = 28.583$ and a standard deviation $\sigma = 3.523$ was obtained on a maximum of 40 points. This result, although still not very representative of the quality of the developed solution, will be used as a reference point for future implementations, always aiming to overcome it.

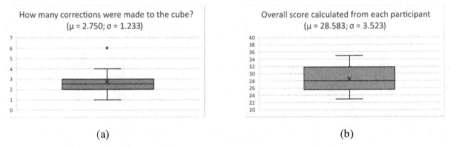

(a)   (b)

Fig. 6. Box charts of: **(a)** The number of corrections made to the cube by the participants; **(b)** The overall score calculated from the participants' answers.

5 Limitations

One of the limitations of this work is the fact that there is no real-world validation. Despite achieving promising results in a simulated and controlled setting, these are not directly transferable to the relevant operational environment, since possible real-world obstacles and drawbacks may not have been taken into consideration. Future implementations will take this into account when performing validation.

Additionally, the conducted experiment to validate our solution has a considerably small population due to time and cost constraints. For a more robust evaluation the experiment should consider a bigger and more diverse population for general use, or a more specific population for a manufacturing setting validation.

Finally, given the innovative nature of the solution proposed here, there are no alternatives yet in the literature that offer a term of comparison. As such, any argument that claims to compare our solution with other alternatives is merely an assumption that would be difficult to support. That said, using a global metric to evaluate the solution will allow us to validate the assumptions made here in future work by directly comparing it to existing approaches.

6 Conclusion and Future Work

This paper proposes a framework for HRI that focuses on the use of robotic gestures to enable a robot of communicating with a user in a manufacturing environment. The main contributions of this work can be summarized as follows. A base project from Unity was modified in order to implement the proposed framework which was validated through an experiment involving 12 participants. Furthermore, a global scoring methodology was created to enable the direct comparison of this solution with different future approaches. The results obtained from the conducted experiment prove that although not as intuitive as initially thought, the presence of robotic gestures in HRI scenarios proves to be a useful addition.

With this in mind, and answering the research question raised in Sect. 1, it is possible to verify that with the integration of robotic gestures as social cues to a robot's movement, there is an improvement to the interaction between a human and a robot. In addition, it is expected that the shortcomings and limitations of this solution will serve to drive any future work in the HRI topic with a focus on robot feedback. For better visualization of the implemented solution, animations containing examples of the robot's behavior can be found here: https://bit.ly/3oRtLoV.

As future work, many aspects of this implementation can be improved upon. The circular path above the object cannot always be feasible due to reachability constraints, for that it is suggested to modify the gesture to accommodate such restraints. As stated in Sect. 4, one aspect to improve is the translation of movement in the robot's gestures where some participants reported difficulties in perceiving how much the robot wanted them to rotate the cube. By generating the path according to how much the user has to rotate the cube this can be avoided, although, another issue can be raised since for minimal corrections the path would most likely be incomprehensible. Finally, as a step forward to this implementation, different gestures for different use-cases will be implemented to improve the robustness of the solution.

References

1. Goel, R., Gupta, P.: Robotics and Industry 4.0. In: Nayyar, A., Kumar, A. (eds.) A Roadmap to Industry 4.0: Smart Production, Sharp Business and Sustainable Development, pp. 157–169. Springer, Cham (2020). https://doi.org/10.1007/978-3-030-14544-6_9
2. Matheson, E., Minto, R., Zampieri, E.G.G., Faccio, M., Rosati, G.: Human–robot collaboration in manufacturing applications: a review. Robotics 8, 100 (2019)
3. Berg, J., Lu, S.: Review of interfaces for industrial human-robot interaction. Curr. Robot. Rep. 1(2), 27–34 (2020). https://doi.org/10.1007/s43154-020-00005-6
4. Erel, H., Tov, T.S., Kessler, Y., Zuckerman, O.: Robots are always social. ACM 5, 1–6 (2019). https://doi.org/10.1145/3290607.3312758

5. Fechter, M., Foith-Förster, P., Pfeiffer, M.S., Bauernhansl, T.: Axiomatic design approach for human-robot collaboration in flexibly linked assembly layouts. Proc. CIRP **50**, 629–634 (2016). https://doi.org/10.1016/j.procir.2016.04.186

6. Maksymova, S., Matarneh, R., Lyashenko, V.V., Belova, N.V.: Voice control for an industrial robot as a combination of various robotic assembly process models. J. Comput. Commun. **5**(11), 1–15 (2017). https://doi.org/10.4236/jcc.2017.511001

7. Neto, P., Simão, M., Mendes, N., Safeea, M.: Gesture-based human-robot interaction for human assistance in manufacturing. Int. J. Adv. Manuf. Technol. **101**(1–4), 119–135 (2018). https://doi.org/10.1007/s00170-018-2788-x

8. Fang, H.C., Ong, S.K., Nee, A.Y.C.: Novel AR-based interface for human-robot interaction and visualization. Adv. Manuf. **2**(4), 275–288 (2014). https://doi.org/10.1007/s40436-014-0087-9

9. Andronas, D., Apostolopoulos, G., Fourtakas, N., Makris, S.: Multi-modal interfaces for natural human-robot interaction. Proc. Manuf. **54**, 197–202 (2021). https://doi.org/10.1016/j.promfg.2021.07.030

10. Berg, J., Lottermoser, A., Richter, C., Reinhart, G.: Human-robot-interaction for mobile industrial robot teams. Procedia CIRP **79**, 614–619 (2019). https://doi.org/10.1016/j.procir.2019.02.080

11. Clair, A.S., Mataric, M.: How robot verbal feedback can improve team performance in human-robot task collaborations. IEEE Comput. Soc. **3**, 213–220 (2015)

12. Lohse, M., Rothuis, R., Gallego-Perez, J., Karreman, D.E., Evers, V.: Robotgestures make difficult tasks easier: the impact of gestures on perceived workload and task performance. ACM **4**, 1459–1466 (2014). https://doi.org/10.1145/2556288.2557274

13. Unity-technologies/robotics-object-pose-estimation. https://github.com/Unity-Technologies/Robotics-Object-Pose-Estimation/

14. Coleman, D., Sucan, I., Chitta, S., Correll, N.: Reducing the barrier to entry of complex robotic software: a move it! case study. arXiv preprint arXiv:1404.3785 (2014)

15. Tremblay, J., To, T., Sundaralingam, B., Xiang, Y., Fox, D., Birchfield, S.: Deepobject pose estimation for semantic robotic grasping of household objects. arXiv preprint arXiv:1809.10790v1 (2018)

16. Doosti, B., Naha, S., Mirbagheri, M., Crandall, D.J.: Hope-net: A Graph-Based Model for Hand-Object Pose Estimation, pp. 6608–6617 (2020). http://vision.sice.indiana.edu/projects/hopenet

17. Xiang, Y., Schmidt, T., Narayanan, V., Fox, D.: PoseCNN: a convolutional neural network for 6D object pose estimation in cluttered scenes. arXiv preprint arXiv:1711.00199v3 (2017)

18. Tobin, J., Fong, R., Ray, A., Schneider, J., Zaremba, W., Abbeel, P.: Domainrandomization for transferring deep neural networks from simulation to the real world arXiv preprint arXiv:1703.06907 (2017)

19. Kuffner, J., LaValle, S.: Rrt-connect: An Efficient Approach to Single-Query Path Planning, vol. 2, pp. 995–1001. IEEE (2000). http://ieeexplore.ieee.org/document/844730/

20. Karaman, S., Frazzoli, E.: Sampling-based algorithms for optimal motion planning. arXiv preprint arXiv:1105.1186 (2011)

Electric Systems and Machines

Exploring Electric Vehicles Energy Flexibility in Buildings

Daniel Viana Dias[1,2(✉)], Rui Amaral Lopes[1,2], and João Martins[1,2]

[1] NOVA School of Science and Technology (FCT NOVA), Caparica, Portugal
dv.dias@campus.fct.unl.pt, {rm.lopes,jf.martins}@fct.unl.pt
[2] Centre of Technology and Systems (CTS UNINOVA), Caparica, Portugal

Abstract. The large-scale integration of electric vehicles presents a challenge for the management of electrical distribution grids. These vehicles differ from conventional ones mainly in the need for charging. Due to user behavior, most vehicles charge simultaneously, leading to possible negative impacts on the electrical distribution grid. The digitalization of grid management can support solutions designed to mitigate those impacts through smart charging strategies. Even considering user comfort, charging of electric vehicles can be controlled thus providing energy flexibility to the building. This energy flexibility can be exploited to achieve different objectives, such as reducing end-user electricity costs while minimizing charging peak load. This paper addresses the impacts of large-scale integration of electric vehicles on a building's electricity consumption and the development of a charging management strategy to mitigate possible negative impacts. The study considers a building and a car park located in NOVA School of Science and Technology, Portugal. Multiple combinations of possible charging power values, electric vehicle penetration ratios and parking times are considered.

Keywords: Electric vehicles · Energy flexibility · Demand side management · Smart charging

1 Introduction

In recent years, the relevance of Electric Vehicles (EVs) has grown significantly with integration levels increasing exponentially [1]. This is as a result of the incentives provided by several countries in this sector [2]. In addition to these incentives, the growing awareness of the population regarding climate change contributes to the increased uptake of electric vehicles as they are associated with lower greenhouse gas emissions over their life cycle compared to conventional fossil fuel vehicles [3, 4]. These vehicles are expected to play a larger role on our lives in the future with the European Union expecting at least 40 million EVs on the road in Europe by 2030 [5]. However, EVs do not refuel as their fossil-fuelled counterparts as their batteries need to be charged. This charging can introduce several challenges to the management of the electricity distribution grid, such as voltage drop or high peak loads. These effects are aggravated when uncoordinated charging is observed [6].

© IFIP International Federation for Information Processing 2022
Published by Springer Nature Switzerland AG 2022
L. M. Camarinha-Matos (Ed.): DoCEIS 2022, IFIP AICT 649, pp. 135–148, 2022.
https://doi.org/10.1007/978-3-031-07520-9_13

By exploring the energy flexibility provided by EVs these negative effects can be mitigated. In this case, energy flexibility is defined as the amount of power demand that needs to be modified at each instant in order to achieve the desired load profile, while taking into account the specific objectives to be achieved and the user's comfort needs [7–9]. In order to utilize the energy flexibility made available by an electric vehicle within a system, the charging process must be coordinated. This coordination can be accomplished through different control and communication strategies. Typically, two main approaches are considered, namely centralized and distributed. Centralized approaches have greater reliability in controlling charging and can be easily integrated into existing power system control paradigms. However, these strategies require a greater amount of information and are most often not as scalable as distributed strategies.

Distributed strategies require more information exchange, but the decision problem is confined to an electric vehicle [10]. Distributed strategies can allow users to more easily interfere in the decision process [11, 12]. Some coordination strategies lie in a middle ground between centralized and distributed coordination, since they can incorporate centralized control, but limit the size of the control problem to defined areas of the system. This approach split the optimization problem into a set of interconnected local optimizations. Under this context, machine learning and artificial intelligence provide new tools to implement optimization strategies [13–15].

These optimizations can have different goals with peak power reduction [16], cost reduction [17] and charging capacity optimization [12, 18] being the most common ones [10]. In this study, peak power reduction is the main impact under analysis. As such, the presented results focus on this effect, but other impacts are considered as well.

2 Methodology

This section describes the methodology used to assess the impacts of EV integration on a specific building's electricity consumption and the EV charging management strategy that can be used to mitigate possible negative impacts.

2.1 Impact Assessment

This methodology aims to simulate the charging of EVs and evaluate the impacts of the charging process on a specific building's electricity consumption. In this case it is considered that the building under analysis has an associated parking lot where the users park their cars and charging is allowed. Considering the car parking facility occupancy data, the building's electricity consumption, the model of the EV and a dataset to model the mobility it is possible to determine the vehicles charging patterns and impacts.

The methodology can be summarized with four main steps. Firstly, it is necessary to determine when the EV arrives at the parking lot (the parking occupancy data is used in this step). This process starts by defining the number of EVs entering the park and the respective entering instant. This step is carried out by the $EV_{entries}$ process, which receives through Ent_{park} all the entry times of vehicles in the park and through $\%_{pen}$ the desired percentage of electric vehicles. Considering these inputs, the process randomly selects n entry times corresponding to EVs where n is defined by Eq. 2.1. The value n is approximated since the EVs selection is random. All other entry values are considered to be from conventional fossil fuel vehicles without the need for charging.

$$n \approx \%_{\text{Pen}} * \text{Length}(\text{Ent}_{\text{Park}}) \tag{2.1}$$

Secondly, the State of Charge (SoC) upon arrival is necessary. In a real-world scenario this information can be provided by the user or by the EV but in this case it is determined through the vehicle's specific consumption and distance traveled. The distance traveled is determined using the mobility dataset. The distances are generated by $Distances_{EV}$ and are based on the data contained in $Mobility_{Data}$. This allows for different user mobility patterns to be considered. The process $Generate_{EV}$ generates the structures EV_{Gen} that define the electric vehicles to be considered. The possible models are provided by the input $Models_{EV}$ which contains the vehicle's maximum battery capacity EV_{Bat}, the energy consumption per km EV_{Cons}, the compatible charging powers P_a and the proportion of each vehicle in the set of EVs. It is considered that the distance travelled is the total distance since the vehicle's last full charging cycle thus, the SoC on the moment the EV enters the park is given by Eq. 2.2.

With these values it is possible to determine the EV charging load profile EV_{Load}. This is done through Eq. 2.3 and Eq. 2.4. Equation 2.3 provides the charging duration for each vehicle assuming that it charges at a constant power P_c until it reaches full charge. The diagram is constructed assuming that there is no consumption before the vehicle enters the park at instant t_i. Charging is considered to start at the moment the vehicle is connected to the charger (for simplicity this is assumed to be the same instant the vehicle enters the park t_i). In order to simplify the methodology, consumption is assumed to be constant and equal to P_c from the moment of start to the end of charging. Charging ends when the t_c duration is exceeded, where t_c is the required charging duration to reach maximum charge. Once charging is completed, the vehicle can remain in the park indefinitely, but there is no more consumption, thus returning the power to zero until the vehicle leaves the park.

$$\text{SOC} = 1 - \frac{EV_{\text{Dist}} * EV_{\text{Cons}}}{EV_{\text{Bat}}} \tag{2.2}$$

$$t_c = \frac{(1 - \text{SoC}) * EV_{\text{Bat}}}{P_c} \tag{2.3}$$

$$EV_{\text{Load}}(t) = \begin{cases} 0, & t < t_i \\ P_c, & t_i \leq t \leq t_i + t_c \\ 0, & t > t_i + t_c \end{cases} \tag{2.4}$$

Then, the load profile of the EV must be added to the building's profile ($Building_{Load}$). This needs to be repeated for all vehicles considered in the simulation, resulting in the total load the building has to satisfy (i.e., building demand plus all charging processes) ($Total_{Load}$). Lastly, the resulting profile can be analyzed, and the impacts of the EV charging assessed.

The process $Extract_{Features}$, as the name indicates, extracts several features of the load diagram. This process can receive any load diagram but, in this case, $Total_{Load}$ is used. This process analyses the load diagram and extracts features such as peak-power P_{max}, average power P_{avg} and total consumption C_{total}. This analysis may have time horizons equal to or lower than the load diagram under analysis. For example, the diagram under analysis may have a one-week horizon and only one day of that week be analyzed. This process can also accept another load and compare both. In this case, the building load without vehicle charging is also received by the process. This process not only returns the values of the selected indicators but also the growth factor of each of these against the load diagram without charging. It is also possible to analyze costs with this process if the hourly rate of the building under review is available. Figure 1 presents a diagram for the described methodology, considering the processes involved and the input/outputs datasets.

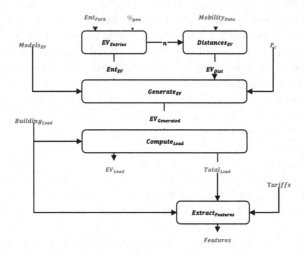

Fig. 1. Block diagram of the impact assessment methodology. Inputs are highlighted in green, outputs in red. (Color figure online)

2.2   Charging Management

The typical charging process for Electric vehicles is: (i) Connect to the charger and start the charging process; (ii) Charge for a specified period; (iii) Stay idle until the user arrives. Since the charging duration is usually smaller than the time the vehicle remains parked is possible to offer energy flexibility to the building the charger is connected to. In order to utilize the energy flexibility provided by electric vehicles, a charging management strategy is presented here. The goal of this management strategy is to determine the optimal charging start instant for a vehicle entering the park. In the moment the vehicle enters the park the optimum instant for the charging start, t_τ, is calculated. The vehicle will then remain idle and only start charging at that moment.

Considering the previous methodology, the charging management has its starting point in the structure $EV_{Generated}$. This structure represents the vehicle at the moment of arrival, it contains the time of the entry of the vehicle t_i, as well as its initial SoC, charging power P_c and car model description. The departure time of the vehicle, t_o, is the sum of the arrival time with the considered permanence time.

Similar to the previous methodology, this data is used to calculate the vehicle's charging duration through Eq. 2.3. If the charging duration is greater than or equal to the vehicle's permanence, the charging in question is assumed to be unmodifiable and the base load profile for this vehicle is considered (i.e., the vehicle maintains the charging start time as the moment of entry into the park). This represents a scenario where there is no energy flexibility. On the other hand, if the vehicle charging can be modified then an algorithm is used to find the best instant to start the charging process.

The optimization function also receives the building's consumption forecast for the period the vehicle will remain parked. This forecast includes the building load forecast and the charging profiles of all vehicles that have previously entered the park. Taking into account the instant of arrival t_i, instant of departure t_o and the charging duration t_c it computes through Eq. 2.5 the maximum delay value in which it is still possible to reach the desired SoC at the end of the charging process, t_l.

$$t_l = t_o - t_i - t_c \tag{2.5}$$

$$EV_{Load}(t) = \begin{cases} 0, & t < t_i + t_s \\ P_c, & t_i + t_s \leq t \leq t_i + t_s + t_c \\ 0, & t > t_i + t_s + t_c \end{cases} \tag{2.6}$$

In the moment the vehicle enters the park, the load diagram is defined. The main difference in this case is that the load diagram will be shifted by t_s intervals. For each delay value t_s between 1 and t_l, a different charging load diagram is calculated through Eq. 2.6 and added to the building load forecast. A function is then used to calculate a cost value for each delay value and the optimization function chooses the delay value that has the lowest cost. The possible delay values start at 1 timestep since the optimization algorithm is not instantaneous. This procedure is repeated each time a new electric vehicle enters the park.

In this case, the cost function was considered to be the maximum power value within the vehicle's parking period. As such, the optimization function will choose the delay value where the peak power value is minimal. If multiple values have the same cost as the optimal one the lowest value is chosen. This allows for the vehicle achieve the desired SoC sooner giving more freedom to the user. The flowchart describing this charging management strategy is shown in Fig. 2.

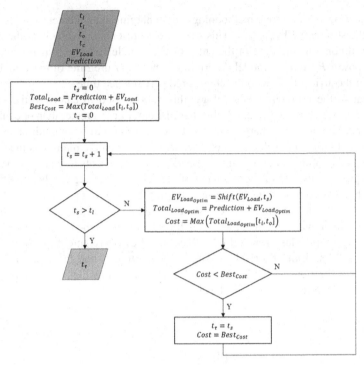

Fig. 2. Vehicle optimization function flowchart

3 Results and Analysis

The results reported in this section were obtained through a case study considering real data associated to a car park and a building located at NOVA School of Science and Technology (FCT NOVA), Portugal. As users of the building are typically students, professors, or staff members, 4, 8 and 12 h were considered as vehicle parking time. The charging power considered were 3.7, 7.4, 10 and 22 kW as these are the more typical ones, as indicated by the report of the European Energy Agency presented in [19].

3.1 Case Study Data

The case study presented focuses on the building of the Department of Electrical and Computer Engineering (DEEC). The building load was obtained using a smart meter installed in the building. Its consumption consists mainly of lighting, personal computers, servers and computers installed in the laboratories. Although there are also electric motors and water pumps in the building, these are not regularly used. As this building is mainly used for academic purposes, its load diagram shows higher consumptions on weekdays, as shown in Fig. 3, which presents the building's load profile for a specific week during school time. The building consumption follows a clear pattern. The consumption starts to increase at the early hours of weekdays, around 7:00 h, with peak consumption values over 100 kW around 14:00 h–15:00 h, and then reduces to the lower values in the evening. It is also possible to see a reduction in consumption on Wednesdays, as these are days with a lower number of classes. This causes a reduction in the number of users of the department thus reducing its consumption. In this case, the peak values are usually between 75 and 80 kW. The consumption on the weekends is lower since the number of users is lower and only the most basic loads are active, such as lighting and servers (it fluctuates between 40 kW and 60 kW in these cases).

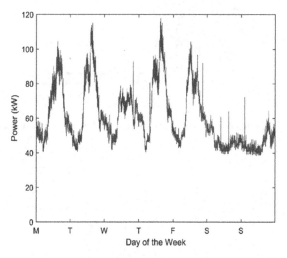

Fig. 3. DEEC building's load diagram.

As explained before, one input required to simulate the charging of an EV is the vehicle's state of charge. To calculate the state of charge it is necessary to estimate the distance travelled by the EV. The distances are estimated through a probability distribution. The data source used was the study present in [20]. This study monitored 49 drivers who usually circulate in Lisbon area. The drivers were between the ages of 18 and 66 and were of both sexes, allowing for a broad and varied sample. The drivers were monitored from April to September 2010 in monitoring cycles with a duration of one week. These distances were used to create a histogram to determine the distance travelled by each vehicle. As the total number of entries in the parking lot were 1322 it was decided that $Distances_{EV}$ should be able to generate at least 1500 distance values with a similar distribution. The comparison between the histograms of the original values and the values generated for 1500 vehicles is presented in Fig. 4.

The entrances of electric vehicles were obtained from data provided by the FCT-NOVA security division. The security division provided the entrance data in the chosen park and the users belonging to DEEC were selected. The data provided correspond to the same week of Fig. 3. Figure 5 presents the occupation of the park with stay times of 4, 8 and 12 h. It is possible to verify a lower occupancy on Wednesdays, which matches with the lower consumption in Fig. 3.

Finally, it is necessary to define the vehicle models to consider in the case study. It is necessary to define the specific consumption per km, the capacity of the battery, the possible charging powers compatible with the vehicle and the frequency of respective

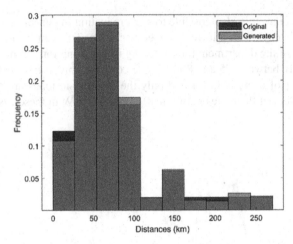

Fig. 4. Comparison between the original and generated histograms.

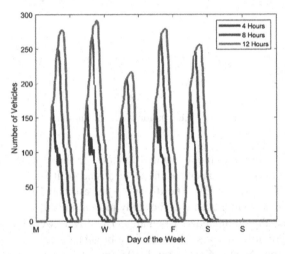

Fig. 5. Parking lot occupation with the considered user stay duration.

vehicle in the considered fleet. The models considered are the same as those described in [21, 22] and are presented in Table 1. It is considered that the vehicles are evenly distributed in the fleet, so the *Generate$_{EV}$* process randomly chooses one of the four available models.

Table 1. Vehicle models considered in the case study

Model	Battery capacity (kWh)	Specific consumption (Wh/km)	Allowed charging power (kW)
Minivehicle	17,7	146	3,7; 7,4; 10; 22
Medium vehicle	24,4	170	
Large vehicle	42,1	185	
Premium vehicle	59,9	207	

3.2 Impacts of EV Charging

Initially, the impact assessment methodology was applied to 50 scenarios. Each scenario is defined by a charging power and a percentage of penetration. The considered scenarios included all vehicles charging at the same power and also a set of scenarios with random charging powers from among those considered. Penetration percentages range from 10% to 100%, with increments of 10%. The time horizon was a full week with one minute resolution. All scenarios were computed using MATLAB. Figure 6 presents the comparison between the following indicators considered for different EV penetration levels: peak power P_{max} and total consumption C_{total}.

As expected, the total power consumption in all scenarios is independent of the chosen load power and increases with the number of electric vehicles. Total building consumption without EVs charging is 10.07 MWh and with 100% EVs penetration is 27.04 MWh. The impacts of charging are much more evident when considering peak power. Since the case study considered is from a university, users' entrances to the park are usually relatively close. This causes most EVs to charge simultaneously, resulting in a sudden increase in building consumption. This event is clearly visible in Fig. 7 where the consumption associated with vehicle charging dwarfs the buildings base consumption. It is possible to see an increase from 49.29 kW at 7:00 to 312.83 kW at 7:30 and to 901.5 kW at 9:30 on Monday when considering a scenario with 100% EV penetration level. This growth is more dramatic in scenarios where the charging power is higher. This rise may be of concern since the power distribution grid may lack the ability to handle such variations. However, in scenarios with lower charging power, although the maximum peak value is lower, the peak duration is longer as vehicles remain charging for longer periods. Considering the energy tariffs for medium voltage power installations available at [23], contracted power costs is 0,0862 €/kW.day. The contracted power costs without EVs is €10.14 per day. If the same rates are applied to the 3.7 kW charging power scenario and 20% penetration this value increases to €18.18. With 100% EV penetration the daily value would be €53,87. As seen in Fig. 6, the 3.7 kW scenario produces the lowest peak power in all scenarios whereas 22 kW scenario produces the highest. This is due to most of the charging periods being simultaneous. If charging was performed with 22 kW instead of 3.7 kW the values for the daily contracted power would be 31,55 € for 20% and € 88,36 for 100% EV penetration. This shows that EVs load management is required not only to reduce peak loads but also the costs associated with contracted power.

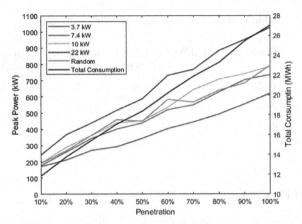

Fig. 6. Peak power and total energy consumption for different charging powers and EV penetration levels.

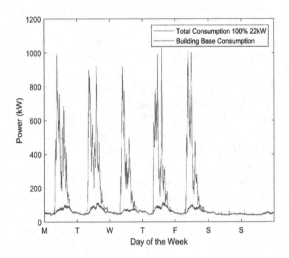

Fig. 7. Building's load diagram with 100% EV penetration and 22kW

3.3 Benefits of Energy Flexibility Usage

Collected results show that the charging management strategy can decrease building's peak load and associated costs. As can be seen from Fig. 8, peak power is reduced by at least 20% when the load management strategy is applied. It is also possible to note that the load profile is significantly smoother. This is due to the optimization function shifting the charging to later periods in an attempt to not increase the peak power. When considering all scenarios, a considerable reduction in peak power is observed as presented by Fig. 9. Although total energy consumption remains the same, the problem of high-power peaks is mitigated by the management strategy. Previously, an increase in the number of EVs produced a significant increase in peak power but now as the charging periods are distributed throughout the day the increase in peak power is not as significant. As an example, with 22 kW as the considered charging power, by increasing the penetration of EVs from 20% to 30%, EV the peak power increased from 366.61 kW to 439.19 kW but in the case of 12-h coordinated charging, this increase in the number of EVs translates into increasing the peak value from 140.21 kW to 171.74 kW. Even though in both cases the increase is around 20%, the values are significantly lower in the scenario with the management strategy. Even scenarios with higher charging power have peak values very close to those with lower power values. For example, prior to charging management, the 100% penetration scenario with 3.7 kW has a peak of 621.69 kW and with 22 kW has a peak of 1027.30 kW. With load management, these values are reduced to 366.75 kW and 324.23 kW, respectively. The results show that this management strategy presents better results when penetration and charging power are increased. Higher charging power values can produce lower peak values when charging is managed. This is due to lower charging power values resulting in longer charging periods and more simultaneous charging. As the number of vehicles increase the proportion between the consumption of the vehicles and the building also increases and the impact of the optimization is more evident. This presents an opportunity for this management strategy since high-power charging is increasingly available and the number of EV purchases increases yearly.

An important factor to also consider is the parking duration. The longer the stay the better the results. The 12-h scenario presents the greatest improvement in reducing peak power due to the increased distribution of charging periods. This effect is most evident at higher charging power values as charging durations are shorter. At lower charging powers, the charging duration is increased which can lead to some vehicles still charging simultaneously. However, this distribution can stretch the consumption into later hours. As mentioned above, this management is only possible due to the existence of energy flexibility in the charging of electric vehicles.

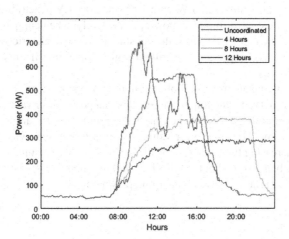

Fig. 8. Comparison between consumption diagram with and without charging management for Monday.

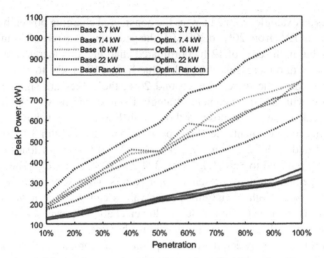

Fig. 9. Comparison of the peak power in scenarios with and without charging management with 12 h of user stay time.

4   Conclusions

The collected results show that some of the main impacts of increased EV penetration in a vehicle fleet are the increase in peak power and total energy consumption. Even though both increase with the number of vehicles, peak power values vary with the chosen charging power while the total consumption does not. The increase in peak power is amplified when the charging power is increased. This shows that the integration of high-power chargers into a building can be detrimental even in low EV penetration scenarios. The uncoordinated charging at 22 kW with 10% and 20% EV penetration represents an increase of 41% and 73% of the peak power, respectively, when compared to the uncoordinated charging with 3.7 kW. Thus, the constant increase in electric vehicle adoption might impose negative impacts on distribution grids operation if only uncoordinated charging is available.

When charging management is applied, improvements in the peak power values for all scenarios are observed. One important result is that peak power values are not related with the chosen charging power. When higher charging powers are considered, such as 10 kW and 22 kW, the peak power value is similar to the ones with lower charging power values. Increasing the parking time also provided better results as expected, with charging periods being spread out. With 8 h of parking time, the power peak values start to converge and the relation between charging power and peak power value is no longer relevant.

References

1. EV-Volumes - The Electric Vehicle World Sales Database. https://www.ev-volumes.com/country/total-world-plug-in-vehicle-volumes/. Accessed 30 Mar 2022

2. EEA: Electric vehicles from life cycle and circular economy perspectives, no. 13 (2018). https://doi.org/10.2800/77428
3. Kester, J., de Rubens, G.Z., Sovacool, B.K., Noel, L.: Public perceptions of electric vehicles and vehicle-to-grid (V2G): insights from a Nordic focus group study. Transp. Res. Part D Transp. Environ. **74**, 277–293 (2019). https://doi.org/10.1016/J.TRD.2019.08.006
4. Ziefle, M., Beul-Leusmann, S., Kasugai, K., Schwalm, M.: Public perception and acceptance of electric vehicles: exploring users' perceived benefits and drawbacks. In: Marcus, A. (ed.) DUXU 2014. LNCS, vol. 8519, pp. 628–639. Springer, Cham (2014). https://doi.org/10.1007/978-3-319-07635-5_60
5. Energiewende, "European Energy Transition 2030: The Big Picture". https://www.agora-energiewende.de/en/. Accessed 29 Mar 2022
6. Dubey, A., Santoso, S.: Electric vehicle charging on residential distribution systems: impacts and mitigations. IEEE Access **3**, 1871–1893 (2015). https://doi.org/10.1109/ACCESS.2015.2476996
7. Reynders, G., Lopes, R.A., Marszal-Pomianowska, A., Aelenei, D., Martins, J., Saelens, D.: Energy flexible buildings: an evaluation of definitions and quantification methodologies applied to thermal storage. Energy Build. **166**, 372–390 (2018). https://doi.org/10.1016/j.enbuild.2018.02.040
8. Junker, R.G., et al.: Characterizing the energy flexibility of buildings and districts. Appl. Energy **225**, 175–182 (2018). https://doi.org/10.1016/j.apenergy.2018.05.037
9. D'hulst, R., Labeeuw, W., Beusen, B., Claessens, S., Deconinck, G., Vanthournout, K.: Demand response flexibility and flexibility potential of residential smart appliances: experiences from large pilot test in Belgium. Appl. Energy **155**, 79–90 (2015). https://doi.org/10.1016/j.apenergy.2015.05.101
10. Al-Ogaili, S., et al.: Review on scheduling, clustering, and forecasting strategies for controlling electric vehicle charging: challenges and recommendations. IEEE Access **7**, 128353–128371 (2019). https://doi.org/10.1109/ACCESS.2019.2939595
11. Schuller, A.: Charging coordination paradigms of electric vehicles. In: Rajakaruna, S., Shahnia, F., Ghosh, A. (eds.) Plug In Electric Vehicles in Smart Grids, pp. 1–21. Springer, Singapore (2015). https://doi.org/10.1007/978-981-287-317-0_1
12. Dudek, E.: The flexibility of domestic electric vehicle charging: the electric nation project. IEEE Power Energy Mag. **19**(4), 16–27 (2021). https://doi.org/10.1109/MPE.2021.3072714
13. Deb, S.: Machine learning for solving charging infrastructure planning: a comprehensive review. In: 5th International Conference on Smart Grid and Smart Cities, ICSGSC 2021, pp. 16–22, June 2021, https://doi.org/10.1109/ICSGSC52434.2021.9490407
14. Shahriar, S., Al-Ali, A.R., Osman, A.H., Dhou, S., Nijim, M.: Machine learning approaches for EV charging behavior: a review. IEEE Access **8**, 168980–168993 (2020). https://doi.org/10.1109/ACCESS.2020.3023388
15. Wan, Z., Li, H., He, H., Prokhorov, D.: Model-free real-time EV charging scheduling based on deep reinforcement learning. IEEE Trans. Smart Grid **10**(5), 5246–5257 (2018). https://doi.org/10.1109/TSG.2018.2879572
16. Zhong, J., Xiong, X.: An orderly EV charging scheduling method based on deep learning in cloud-edge collaborative environment. Adv. Civ. Eng. **2021** (2021). https://doi.org/10.1155/2021/6690610
17. Saner, B., Trivedi, A., Srinivasan, D.: A cooperative hierarchical multi-agent system for EV charging scheduling in presence of multiple charging stations. IEEE Trans. Smart Grid **13**(3), 2218–2233 (2022). https://doi.org/10.1109/TSG.2022.3140927
18. Liu, J., Lin, G., Huang, S., Zhou, Y., Li, Y., Rehtanz, C.: Optimal EV charging scheduling by considering the limited number of chargers. IEEE Trans. Transp. Electrification **7**(3), 1112–1122 (2021). https://doi.org/10.1109/TTE.2020.3033995

19. EEA: Electric Vehicles in Europe. European Environmental Agency Report No 20/2016, no. 20 (2016). https://doi.org/10.2800/100230

20. Pereira, N.B.R.C.: Eficiência Energética No Sector Dos Transportes Rodoviários: Metodologia Para Quantificação Do Excesso De Energia Consumida Devido Ao Factor Comportamental Na Condução De Veículos Automóveis Ligeiros. Faculdade de Ciências e Tecnologia, p. 14 (2011)

21. Ellingsen, L.A., Singh, B., Programme, I.E., Strømman, A.H.: Supplementary data for the size and range effect: lifecycle greenhouse gas emissions of electric vehicles. Environ. Res. Lett. **11**(5), 054010 (2016). https://doi.org/10.1088/1748-9326/11/5/054010

22. European Environment Agency: Electric vehicles from life cycle and circular economy perspectives TERM 2018: transport and environment reporting mechanism (TERM) report EEA report no 13/2018, no. 13 (2018)

23. Entidade Reguladora dos Serviços Energéticos: Tarifas e preços para a energia elétrica e outros serviços em 2022 e Parâmetros para o período de Regulação 2022–2025 (2021)

A Rule-Based Method for Efficient Electric Vehicle Charging Scheduling at Parking Lots

George Konstantinidis[✉], Emmanuel Karapidakis, and Alexandros Paspatis

Department of Electrical and Computer Engineering, Hellenic Mediterranean University,
71410 Heraklion, Greece
`{gkons,karapidakis,agpaspatis}@hmu.gr`

Abstract. Electromobility is being promoted to reduce the greenhouse gas emissions. To this extend, and through the technical advancement of electric vehicles (EVs), EVs are increasing in a fast pace. However, their charging could impose problems to the distribution network, local substations and transformers. This holds true especially in charging stations with a high number of EV chargers, such as the parking lots. To address this, a rule-based algorithm is proposed in this paper to minimize the charging cost, participate in a demand response program, and simultaneously satisfy the technical and operational constraints of the EVs and parking lot's local transformer. The proposed rule-based algorithm is compared with the case of uncoordinated charging and with an optimization-based charging schedule based on the particle swarm optimization (PSO). The obtained results indicate that even if the charging cost with the proposed algorithm is not significantly reduced compared to the PSO charging strategy, the executed time is significantly lower. Comparing with the uncoordinated charging, the proposed algorithm has a lower charging cost and a similar execution time.

Keywords: Electric vehicles · Energy management system · Demand response · Efficient charging scheduling · Vehicle-to-grid · Distribution network

1 Introduction

1.1 Motivation

In the effort of reducing the greenhouse gas (GHG) emissions, the increase in the electrification of the transportation sector is a crucial factor, as the sector represents 21.5% of Europe's GHG emissions [1]. EVs penetration is increasing year by year and their charging concerns the scientific community and distribution system operators, as it could create new congestion and demand peaks, voltage quality problems etc. Especially, the parking lots (PLs) that would facilitate a considerable number of EV chargers, making them a potential "troublemaker" for the operation of the grid. However, many of the issues that EVs charging creates, could be addressed by coordinating their charging or even Vehicle-to-Grid (V2G) services [2].

© IFIP International Federation for Information Processing 2022
Published by Springer Nature Switzerland AG 2022
L. M. Camarinha-Matos (Ed.): DoCEIS 2022, IFIP AICT 649, pp. 149–157, 2022.
https://doi.org/10.1007/978-3-031-07520-9_14

1.2 PhD Work Relation to the Conference Theme

Energy, which is one of the topics of interest of the Advanced Doctoral Conference on Computing, Electrical and Industrial Systems 2022, is a very interesting subject, especially in crisis time periods. The energy demand is increasing more and more through the years. Energy management in order to exploit the available energy and electric grid efficiency is imperative if we aim to keep a sustainable future. This is the reason why this PhD work deals with the electricity distribution and the required coordination of the EV chargers in the electricity network. The work in this paper consists a part of this PhD project and gives an insight into managing EV charging at a PL.

1.3 Literature Review

Smart charging of EVs at PL has thoroughly been examined in the literature taking into consideration various methodologies, scenarios and objectives. Coordinating the EV charging process in order to prevent the overloading of the PL's local transformer and generally the local distribution grid while at the same time achieving minimization of the charging costs is a challenging but possible task, as the EV's charging load could be characterized as shiftable and interruptible.

In this sense, the authors in [3], developed a centralized charging schedule of EVs at a PL and used the Advanced Interactive Multidimensional Modeling System software to maximize the profit of the PL. Realistic mobility/parking patterns were taken into consideration but only slow charging was considered. The main objective in [4] was the valley filling and peak shaving of power consumption in a non-residential system. It was achieved by scheduling suitable the EV charging and discharging. In [5], a real-time fuzzy logic based charging scheme with V2G capability was proposed in order to manage the charging loads of EVs in a PL and to minimize the charging costs. The charging/discharging priority of each EV was calculated depending on the state-of-charging (SoC), remaining charging time and electricity price. In [6] the authors developed a particle swarm optimization (PSO)-based EV charging schedule considering the discharging of EV's. Their objective was to minimize the cost and the charging time at different scenarios, i.e., considering electricity price, and microgrid total cost. In [7], an EV charging schedule is proposed and PSO is used to minimize the PL charging cost. In [8], a simple multi-parameter method was developed in order to minimize the EVs charging cost at a PL, considering electricity price and distribution load. Moreover, PSO was used to obtain the charging schedule of EVs.

Indeed, classical optimization-based approaches have been examined in many studies. However, some rule-based approached for coordinating EV charging schedule have also been discussed. In particular, rule-based algorithms may be preferred for the implementation of energy management schemes, as they provide exact solution to the desired output conditions, computationally efficiency and are preferable for real-time applications [9]. In particular, in [10], the authors developed a rule-based energy management scheme for EV charging in order to provide uninterrupted charging at a constant price under a different number of office working days. Valley filling of power consumption and the financial model for a PL with photovoltaic and energy storage system was examined, too. Finally, V2G technology could reduce the payback period of the existing system but, the satisfaction of the charging targets of all EVs are not guaranteed. In [11], a simplified charging strategy is proposed to improve the load profile for commercial building microgrids accommodating PV and EV. The proper allocation of PV power and EV charging was assigned according to priority rules without taking into consideration V2G services.

1.4 Contributions

The main contributions of this paper are summarized as follows:

- The EV charging scheduling algorithm proposed in this paper is simple and efficient. No forecast or other possibly expensive devices for the optimal solution calculation are needed.
- The algorithm takes into consideration all the constraints of the EV charging process (minimum and maximum SoC, charging rate limitation) and satisfies the charging requirements of all EVs. Moreover, the proposed charging strategy is compared with an optimization-based charging strategy (PSO) and an uncoordinated charging giving better results. More specifically, it is faster enough than the PSO charging scheduling and furthermore delivers better cost results compared to both basic charging strategies (PSO and uncoordinated).
- The proposed charging algorithm can participate in demand response (DR) program by reducing PL's total consumption. The amount of power that can be reduced, without violating any charging constrains, can be easily estimated.

2   Parking Lot Model and System Parameters

To evaluate the effectiveness of the proposed charging method, over the standard optimization algorithm of particle swarm optimization (PSO) as well as the case of uncoordinated charging, we model a representative PL equipped with EV chargers.

2.1   Parking Lot Model

A PL with EV chargers, adequate to serve all the incoming EV, was assumed. The arrivals, parking duration of the EVs and residual state of charge of each arriving EV (SoC_{Arr}) were estimated as in [12].

2.2   EV and Charger Type

Ten representative model of EVs were used (Tesla Model 3, Renault Zoe, Hyundai Kona Electric, Nissan Leaf, Volkswagen e-Golf, Peugeot e-208, Audi e-Tron, Kia e-Niro, BMW i3, Volkswagen e-Up!). Their possibility of appearance of each type of EV in the parking lot is estimated from [13], depending on their sales. In addition, the PL was considered to include four types of EV charging stations. Their types and power rate are shown in Table 1. It was considered that all charging stations and EVs could support bidirectional energy flow. Finally, the charging efficiency (ce) was considered 0.93 and it represents the losses from cabling, EV battery and conversion losses during the charging and discharging process.

Table 1. Chargers types and power rate.

Charger type	Power limit
1-ph-32A (AC)	$-7.4\,\text{kW} \leq \text{Power} \leq 7.4\,\text{kW}$
3-ph-16A (AC)	$-11\,\text{kW} \leq \text{Power} \leq 11\,\text{kW}$
3-ph-32A (AC)	$-22\,\text{kW} \leq \text{Power} \leq 22\,\text{kW}$
Combined Charging System (DC)	$0\,\text{kW} \leq \text{Power} \leq 100\,\text{kW}$

3   The Benchmark and Proposed Charging Strategies

Depending on the charging strategy that would be applied, the economical and operational benefits are varied. For developing the proposed strategy, the time horizon was divided into time slots with length $\Delta t = 1$ h.

3.1   Charger Type and Power Limit Selection

Depending on the parking duration and EV's charging power converter, a suitable charger type was selected to be plugged in. As a first step, it is checked in which AC charger type could be plugged in depending on the EV's AC charging power converter. Follows the check if the EV would charge at an AC charger, that was chosen in the previous step, or at a DC charger as shown in Eq. (1). If the EV is connected to a DC charger, discharging is not considered as an option.

$$\text{Charger} = \begin{cases} \text{AC charger, } E_{max}(i) \geq E_t(i) \\ \text{DC charger, otherwise} \end{cases}, \forall\, i \in EV \qquad (1)$$

where $E_{max}(i)$ is the maximum energy that the specific type of charger could give to the ith EV if it operates with its nominal power during the parking duration and $E_t(i)$ is the energy required for the ith EV to reach its desirable SoC. The power limit of each charger is depending on its charger type and the EV's on-board charger limitations, and it is estimated in the following Equation:

$$-P_{limit}^{Charger}(i,t) \leq P(i,t) \leq P_{limit}^{Charger}(i,t),\ t_A(i) \leq t < t_D(i), \forall\, i \in EV \qquad (2)$$

where $P_{limit}^{Charger}$ is the nominal power of the ith EV's charger at the t time slot, t_A and t_D is the arriving and departure time of the ith EV, respectively. In the sequel, the two benchmark (uncoordinated and PSO) strategies as well as the proposed rule-based algorithms are presented.

3.2   CS1: Benchmark Uncoordinated Charging

As uncoordinated charging is defined the process where the EV users arrive at the PL, plug in their EV and the charging process starts immediately with the maximum power of their EVs charging power limitations.

3.3 CS2: Benchmark PSO Charging

The PSO function of Matlab was used to optimize the charging process of the EVs in the PL. The objective function that was used takes the form:

$$F(i) = \min\left(\sum_{t_A}^{t_D - 1} P(i, t) \cdot T \cdot (ce\ cha(t) - dis(t)) \cdot EP(t) \right), \forall\ i\ \in EV \qquad (3)$$

where *cha* and *dis* are binary variables and set to 1 when the EV charge or discharge, respectively. The battery stored energy constraints of the lower and upper limits are taken into consideration during the whole process. As battery lower and upper limit are considered the 20% and 100% of the battery capacity of the EV, respectively. Furthermore, the desirable state of charging is shown in Eq. (4).

$$\sum_{t=Arr}^{Dep - 1} P(i, t) \cdot \Delta t \cdot (ce\ cha(t) - dis(t)) + E_A(i) = E_t(i),\ t_A(i) \leq t < t_D(i), \forall\ i\ \in EV$$
$$\qquad (4)$$

where E_A is the residual energy of the ith arriving EV's battery.

3.4 CS3: Proposed Rule-Based Algorithm

The idea of using rule-based charging strategy is simple. More specifically, it is assigning the charging process in the time slots where the electricity price is low and the discharging of the battery of the EVs the time slots where the electricity price is high.

At first, the time slot with the lowest electricity price is searched and it is assigned the maximum power or part of the charger power limit depending on the SoC_t. In case that it requires another time slot to satisfy the charging target, the same process takes place until the EV reaches the desirable departure SoC.

As a next step, it is checked if the discharging process is profitable. Then, an opposite process takes place. Particularly, the time slot with the lowest and highest electricity price and, in which the charger does not operate in its nominal power are identified in order to perform charging in the first and discharging (V2G) to the second.

Furthermore, in case that the PL has a power limitation, e.g., due to a local MV/LV transformer, an extra check is added to the proposed rule-based algorithm. Note that the EVs were divided into two categories, flexible and inflexible, depending on their capability to change their charging schedule without delaying their departure. After the charging scheduling in each time slot has been completed, the total power consumption of the PL is calculated. In the case that consumption exceeds the power limit (when assuming one), the following process takes place. At first, the flexible and inflexible EVs are estimated. Inflexible EVs are defined those that the PL's power violation happens at the last time slot of their charging. At the power limit violation time slot, the available power is proportionally distributed to the flexible EVs, following the Equation. Note that, available power is defined by the power limit minus the sum of the inflexible EV charger power.

$$P(i, t) = P_{Flex}^{old}(i, t) \cdot \frac{P_{Lim}}{P_{Flex}(t)},\ t\ \in T_{Violation},\ \forall\ i\ \in EV_{Flex} \qquad (5)$$

where P_{Flex}^{old} is the charging power that was assigned to the charger of the ith flexible EV at the t time slot before the PL's power violation check is triggered, P_{Flex} is the sum of all flexible EVs' charging power at the power violation time slot, P_{Limit} is the available power, as it was explained above, $T_{Violation}$ is the time slot that the power violation occurs and EV_{Flex} is the flexible EVs. In addition, inflexible EVs where also those EVs which, when their charging schedule change in the power violation time slot, they cannot reach their charging target with the new charging scheduling. In Fig. 1, the process that takes place when power violation happens is described. Note that in the step "New charging scheduling", the EVs' charger power that it is estimated in Eq. (5) at the time slot that the power violation happens is assigned. Moreover, for the remaining parking duration the charging schedule of the EV is calculated as it was explained above, before the power violation happens. Finally, the power limit of the PL is insufficient when all EV characterized as inflexible. In particular, there is not adequate power in order to cope with the power limit violation without delaying the departure or not satisfying the SoC target of some EVs. In this way, it can be estimated the lowest power limit of the PL, which can be assigned to the PL, without changing the EV drivers' preferences.

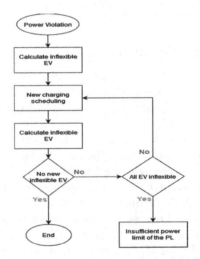

Fig. 1. Charging process when the power limit of the PL is violated.

4   Results

To evaluate the performance and efficiency of the proposed strategy multiple scenarios were created. The simulations were conducted in a computation system with processor Intel(R) Core (TM) i5-3470 CPU @ 3.20 GHz and RAM 8 GB. The electricity price time series were obtained from the independent power transmission operator (IPTO), Greece [21] and they are shown in Fig. 2.

4.1   Comparison Between Charging Strategies

The PL's local transformer capacity was not taken into consideration when the charging strategies were compared. The proposed algorithm for the charging of the EVs at a PL showed a better efficiency than the other two charging strategies in all scenarios. The mean charging cost of the proposed charging strategy for 10 operation scenarios is 0.99% and 6.25% better than that of CS1 and CS2, respectively. Although the charging cost when the proposed charging strategy was applied was lower, it did not show considerable difference compared with the PSO case. However, the mean executed time for each EV, at all the examined period, of the proposed charging strategy was 0.014 s and in the case of PSO 13 s.

Hence, it can be concluded that the proposed charging strategy could be applied in real-time problems with uncertainties as it can respond faster by calculating the EV charging schedule at short time periods. Finally, no expensive device for the calculation process is needed because of the simplicity of the algorithm.

4.2   CS3 When the PL's Transformer Capacity was Considered

The nominal power of the PL's local transformer was considered 1500 kVA. The operation scenarios had similar results, so a random scenario was chosen to show the behavior of the CS3 when the PL's transformer and DR program were considered. During the examined period 715 EVs were charged. The PL's active power when CS3 is applied and i) no power limit is considered (case A), ii) power limit of the transformer (case B) and iii) power limit of the transformer and DR (case C) are considered, is depicted in Fig. 2.

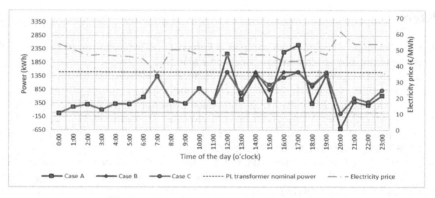

Fig. 2. PL's active power and electricity price.

In case A, it can be observed in Fig. 2 that the PL's active power and electricity price are correlated, as the charging process was mostly arranged when the electricity price was low, while the discharging process correspondingly occurred when the electricity price was high. In addition, the charging cost of the PL was 887.49 EUR.

In case B, it can be observed in Fig. 2 that the PL's active power and electricity price are correlated as long as the power limit of the PL is not violated. Moreover, it can be observed that the power that was reduced, because of the power limit, was shifted in the next or the previous time slots. The energy sold to the grid was reduced because there was not enough available power to charge the batteries adequately and later discharge (V2G) them at the time slots that it would be profitable. Additionally, the charging cost of the PL was 901.63 EUR, and it was, as expected, higher than the case A. This happened for two reasons, the energy that was sold to the grid was lower, and by applying the power limit it was not fully exploit the time slot in which the electricity price was low. Case C was similar with case B. In addition, at 14:00 and 16:00 o'clock the PL's active power limit was reduced at 1400 kVA and 1300 kVA as a demand response service, respectively. In this case, the charging cost of the PL was 902.65 EUR. The application of the transformer capacity and DR did not affect considerable (1.68%) the daily charging cost, but it is a more realistic case as the PLs have power limitation. Furthermore, demand response program could return profits as it is a service that the client who use it, is getting paid for it.

5   Conclusion

In this paper, a rule-based algorithm for coordinated charging of EVs at a PL is proposed. To evaluate the performance of the proposed algorithm, it has been compared with two charging strategies which use the PSO function of Matlab as well as the case of uncoordinated charging. Results show that the proposed algorithm achieved the minimum charging cost, satisfied all the constraints and at the same time the executed time was short enough to be applied at short time slots as a demand response tool and support the distribution network.

References

1. Greenhouse gas emissions from transport in Europe. https://www.eea.europa.eu/ims/greenhouse-gas-emissions-from-transport. Accessed 2 Mar 2022
2. Sarabi, S., Davigny, A., Courtecuisse, V., Riffonneau, Y., Robyns, B.: Potential of vehicle-to-grid ancillary services considering the uncertainties in plug-in electric vehicle availability and service/localization limitations in distribution grids. Appl. Energy **171**, 523–540 (2016)
3. Kuran, M.Ş, Carneiro Viana, A., Iannone, L., Kofman, D., Mermoud, G., Vasseur, J.P.: A smart parking Lot management system for scheduling the recharging of electric vehicles. IEEE Trans. Smart Grid. **6**(6), 2942–2953 (2015)
4. Ioakimidis, C., Thomas, D., Rycerski, P., Genikomsakis, K.: Peak shaving and valley filling of power consumption profile in non-residential buildings using an electric vehicle parking lot. Energy **148**, 148–158 (2018)
5. Yao, L., Damiran, Z., Lim, W.H.: A fuzzy logic based charging scheme for electric vechicle parking station. In: 16th IEEE International Conference on Environment and Electrical Engineering (EEEIC). Florence, Italy (2016)
6. Savari, G.F., Krishnasamy, V., Sugavanam, V., Vakesan, K.: Optimal charging scheduling of electric vehicles in micro grids using priority algorithms and particle swarm optimization. Mob. Netw. Appl. **24**(6), 1835–1847 (2019). https://doi.org/10.1007/s11036-019-01380-x
7. Wu, H., Pang, G.K.H., Choy K.L., Lam, H.Y.: A scheduling and control system for electric vehicle charging at parking lot. In: 11th Asian Control Conference (ASCC). Gold Coast, QLD, Australia (2017)

8. Konstantinidis, G., Kanellos, F.D., Kalaitzakis, K.: A Simple multi-parameter method for efficient charging scheduling of electric vehicles. Appl. Syst. Innov. **4**(3), 58 (2021)
9. Peng, J., He, H., Xiong, R.: Rule based energy management strategy for a series–parallel plug-in hybrid electric bus optimized by dynamic programming. Appl. Energy **185**, 1633–1643 (2017)
10. Bhatti, A., Salam, Z.: A rule-based energy management scheme for uninterrupted electric vehicles charging at constant price using photovoltaic-grid system. Renew. Energy **125**, 384–400 (2018)
11. Liu, N., et al.: A heuristic operation strategy for commercial building microgrids containing EVs and PV system. IEEE Trans. Industr. Electron. **62**(4), 2560–2570 (2015)
12. Konstantinidis, G., Karapidakis, E., Paspatis, A.: Mitigating the impact of an official PEV charger deployment plan on an urban grid. Energies **15**(4), 1321 (2022)
13. European sales 2020 EV and PHEV. https://carsalesbase.com/european-sales-2020-ev-phev/. Accessed 21 Feb 2022
14. Independent Power Transmission Operator, Data. https://www.admie.gr/en/market/market-statistics/detail-data. Accessed 21 Feb 2022

A Novel Photovoltaic Maximum Power Point Tracking Method Using Feedback Conductance Integral Compensation

Sergio André[1,2,3](✉), J. Fernando Silva[2,3], Sónia F. Pinto[2,3], and P. Miguens Matutino[1,3]

[1] ISEL - Instituto Superior de Engenharia de Lisboa, R. Conselheiro Emídio Navarro, 1959-007 Lisboa, Portugal
{sergio.andre,pedro.miguens}@isel.pt
[2] Instituto Superior Técnico, Universidade de Lisboa, DEEC, AC Energia Av. Rovisco Pais, 1049-001 Lisbon, Portugal
{fernando.alves,sonia.pinto}@tecnico.ulisboa.pt
[3] INESC-ID, Rua Alves Redol, 1000-029 Lisboa, Portugal

Abstract. Environmental concerns are driving significant research in energy-efficient devices, namely in the photovoltaic (PV) area. Recent scientific papers focus in photovoltaic cells modeling, converter topologies to directly interconnect low voltage solar modules to high voltage inverters, and maximum power point tracking (MPPT) methods able to extract the maximum energy from PV assemblies.

Several research works are aimed at increasing the amount of energy extracted from PV panels, by introducing novel MPPT strategies. Some works propose promising MPPT methods and improved results. However, they often lack comparisons with already existing MPPT techniques. This paper proposes a novel MPPT technique based on the integral feedback of the conductance. Additionally, a comparison with some of the most well-known MPPT algorithms is presented, such as the classic perturb and observe, incremental conductance and the most recent techniques based on fuzzy logic and neural networks. The comparative analysis of the MPPT algorithms is made based on parameters as complexity and performance, under different test conditions.

Keywords: Maximum Power Point Tracking (MPPT) · Photovoltaic · Solar energy · Linear integrator

1 Introduction

With the increase of the environmental metrics and the growing necessity to reduce pollution from fossil fuels, adoption of renewable energy production technologies has been growing over the last decades [1]. This has driven researcher interests to the search of new methods of maximizing the power production of PV installations [2].

© IFIP International Federation for Information Processing 2022
Published by Springer Nature Switzerland AG 2022
L. M. Camarinha-Matos (Ed.): DoCEIS 2022, IFIP AICT 649, pp. 158–166, 2022.
https://doi.org/10.1007/978-3-031-07520-9_15

The tracking of the Maximum Power Point (MPP) of a photovoltaic (PV) panel is a difficult task due to the non-linearity of P-V Curves and the varying response in produced power in respect to the irradiance, temperature, solar incidence angle and output load [3].

MPP can be calculated based on several existing methods; mostly presented in [4]. The Maximum Power Point Tracking (MPPT) algorithms are generally divided into offline and online tracking [5]. The offline methods are generally simpler methods such as the fractional Open Circuit Voltage (OCV) or fractional Short Circuit Current (SCC) [5]. These strategies are classified as offline due to its necessity to disconnect the load during some time to measure the OCV or SCC to compute the present MPPT. Furthermore, the offline methods are not truly MPPT methods because of their inability to continuously track the most efficient operating point of a given PV cell.

The online MPPT methods allow continuous tracking of the MPP considering different conditions such as the temperature or irradiance, not requiring the disconnection of the PV panels. One of the best-known methods in industry and academia is Perturb and Observe (P&O) [6–7], immensely used in commercial products due to its simplicity and low computational requirements [7]. Another well-known MPPT method is the Incremental Conductance (INC) [8], that appears in literature with a lot of modifications in its search algorithm, some of them with adaptive step size [8].

During the decades of 90s and 00s, with the increase of computing power, more complex controllers like Fuzzy Logic (FL) [3], neuro-fuzzy controllers [9], Artificial Neural Networks (ANN) [1], and more recently reinforcement learning [10] have been proposed in the literature to track the MPP.

This paper proposes a new method which combines the incremental conductance concept with a classic linear integral compensator. The main advantage is the possibility of using linear control theory to estimate the integral compensator gain. The proposed MPPT controller is compared with four of the most popular MPPT algorithms in terms of power extracted from the PV panel, response time, and oscillations around the MPP. These analyzed MPPT strategies are: P&O, INC, FL, and ANN. All these methods are tested using time varying irradiance conditions.

The paper is organized as follow: Sect. 2 presents the relationship with the conference theme. Section 3 presents the topology presented for the evaluation of the MPPT methods under study that are described in Sect. 4. Then, simulation results are presented in Sect. 5. Finally, Sect. 6 presents conclusions and future work.

2 Relationship to Technological Innovation for Digitalization and Virtualization

Nowadays, the society we live in is increasingly competitive and focused on optimizing systems and energy efficiency [1], with microgrids having a highly important role in this development. These microgrids are closely associated with the optimization of renewable energy sources such as wind turbines and PV due to their intermittent nature.

MPPT controllers are commonly used in the production of electricity from renewable energy sources [10], which are mandatory to provide clean power to systems running digital twin models of technological processes. Digital twins and virtualization replace the authentic physical experience or assets with digital models, while needing and contributing to renewable energy extraction efficiency. With the technological advances of the last two decades, it is increasingly evident that the implementation of digital twins and virtualization in embedded systems is often associated with concepts such as Internet of Things (IoT) and smart grids, being connected to central servers that control the microgrid power flow sending setpoints for the converters to optimize and adjust their operation.

Furthermore, the algorithms and methods presented in this paper are part of the digitalization and virtualization paradigm. The proposed new method aims to be implementable in inexpensive digital embedded systems with low computational power and low energy consumption, based on increasing the overall efficiency of the digital control and power systems. The experimental part is not yet included in this work, and this implementation is one of the points of future study.

3   PV Panel and Power Converter

For the study of the MPPT methods, a topology with a PV connected to a Boost converter that powers a resistive load is used as shown in Fig. 1a. Herein, the inductor value L is 550 μH and capacitors value C_{in} and C_{out} values are 150 μF. The PV panel considered in the simulations is the A10J-M60-240 from A10 Green Technology, with a maximum power of 240.54 W, being the characteristic P-V curve in Fig. 1b. The converter step-up topology was implemented due to its simplicity and common use in PV applications [11].

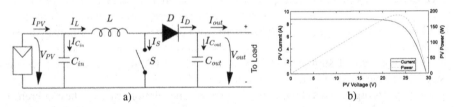

Fig. 1. a) Electric schematic of implementation, PV panel and boost converter; b) Typical Power-Voltage Characteristic of Photovoltaic Panels

The boost converter is used in this scenario to control the extracted current from the PV panel and at the same time increase the voltage. This is beneficial for future development when the boost will be connected to an inverter and inject power into a grid or a microgrid.

Voltage ripple in capacitor C_{in} at the PV terminals should be as small as possible since the MPP is dependent on voltage and current, and voltage as well as current ripples causes power losses. For this, the PV output capacitor should have enough capacitance to steady the PV output voltage and support the system during several switching periods.

4 Well-Known MPPT Control Methods

MPPT algorithms track the MPP in the power-voltage curves of PV panels. These curves are non-linear and strongly dependent on solar irradiance and temperature [2]. Consequently, MPPT algorithms should have a great elasticity to adjust and search for the MPP. Besides, the MPP in the characteristic power-voltage curve of a PV panel (Fig. 1b) is not a stable point.

One of the proposed algorithms is the P&O that affects the duty cycle (D) of the converter by a constant ΔD. To note that a bigger ΔD increment or decrement causes bigger limit cycles and consequently a bigger ripple in PV voltage and current, similarly a lower ΔD causes a lower ripple but slow convergence rate. Another disadvantage of this algorithm occurs in cases of a gradual increase in irradiance [7].

On this work, three different P&O algorithms are considered: the first one uses a fixed step (P&O) [6], while the others use two adaptive algorithms based on dP_{PV}/dV_{PV} (P&O Adapt) and $\log_{10}(dP_{PV}/dV_{PV})$ (P&O Adapt Log) [6].

INC is another very well know method in literature, and it is based on finding the V_{PV}, I_{PV} point where the power derivative relatively to the voltage is zero:

$$\frac{dP_{PV}}{dV_{PV}} = 0 \tag{1}$$

Considering the typical P-V curve, when the dP_{PV}/dV_{PV} is greater than zero the system is on the left side of MPP and the duty cycle should be decreased and when dP_{PV}/dV_{PV} is lower than zero, the system is working on the right side of MPP and duty cycle should be increased.

Considering the power given by $P_{PV} = V_{PV}I_{PV}$, from (1) the PV panel conductance (I_{PV}/V_{PV}) can be related to its incremental value (dI_{PV}/dV_{PV}). Sometimes, the INC approach also presents problems during variations of irradiance. When the irradiance changes the algorithm sometimes compute the dI_{PV}/dV_{PV} with the wrong values, which results in slower transient response and consequently in a momentaneous loss of power [12]. The INC algorithm herein implemented uses fixed and adaptive step based on dP_{PV}/dV_{PV} and $\log_{10}(dP_{PV}/dV_{PV})$ [8], namely INC, INC Adapt and INC Adapt Log, respectively.

Application of neural networks (NN) in MPPT is depicted in [8]. These networks are trained with irradiance and temperature as input data. Herein, a table with irradiance, temperature, and the corresponding outputs (V_{mpp}, I_{mpp}, and P_{mpp}) were used as data to train a NN with 10 neurons in a single hidden layer.

As the ANN used in this study is trained with irradiance and temperature to obtain a reference current and these parameters are different for each PV, for each it is necessary to create a different NN.

FL uses rules designed using linguistic variables to control complex systems [12]. This type of control typically doesn't need a mathematical model of the system under control. Instead, FL needs an expert on the system dynamics behavior to devise just a few membership functions and linguistic rules based on the knowledge of the system dynamics.

Regarding the MPPT based on FL, there are multiple implementations in the literature. Herein, it is considered [3], where six possible solutions for FL implementation in
MPPT can be found.

To design a FL MPPT algorithm, the discrete form of dP_{PV}/dV_{PV}, represented as
$S(k)$ and its discrete time derivative $\Delta S(k)$ are used [3].

For the implementation of FL, the Mamdani method was used as an inference engine
and a center of gravity algorithm was used in the defuzzification process. The fuzzy rules
are presented in [3] and the input and output membership functions can be found in Fig. 2.
All the membership functions were adjusted from [3] and uniformized to generalize to
different approaches or different topologies.

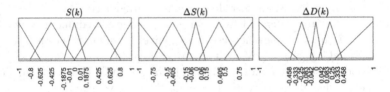

Fig. 2. Fuzzy logic membership functions.

5   Incremental Conductance with Linear Integral Compensator (LIC-INC)

The proposed approach is based on the INC algorithm, obtained from (1), written as
$V_{PV} \frac{dI_{PV}}{dV_{PV}} + I_{PV} = 0$.

This form can be written as in a negative feedback system ($V_{PV} \frac{dI_{PV}}{dV_{PV}} - (-I_{PV}) =
0$). Moreover, during convergence, it can be admitted that the algebraic sum of the
incremental conductance value dI_{PV}/dV_{PV} with the conductance I_{PV}/V_{PV} will not be
zero, presenting some tracking error e_{MPPT}, or $V_{pv} \frac{dI_{pv}}{dV_{pv}} - (-I_{pv}) = e_{MPPT}$, re-written
in (2). The tracking error value e_{MPPT} will be enforced to zero within a finite amount of
time.

$$\frac{dI_{PV}}{dV_{PV}} - \left(-\frac{I_{PV}}{V_{PV}}\right) = \frac{e_{MPPT}}{V_{PV}} \tag{2}$$

Considering the Boost DC/DC converter, driven by a current controller to track the
input current $i_{L_{ref}}$ at high frequency, it is possible to consider the boost inductor current
$I_L \approx I_{L_{ref}}$. For simplicity, the panel current I_{PV} is here considered to follow the i_L current
with a first order low pass filter dynamics with pole at $-1/(sTc)$. Then, $-I_{PV}/V_{PV}$ is
(3):

$$-\frac{I_{PV}}{V_{PV}} \approx -\frac{I_{L_{ref}}}{V_{PV}} \frac{1}{1 + sTc} \tag{3}$$

A linear integral controller K_i/s returning the set-point value $I_{L_{ref}}/V_{PV}$, can then be
devised (Fig. 3) to ensure MPPT tracking (zero steady-state error).

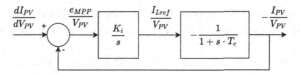

Fig. 3. Block Diagram of the novel linear integral compensator MPPT method.

To compute the integral gain K_i, the closed loop transfer function of the linear integral compensator MPPT represented in Fig. 3 is written in (4).

$$\frac{-\frac{I_{PV}}{V_{PV}}}{\frac{dI_{PV}}{dV_{PV}}} \approx \frac{-\frac{K_i}{T_c}}{s^2 + \frac{s}{T_c} - \frac{K_i}{T_c}} \tag{4}$$

Comparing the denominator of the closed loop transfer function to the canonical form denominator of a second order system $s^2 + 2\xi\omega_n + \omega_n^2$, it is obtained (5), where it is seen that for stability K_i should be negative definite, $K_i < 0$.

$$\omega_n^2 = -\frac{K_i}{T_c}; K_i = -\frac{1}{2\xi^2 T_c} \tag{5}$$

The time constant T_c can be estimated considering the capacitor at the output of the PV panel. This capacitor in the diagram of Fig. 1 is the capacitor of input of boost converter represented by C_{in}. Considering an equivalent MPPT resistor given by $R_{PV} = V_{PV}/I_{PV}$, and determining the equivalent resistor value in the MPP, T_c can be written as (6).

$$T_c = C_{in}R_{pv} = C_{in}\frac{V_{MPP}}{I_{MPP}} \tag{6}$$

6 Simulation Results

The MPPT implementations were submitted into four test types, each one with different irradiance variations as: i) The step test was made with 3 values of irradiance: at the beginning the irradiance is 400 W/m^2, at 0.133 s this value is increased to 1000 W/m^2 and a second transition occurs at 0.266 s with a final value of 600 W/m^2; ii) The fast test has an initial irradiance value of 400 W/m^2, it is increased to 1000 W/m^2, stabilizes for 0.1 s and decreases from this value to 300 W/m^2; iii) The slow test irradiance values are 600 W/m^2, 700 W/m^2 and in final reaches 600 W/m^2, iv) steady state test was implemented under a irradiance value of 1000 //m^2.

In Fig. 4 are presented the results of each algorithm for step variations. The figures of fast, slow and steady state tests are not depicted here due to lack of space, and its similarity. However, on Table 1 all the results are summarized.

Table 1 shows the effectiveness of the studied methods including the integral linear compensator. The effectiveness shown in table does not include the efficiency of the boost converter.

The results obtained from this study demonstrate that the methods presented have distinct responses when subjected to different variations of irradiance. It can also be verified that there is no perfect MPPT algorithm but all of them have effectiveness above 99% in steady state. In terms of analysis of response times and oscillation in the voltage and current of the PV, it is seen that the algorithm that faster reaches the MPPT value is the ANN. However, this algorithm needs training data from the PV panels to be trained beforehand, thus having high dependence on the panel characteristics. In addition this algorithm needs, as inputs, the irradiance and the temperature that are parameters whose measurement is more complex.

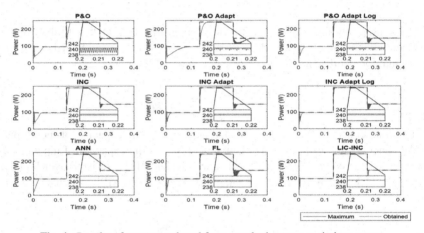

Fig. 4. Results of power produced from panel when step variations occur.

By analysis of Table 1, the algorithms with greater effectiveness are the ANN in steady state and the new proposed method in situations of irradiance variation.

Table 1. Results of MPPT efficiency for different algorithms and tests implemented.

Algorithm	*i*) Step variation	*ii*) Fast variation	*iii*) Slow variation	*iv*) Steady state
P&O	96.19%	97.61%	94.51%	99.67%
P&O adapt	93.36%	92.01%	94.97%	99.90%
P&O adapt log	98.36%	97.47%	98.42%	99.90%

(continued)

Table 1. (*continued*)

Algorithm	*i*) Step variation	*ii*) Fast variation	*iii*) Slow variation	*iv*) Steady state
INC	97.36%	98.36%	96.52%	99.98%
INC adapt	98.60%	98.02%	97.44%	99.86%
INC adapt log	98.81%	96.44%	98.65%	99.86%
FL	98.28%	98.20%	98.96%	99.88%
ANN	98.68%	98.79%	98.81%	**100.00%**
LIC-INC (proposed)	**99.24%**	**99.09%**	**99.62%**	99.98%

7 Conclusion

Observing the results, it is possible to conclude that the proposed algorithm has good tracking capabilities since the controller manages to maintain the search for the MPP even with different conditions.

This new method shows very good characteristics of speed in tracking the MPP and a very accurate detection of this point, however the controller generates some disturbances on voltage, current and consequently on power produced by the control objective dP_{PV}/dV_{PV}.

As future work is expected the test of this algorithm in partial shading to verify its ability to detect global MPP. Furthermore, this new method can also be combined with a NN or a deep learning algorithm to optimize the problems arising from dP_{PV}/dV_{PV} generated outliers.

The linear integral compensator method can use linear control theory to estimate the integral gain. This method can be used to improve the INC algorithms.

Acknowledgments. This work was supported in part by Portugal funds through Fundação para a Ciência e Tecnologia (FCT) with project reference UIDB/50021/2020 and by project PTDC/EEI-EE/32550/2017.

References

1. Elobaid, L.M., Abdelsalam, A.K., Zakzouk, E.E.: Artificial neural network-based photovoltaic maximum power point tracking techniques: a survey. IET Renew. Power Gener. **9**(8), 1043–1063 (2015)
2. Heidari, M.: Improving efficiency of photovoltaic system by using neural network MPPT and predictive control of converter. Int. J. Renew. Energy Res. (IJRER) **6**(4), 1524–1529 (2016)
3. Shiau, J.K., Wei, Y.C., Chen, B.C.: A study on the fuzzy-logic-based solar power MPPT algorithms using different fuzzy input variables. Algorithms **8**(2), 100–127 (2015)
4. Hassani, M., Mekhilef, S., Hu, A.P., Watson, N.R.: A novel MPPT algorithm for load protection based on output sensing control. In: 2011 IEEE Ninth International Conference on Power Electronics and Drive Systems. pp. 1120–1124. IEEE (2011)

5. Hanzaei, S.H., Gorji, S.A., Ektesabi, M.: A scheme-based review of MPPT techniques with respect to input variables including solar irradiance and PV arrays' temperature. IEEE Access **8**, 182229–182239 (2020)
6. Killi, M., Samanta, S.: Modified perturb and observe MPPT algorithm for drift avoidance in photovoltaic systems. IEEE Trans. Industr. Electron. **62**(9), 5549–5559 (2015)
7. Ahmed, J., Salam, Z.: An improved perturb and observe (P&O) maximum power point tracking (MPPT) algorithm for higher efficiency. Appl. Energy **150**, 97–108 (2015)
8. Tey, K.S., Mekhilef, S.: Modified incremental conductance MPPT algorithm to mitigate inaccurate responses under fast-changing solar irradiation level. Sol. Energy **101**, 333–342 (2014)
9. Harrag, A., Messalti, S.: Ic-based variable step size neuro-fuzzy MPPT improving PV system performances. Energy Procedia **157**, 362–374 (2019)
10. Phan, B.C., Lai, Y.C., Lin, C.E.: A deep reinforcement learning-based MPPT control for PV systems under partial shading condition. Sensors **20**(11), 3039 (2020)
11. Irmak, E., Güler, N.: A model predictive control-based hybrid MPPT method for boost converters. Int. J. Electr. **107**(1), 1–16 (2020)
12. Sera, D., Mathe, L., Kerekes, T., Spataru, S.V., Teodorescu, R.: On the perturb and observe and incremental conductance MPPT methods for PV systems. IEEE J. Photovolt. **3**(3), 1070–1078 (2013)

Reduction of Air-Gap Flux Density Distortion for a 20 kW HTS Induction Motor

Masoud Ardestani[1]([✉]) and Hamid Reza Izadfar[2]

[1] Department of Electrical and Computer Engineering, NOVA School of Science and Technology (FCT NOVA), Caparica, Portugal
ardestani.masoud90@gmail.com
[2] Department of Electrical and Computer Engineering, Semnan University, Semnan, Iran
hrizadfar@semnan.ac.ir

Abstract. Nowadays, High-Temperature Superconducting (HTS) electric machines are widely used in industry due to the unique properties of HTS materials. Besides, the effect of space harmonics is a very serious challenge that must be considered in the design of HTS electric machines. In this paper, a high-temperature superconductor- induction/synchronous machine (HTS-ISM) with 20 kW power is provided to reduce air-gap flux density distortion. For a precise comparison, the main parameters of the machine are studied under the same conditions such as frequency, core material, pole number, critical current density, and voltage by the Finite Element Method. In addition to winding arrangement, the geometrical parameters of the machine also affect the space harmonics, so by modifying each of these parameters, the amount of Total Harmonic Distortion (THD) is obtained in each case. In the proposed model, the amount of THD is significantly reduced, which makes the air-gap flux density more sinusoidal. Torque ripple has also been improved in the proposed machine.

Keywords: High-temperature superconductor · Air-gap flux density · Harmonic component · Total harmonic distortion · Finite element method

1 Introduction

Today, the development of High-Temperature Superconductor (HTS) machines has increasingly drawn the attention of researchers [1–4]. These types of HTS machines can be used in different applications such as ship propulsion [5], electric vehicles [6], wave energy converters [7], wind energies [8], and so on. However, although superconducting electric machines have been increasingly used in various industries and have unique properties, they are not immune to harmonics, Nevertheless, superconducting machines perform better than conventional machines against harmonic distortion [9]. The problem of harmonics is the main issue in electric machines that must be considered in the design since it affects the performance of electric machines, both superconducting, and conventional machines. Generally, harmonics are divided into two categories, time,

© IFIP International Federation for Information Processing 2022
Published by Springer Nature Switzerland AG 2022
L. M. Camarinha-Matos (Ed.): DoCEIS 2022, IFIP AICT 649, pp. 167–183, 2022.
https://doi.org/10.1007/978-3-031-07520-9_16

and space harmonics. Time harmonics are caused by nonlinear loads and power electronics devices, but space harmonics are created inside the electric machines. The space harmonics are related to the design, the type of winding (concentrated or distributed), the full or fractional pitch, and the geometry of the machine such as air-gap length, slot opening, eccentricity, and lamination stack, magnetic saturation, etc. [13–15]. Apart from that, another issue that must be considered in HTS machines is the design and implementation of HTS coils, which is also effective in reducing the distortion of the air-gap flux density, so that the perpendicular flux to their surface is reduced. Since the anisotropy of HTS coils is completely different from copper winding and their characteristics as critical current density are strongly affected by perpendicular fluxes which leads to a decrease in critical current density, an increase in AC losses, and distortion in the air-gap flux density. Therefore, the proper design of an HTS coil in the superconducting machine is very important to reduce the harmonic component of the air-gap flux density [10–13, 30]. One of these machines discussed in this paper is High-Temperature Superconductor- Induction/Synchronous Machine (HTS-ISM), which is an ideal candidate in the electrical transportation industry. Concerning this, a 20 kW HTS induction motor which was designed and built by Japanese researchers [16] examined from the harmonic perspective. In fact, we analyzed a partial HTS induction motor in which superconducting materials only used in the rotor and stator winding are made of copper exactly like a conventional electric motor [16, 19]. On the other hand, since the stator winding was pre-designed as distributed, we have only focused on the motor geometry to reduce the harmonic components in the air-gap. Furthermore, space harmonics in the HTS-ISM cause noise due to the pulsating torque, and increased copper and core losses, which leads to heat and decrease efficiency. For this reason, if the harmonic components of the air-gap can be reduced, the vibration, noise, copper, and core losses of the motor can be decreased [15, 20]. Regarding this, the HTS-ISM air-gap magnetic flux distortion is investigated, and a new structure is proposed to reduce the harmonic component of air-gap flux density. For this purpose, the geometric parameters that were effective on the harmonic component of air-gap flux density were investigated and the most appropriate ones were selected from the THD point of view. Also, with decreasing the harmonic components of the air-gap, the torque ripple has decreased. The rest of the paper is as follows. In Sect. 2, the relation of the conference theme with the paper is given. In Sect. 3 the structure of HTS-ISM will be described. In Sect. 4, the HTS-ISM operation is explained. In Sect. 5, the geometry optimization of HTS-ISM is given. In Sect. 6, electromagnetic analysis of the initial and proposed HTS-ISM is investigated. Finally, the conclusion and future work will be explained in Sects. 7 and 8, respectively.

2   Relation with Technological Innovation for Life Improvement

The technological innovation proposed in this work is related to life improvement by contributing to the development of high-temperature superconducting machines. Superconducting materials allow the development of more compact and light devices with the same power when compared to their conventional counterparts. This has impacts on several sectors, such as industry or transportation. The development of superconducting-based technologies has also direct impact on life improvement, as related to all the links of the energy chain, besides end-use, like generation, transmission, distribution, and storage of electrical energy, fostering the Energy Transition.

3 Machine Structure

The initial machine structure is shown in Fig. 1 [16]. The stator and rotor cores are silicon-steel and laminated. The stator coil is made of copper and the distributed winding is adopted to reduce the harmonic component of the air-gap magnetic flux density [17]. Also, rotor bars with HTS wires (Bi-2223) are located in the rotor slots. Since the core of the motor passes almost all of the main magnetic flux from the slots, it has two major advantages over the air-core motor: 1- There are only self-magnetic fields in the slots i.e., magnetic field leakage due to the current passing through the HTS rotor bars, in other words, there is no external magnetic field in the rotor bars. Therefore, the destructive effects of magnetic fields on the current transport property can be ignored. 2- Reducing the electromagnetic force applied on rotor HTS bars, therefore does not need a complex structure to protect the conductors [26]. The HTS rotor bars are mounted on the top of the rotor near the air-gap to reduce leakage flux [27].

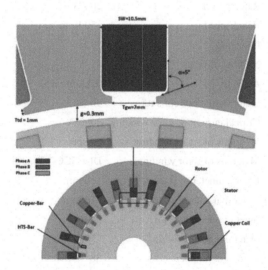

Fig. 1. The structure of the initial machine

Rotor bars are made of eleven HTS tapes, isolated copper bars are also used in the rotor slots for thermal stability, mechanical support, and current pass in the non-superconducting area of the HTS bars [18]. At the time of starting, the motor has to be cooled to 77 k. The length of the cryostat is the length of the shaft with a diameter of 428 mm. The cryostat structure is such that the HTS-ISM can rotate slowly even below the Cryogenic temperature and the cryostat is equipped with a nitrogen reservoir [16]. Since the stator and rotor cores are laminated, the effects of eddy losses are neglected. All the analyses of the proposed and initial machines were carried out under the identical conditions such as the coil number, speed, core materials, and poles number. The specification of HTS wire and the main parameter of the HTS-ISM are presented in Table 1 and Table 2, respectively.

Table 1. Specification of HTS wire

HTS wire	Type H
Width	4.3 ± 0.3 mm
Thickness	0.23 ± 0.23 mm
I_C at 77 k, self-field	190 A
Allowable banding radius	70 mm

Table 2. Main parameter of HTS-ISM

Item	Basic HTS-ISM
Rated power	20 kW
Rated speed	750 Rpm
frequency	50 Hz
Number of poles	8
Air-gap	0.3 mm
Stator number of coils turns	30
Critical current of rotor winding	2090 A
Materials of stator winding	Copper
Materials of rotor winding	DI-BSCCO Type H
Inner diameter of stator	160 mm
Outer diameter of stator	256 mm
Inner diameter of rotor	50 mm
Outer diameter of rotor	159.4 mm
Rotor slot number	38
Stator slot number	24

4   Machine Operation

When AC voltage is applied to an HTS induction motor, the rotor bars are exposed to time-varying magnetic flux due to the MMF caused by the stator winding. On the other hand, since the rotor bars are made of high-temperature superconducting material and type Bi-2223, they show losses against AC fields. Also, another type of loss due to thermal activation occurs in currents below J_c, called Flux creep. In addition, superconducting materials have inherent properties and impurities, so their interaction with time-varying magnetic fields creates a force called the pinning force.

This force keeps in place the vortices that cause losses in superconducting materials. At the opposite point, there is another force called the Lorenz force that wants to move the vortices. When these two forces are equal, that point is the critical current density. Thus, in the initial moments, since the motor has not yet started to rotate and the magnetic field applied to the rotor bars is less than Hc_1, the flux applied to the rotor bars is shielded because of pinning centers and they are not allowed to enter the bars, which this is called initial mode (shielding). At this moment, the magnetic flux inside the rotor bars is zero ($B = 0$). After a while, as the motor starts to rotate due to high slip ($s = 1$), high currents are created in the rotor bars. In this situation, the Lorenz force is greater than the pinning force, which causes the vortices to flow in the rotor bars, and the bars show resistance losses, which is called Flux-Flow or Asynchronous mode. At this moment, rotor bars current also greater than the critical current density of the bars, which is 2090 amps, so the bars are out of superconductivity for a short time. In this case, the motor starts with a slip, which is obtained as follows (1).

$$S = \frac{N_S - N}{N_S} \qquad (1)$$

where, N_s is the synchronous speed and N_r is the speed of rotor. Moments later, due to the reduction of slip, the current of the rotor bars becomes less than the critical current density of the bars and the resistance of the rotor bars becomes almost zero. At this time, the Lorentz force is less than the pinning force, and all magnetic flux is trapped by the pinning centers in the rotor bars, which is called persistent current mode or Synchronous mode. At this time, the rotor is locked with a magnetic field and reaches synchronous speed. In this case, the rotor bars act like PM. In fact, this motor has 3 modes of shielding, asynchronous and synchronous due to the unique properties of superconducting materials that have nonlinear resistance. This nonlinear resistance leads the motor to have high starting torque (due to high resistance) and synchronous torque (due to almost zero resistance) [17, 21, 22, 24, 27, 33].

4.1   The Relationship Between Voltage-Current of Superconductor and Torque-Speed of HTS-ISM

To use a superconductor, its electromagnetic behavior must be described. Quantitative calculation of the electromagnetic behavior of HTS materials is complex because their voltage-current relationship is non-linear. The E-j power-law method uses the nonlinear voltage-current superconductor relation to model it as a nonlinear conductor. The voltage-current curve of the superconductor and torque-speed of HTS-ISM is shown in Fig. 2. the superconductor voltage-current curve can be fit by the power-law given in Eq. 2.

$$E(I) = E_c \left(\frac{I}{I_c}\right)^N \tag{2}$$

where E(I) is the longitudinal voltage drop through the superconductor, E_C is the electric field criterion at $1\mu v/cm$, I is the current in the conductor, I_C is the critical current, and N is the exponent. A higher N-value produces a sharp transition in the V-I curve and demonstrates the quality of the superconductor. High-quality superconductors will have numerous N-value. A superconductor is categorized by a V-I curve or the voltage drop across the length of it as a function of its current. The critical current of the superconductor is defined as the current that produces a voltage drop of $1 \ \mu v/cm$ as depicted in Fig. 2. According to Fig. 2, this motor not only has a slip torque but also synchronous torque. In simple terms, the rotational synchronous mode is achieved in zero resistivity state and rotational slip mode is achieved in the flux-flow state. These exclusive features are due to the nonlinear voltage current of HTS materials [9, 25].

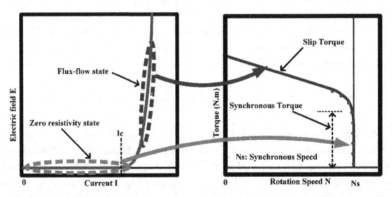

Fig. 2. The voltage-current of superconductor relationship with torque-speed of HTS-ISM [25].

5   Motor Geometry Optimization

Generally, in an electric machine, the geometrical parameters of the machine and the structure of the winding affect the space harmonics. So, by choosing these parameters properly, the effects of the space harmonics, which result in vibration, parasitic torque, noise, and losses, can be reduced. In this section we only focused on the geometrical parameters of the motor because the winding arrangement of the initial motor has been designed as distributed with a short pitch configuration. Therefore, to investigate the air-gap magnetic flux density in terms of harmonic, first, air-gap magnetic flux density was acquired based on FEM with the ANSYS-Maxwell software. After that, the Fourier transform was obtained from the air-gap magnetic flux by MATLAB software, and the

THD value of air-gap flux was attained for each variable which is presented in Fig. 4. The parameters examined are air-gap (g), tooth gap width (Tgw), slot width (Sw), tooth tang angle (α), and tooth tang depth (Ttd) as shown in Fig. 3. Figure 4 (a) shows the rate of THD changes of parameters which their unit is length (air-gap, tooth gap width, slot width, tooth tang depth). Figure 4 (b) also shows the THD value of tooth tang angle parameter for different angles in degree. In addition, an explanation of all the examined parameters is given below. Finally, the THD values for different parameters are given in Table 3.

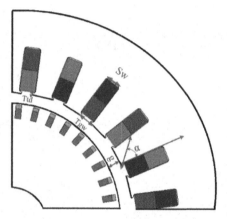

Fig. 3. Examined parameters of HTS-ISM.

5.1 Air-Gap

Air-gap is the most important factor in reducing air-gap magnetic flux density distortion. The length of the air-gap of the initial HTS-ISM is 0.3 mm. By increasing this parameter from 0.3 to 1 mm, the odd harmonics components of the air-gap magnetic flux decreased, the reason behind this, is the variation of permeance which affects the amplitude of the harmonic component [20]. Also, the amplitude of the fundamental component is reduced due to the increase in the air-gap magnetic reluctance. The lowest value of THD belongs to the air-gap of 1 mm.

5.2 Tooth Gap Width

After the air-gap, the gap between the teeth which is called tooth gap width is the most important parameter in reducing THD of the air-gap magnetic flux. By changing this parameter to 5.5 mm, the THD reaches its minimum value which is 0.5064.

5.3 Slot Width

The slot width is designed according to machine limitations such as specific magnetic loading and specific electric loading. As the slot width increases, the specific electric

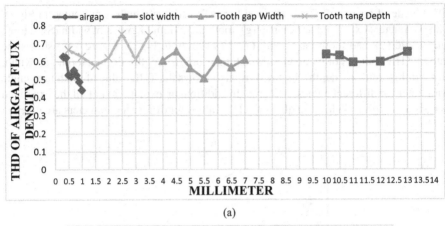

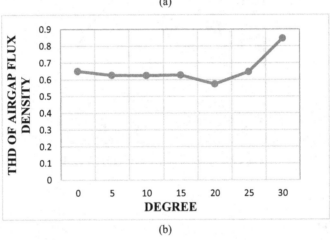

(b)

Fig. 4. The THD values for different parameters a) parameters with different unit lengths b) Tooth tang angle parameter with unit of degree.

loading increases, and by decreasing it, the specific magnetic loading increases. There-fore, the slot width should be selected according to the limitations of the machine such as the standard current density in the stator coil and the maximum allowable magnetic flux density; regarding the need and the limitations of the machine, a compromise should be made between the specific magnetic loading and specific electric loading. To optimally select the dimensions of the slot, Eq. 3 must be satisfied.

$$A_{ss} = \frac{Z_{ss}a_s}{0.4} \qquad (3)$$

where Z_{ss} is the number of conductors, a_s is the conductor cross-section, 0.4 is a constant coefficient and A_{ss} is the slot area. By varying the slot width from 10 to 13 mm, the THD value of the air-gap flux belongs to the slot width of 11 mm with a value of 0.5927.

5.4 Tooth Tang Angle

The tooth tang angle is the angle between the tang and the bottom of the slot. The variation of the THD of tooth tang angle changes in terms of degree is shown in Fig. 4 (b), the lowest of which is at 20°.

5.5 Tooth Tang Depth

Tooth tang depth is the length of the tang. The lowest THD value of the air-gap belongs to the tooth tang depth of 1.5 mm. As shown in Table 3, the minimum THD values for the examined parameters (air-gap, tooth gap width, slot width, tooth tang angle, and tooth tang depth) are 1 mm, 5.5 mm, 11 mm, 20°, and 1.5 mm respectively. Therefore, the proposed machine is designed with these values.

Table 3. THD values for the examined machine parameters in different range.

Examined parameter	Examined parameter variation	THD of air-gap flux density
Air-gap (mm)	0.3	0.6267
	0.4	0.6209
	0.5	0.5252
	0.6	0.5183
	0.7	0.5496
	0.8	0.5229
	0.9	0.4869
	1	0.4415
Tooth gap width (mm)	4	0.6052
	4.5	0.6566
	5	0.5633
	5.5	0.5063
	6	0.61
	6.5	0.5668
	7	0.6096
Slot width (mm)	10	0.6372
	10.5	0.631
	11	0.5927
	12	0.5958
	13	0.6494

(continued)

Table 3. (*continued*)

Examined parameter	Examined parameter variation	THD of air-gap flux density
Tooth tang angle (degree)	0	0.65
	5	0.6267
	10	0.6249
	15	0.6277
	20	0.5736
	25	0.647
	30	0.8456
Tooth tang depth (mm)	0.5	0.6643
	1	0.6267
	1.5	0.5774
	2	0.6184
	2.5	0.7522
	3	0.6111
	3.5	0.7439

6 2D FEM Analysis

Analytical equations cannot be used when the geometry is complicated, and the field condition is not uniform. Numerous numerical methods have been proposed to solve this problem. These numerical methods usually use the FEM and FDM methods to solve the Maxwell equations. FEM is the most popular method for solving partial differential equations. These methods can be categorized by solving the Maxwell equations that are the same: A-V (based on the magnetic vector potential A), T- Ω (based on the current vector potential T), E (based on the electric field E), and H (based on directly solving the magnetic field components) formulations. The final answer to each of these equations is the same.; the only difference is their solutions [27–29]. The numerical model used in this paper for modeling of HTS-ISM is based on solving the set of Maxwell equations in 2D implementing the A-V formulation using the software package ANSYS-Maxwell. Therefore, by solving the partial differential equation (PDE) in 2D, the amount of electric and magnetic fields in each node can be accurately obtained from the Eq. (4).

$$\nabla \times \upsilon \nabla \times A = J_s - \sigma \frac{dA}{dt} - \sigma \nabla v + \nabla \times H_c \qquad (4)$$

where A is the magnetic vector potential, J_s is the source current density (one component in z-direction for 2D), H_C is the coercive magnetic field (A/m) and v is the velocity of the moving part. For a simple definition of the HTS materials, a material called perfect conductor which also exist in the ANSYS-Maxwell Library, is included with a magnetic relative permeability of almost zero.

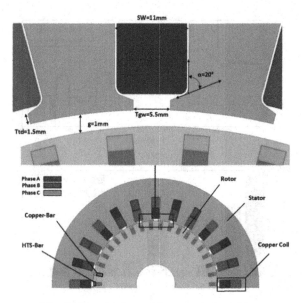

Fig. 5. The structure of the proposed machine.

The proposed machine is designed based on the initial machine as shown in Fig. 5. According to the results of the previous section, the lowest THD values were obtained by changing air-gap, tooth gap width, slot width, tooth tang angle, and tooth tang depth values by 1 mm, 5.5 mm, 11 mm, 20°, and 1.5 mm, respectively. In this section, the electromagnetic parameters of the initial and proposed machine are presented and investigated, such as the distribution of the air-gap magnetic flux and its harmonic components, magnetic flux lines and magnetic flux density distribution, and torque ripple.

6.1 Air-Gap Flux Density Distribution and Harmonic Component

The interaction between the stator and the rotor MMF leads to magnetic flux density in the air-gap of the HTS induction motor. So that the voltage applied to the stator winding, which causes induced current in the cage rotor, creates MMF in the stator and rotor winding, respectively. Space harmonics make the air-gap magnetic flux distorted, so it is not purely sinusoidal. To detect the decrease and increase of air-gap magnetic flux density harmonics, Fourier transforms which are known as the total harmonic distortion (THD) criterion, could be utilized. Generally, the THD relation in terms of air-gap magnetic radial flux (Br) can be defined as below. The tangential flux is ignored.

$$\text{THD} = \frac{\sqrt{\sum_{k=2} \text{Brk}^2}}{\text{Br1}} \tag{5}$$

Where k is an integer and refers to harmonics (k = 1, 2, 3, 4, …), B_{rk} is the K_{th} amplitude of the K_{th} order harmonic and B_{r1} is the fundamental component [26, 30]. pursuant to Eq. (5), the lower the amplitude of the harmonic components, the lower the

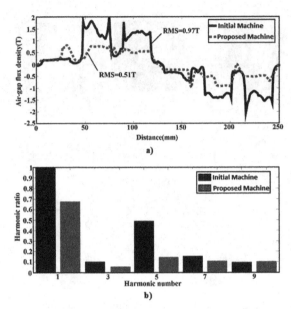

Fig. 6. Air-gap flux density a) air-gap flux density distribution b) air-gap flux density harmonic component.

THD, and the waveform gets closer to the main component, which is a pure sine wave. The distribution of air-gap flux density is shown in Fig. 6 (a). As can be seen, the RMS value of air-gap flux density in the proposed machine is lower than the initial one, and that is the main disadvantage of air-gap increases which leads to reducing the air-gap magnetic flux magnitude. On the other hand, by reducing the air-gap distance the harmonic ratio also decreases significantly. Figure 6 (b) shows the odd harmonic components of the initial and the proposed machines. As shown in Fig. 6 (b), the amplitude of components 3, 5, and 7th decreased, which made the magnetic flux of the air-gap more sinusoidal. Also, the amplitude of the first component, which is the fundamental component is reduced due to the elimination of space disturbing harmonic components. The obtained amount of THD in the proposed machine was 0.4126 and in the initial machine was 0.6267 under 112 Nm load, which was reduced by 34.17% in the proposed machine.

6.2 Magnetic Flux Density Distribution and Magnetic Flux Lines

Figure 7 shows the distribution and flux line density of magnetic flux in the stator and rotor of the initial and proposed machine under a load of 112 Nm. As can be seen from the figure, the magnetic flux density distribution is higher in the initial machine due to the smaller air-gap of the initial machine compared to the proposed machine. On the other hand, since the analysis of both machines was performed under the same conditions, the applied voltage to both machines was equal, which caused a small saturation in the stator teeth of the initial machine. In general, increasing the air-gap increases the magnetizing current of the motor, which causes the motor to draw more current from the grid, so it needs to apply more voltage. The maximum magnetic flux density is set at 2.5 T, which is less than 2.5 T in both machines. Besides, the flux line intensities in the proposed machine are weaker than the initial machine due to the increase in air-gap [31].

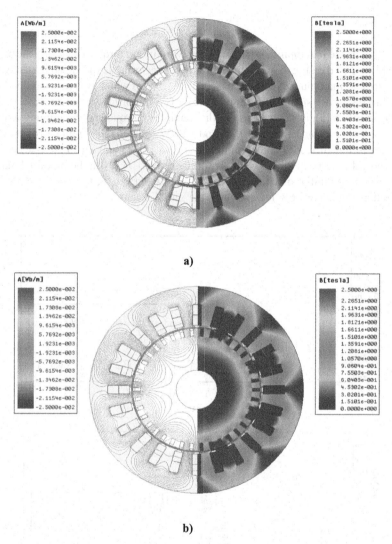

a)

b)

Fig. 7. Magnetic flux lines and magnetic flux density distribution a) initial machine b) proposed machine.

6.3 Torque Ripple

Torque ripple is one of the effects that can be observed in the majority of motors and the reason is the periodical increment and reduction of the output torque in the motor shaft. The amount of torque is often expressed as a percentage, which can be calculated by the difference between the maximum and minimum electromagnetic torques to their average over a period, using the following relation:

$$\text{Torque ripple} = \frac{T_{max} - T_{min}}{T_{avg}} \times 100 \qquad (6)$$

where, T_{max} is the maximum torque, T_{min} is the minimum torque and T_{ave} is the average torque [32]. Based on Fig. 8, when the motor is in synchronous speed and in steady state, a load equal to maximum synchronous torque (112 Nm) which was measured in [16] is applied to the motor shaft at the time of 0.6 s. The motor power, in this case, is about 8.7 kW. In Fig. 8 (a), at 1.3 to 1.4 s (s), the maximum torque and the minimum torque, and average torque are 137.95, 110.79, and 124.37 respectively. Figure 8 (b) shows the maximum torque of 131.77 and minimum torque of 120.11 and a mean torque of 125.94 at 1.3 and 1.4 s, respectively. So that the torque ripple is 9.2% in the proposed machine and 21.8% in the initial machine. As can be seen from Fig. 8, the torque ripple in the proposed machine is 12.6% lower than in the initial machine.

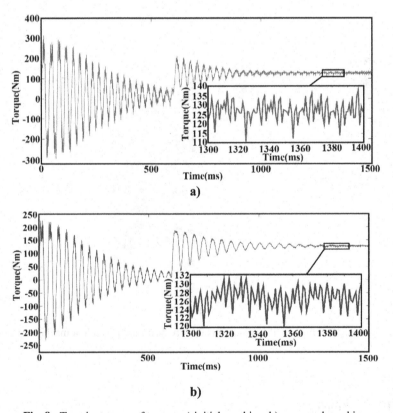

Fig. 8. Transient curve of torque. a) initial machine. b) proposed machine.

7 Conclusions

In this paper, a 20 kW HTS induction motor with the new physical model is presented to reduce the air-gap flux density distortion. The cause of distortion in the air-gap flux density of electric machines is related to space harmonics. These harmonics can be reduced or eliminated by a modification of the winding configuration and motor geometry. Concerning this, we only focused on motor geometry parameters, since the stator winding was predesigned as distributed with a short pitch factor. The geometrical parameters which we investigated were air-gap, tooth gap width, slot width, tooth tang depth, and tooth tang angle, respectively. So that, by changing each of these parameters and selecting the best ones, the optimal model of the machine is obtained from the harmonic point of view. In addition, the most important parameter that reduced the harmonic component of the air-gap flux density was the air-gap changes. Also, all analyses were performed under the same conditions such as voltage, current, pole number, current density, etc. by ANSYS-Maxwell software. Eventually, In the proposed model, THD decreases from 0.6267 to 0.4126 with a decrease of 34.17%. Torque ripple has also decreased from 21.8% to 9.2% by a 12.6% decrease, which results in improving the performance of the machine.

8 Future Work

This HTS motor has been improved by Japanese researchers for many years. Besides, this motor was made in two types of partial and fully HTS induction motors. In the partial structure, HTS materials are used in the rotor, and copper is used only in the stator windings, but in the fully structure, HTS materials are used in both the stator and the rotor. This approach, which is used in this paper to reduce the harmonic component of air-gap flux density, has the potential to be implemented in other structures of HTS induction motors such as fully HTS induction motors or higher power HTS induction motors with both structures (partial and fully) which also built-in recent years. Although in general all parameters must be considered for the design of electric motors and compromise between the parameters is necessary, nevertheless, this approach, regardless of its disadvantages, is a good candidate to reduce the harmonic component of air-gap flux density.

References

1. Umemoto, K., et al.: Development of 1 MW-class HTS motor for podded ship propulsion system. J. Phys. Conf. 234 (2010)
2. Gamble, B., Snitchler, G., Macdonald, T.: Full power test of a 36.5 MW HTS propulsion motor. IEEE Trans. Appl. Supercond. 21, 1083–1088 (2011)
3. Ueno, E., Kato, T., Hayashi, K.: Race-track coils for a 3 MW HTS ship motor. Physica C: Supercond. Appl. 504, 111–114 (2014)
4. Huang, Z., et al.: Control and operation of a high temperature superconducting synchronous motor. IEEE Trans. Appl. Supercond. 3, 235200204–245200204 (2013)
5. Snitchler, G., Gamble, B., Kalsi, S.S.: The performance of a 5 MW high temperature superconductor ship propulsion motor. IEEE Trans. Appl. Supercond. 15, 2206–2209 (2005)

6. Karashima, T., Nakamura, T., Okuno, M.: Multidisciplinary analysis of the transient performance of a 20 kW class HTS induction/synchronous motor cooled with a cryocooler and gaseous air-gap coolant. Cryogenics **99**, 9961–9967 (2019)
7. Ardestani, M., Arish, N., Yaghobi, H.: A new HTS dual stator linear permanent magnet Vernier machine with Halbach array for wave energy conversion. Physica C: Supercond. Appl. **569**, 1353593 (2020)
8. Go, B.S., Sung, H.J., Park, M., Yu, I.K.: Structural design of a module coil for a 12-MW class HTS generator for wind turbine. IEEE Trans. Appl. Supercond. **27**, 1–5 (2017)
9. Kalsi, S.S.: Applications of High Temperature Superconductors to Electric Power Equipment. Wiley, Hoboken (2011)
10. Ikeda, K., et al.: DC and AC current transport characteristics of the HTS stator coils in an HTS induction/synchronous motor. IEEE Trans. Appl. Supercond. **28**(3), 14–18 (2018)
11. Yazdani-Asrami, M., Gholamian, S.A., Mirimani, S.M., Adabi, J.: Influence of field-dependent critical current on harmonic AC loss analysis in HTS coils for superconducting transformers supplying non-linear loads. Cryogenics **113**, 103234 (2021)
12. Wei, L., Nakamura, T., Yoshikawa, M., Itoh, Y., Terazawa, T.: Comparison of different stator winding configurations of fully high-temperature superconducting induction/synchronous motor. IEEE Trans. Appl. Supercond. **30**(4), 4–7 (2020)
13. Lukasik, B., Goddard, K.F., Sykulski, J.K.: Finite element assisted method to reduce harmonic content in the airgap flux density of a high temperature superconducting coreless rotor generator. In: 2008 IET 7th International Conference on Computation in Electromagnetics, pp. 56–57 (2008)
14. On, G.N.: Guidance Note to Control of Harmonics in Electrical Power Systems, American Bureau of shipping ABS plaza 16855 Northchase Drive Houston, TX 77060 USA (2006)
15. Wakileh, G.J.: Harmonics in rotating machines. Electric Power Syst. Res. **66**, 31–37 (2003)
16. Sekiguchi, D., et al.: Trial test of fully HTS induction/synchronous machine for next generation electric vehicle. IEEE Trans. Appl. Supercond. **22**, 5200904 (2012)
17. Karashima, T., et al.: Experimental and analytical studies on highly efficient regenerative characteristics of a 20-kW class HTS induction/synchronous motor. IEEE Trans. Appl. Supercond. **27**, 1–5 (2017)
18. Shimura, H., Nakamura, T., Kitano, H., Nishimura, T., Amemiya, N., Itoh, Y.: Calculated characteristics of HTS induction/synchronous machine below and above its critical temperature. IEEE Trans. Appl. Supercond. **23**, 5201705 (2013)
19. Ardestani, M., Hefaz, H., Arish, N., Yaghobi, H.: Electromagnetic analysis of partial and fully HTS induction motor using finite element method. In: 28th Iranian Conference on Electrical Engineering (ICEE), Tabriz, Iran, pp. 1–5 (2020)
20. Cordier, J.A.: Modelling space harmonics in induction machines for real-time applications. Ph.D. thesis Technical University of Munich (2020)
21. Morita, G., Nakamura, T., Muta, I.: Theoretical analysis of a YBCO squirrel-cage type induction motor based on an equivalent circuit. Supercond. Sci. Technol. **19**, 473–478 (2006)
22. Nakamura, T., Miyake, H., Ogama, Y., Morita, G., Muta, I., Hoshino, T.: Fabrication and characteristics of HTS induction motor by the use of Bi-2223/Ag squirrel-cage rotor. IEEE Trans. Appl. Supercond. **16**, 1469–1472 (2006)
23. Morita, G., Nakamura, T., Muta, I.: Theoretical analysis of a YBCO squirrel-cage type induction motor based on an equivalent circuit. IEEE Trans. Appl. Supercond. J. **19**, 473–478 (2006)
24. Murakami, M.: Magnetic properties of high-temperature superconductors. IEEE Transl. J. Magn. Jpn. **8**(6), 405–414 (1993)
25. Ikeda, K., et al.: Hysteretic rotating characteristics of an HTS induction/synchronous motor. IEEE Trans. Appl. Supercond. **27**, 1–5 (2017)

26. Laksar, J., Sobra, J., Veg, L.: Numerical calculation of the effect of the induction machine load on the air gap magnetic flux density distribution. In: 18th International Scientific Conference on Electric Power Engineering (EPE), pp. 1–6 (2017)
27. Ainslie, M.: Transport AC loss in high-temperature superconducting coils. Ph.D. thesis, University of Cambridge (2012)
28. Yazdani-Asrami, M., Gholamian, S.A., Mirimani, S.M., Adabi, J.: Calculation of AC magnetizing loss of ReBCO superconducting tapes subjected to applied distorted magnetic fields. J. Supercond. Novel Magn. 31(12), 3875–3888 (2018). https://doi.org/10.1007/s10948-018-4695-7
29. Wang, L., Zheng, J., Jiang, F., Kang, R.: Numerical simulation of AC loss in 2G high-temperature superconducting coils with 2D-axisymmetric finite element model by magnetic field formulation module. J. Supercond. Novel Magn. 29(8), 2011–2018 (2016). https://doi.org/10.1007/s10948-016-3523-1
30. Kulkarni, R., Prasad, K., Lie, T.T., Badcock, R.A., Bumby, C.W., Sung, H.J.: Design improvisation for reduced harmonic distortion in a flux pump-integrated HTS generator. Energies 10(9), 1344 (2017)
31. Chen, Q., Liu, G., Liu, Z., Li, X.: Design and analysis of a new fully stator-HTS motor. IEEE Trans. Appl. Supercond. 24, 1–5 (2014)
32. Liu, B., Badcock, R., Shu, H., Tan, L., Fang, J.: Electromagnetic characteristic analysis and optimization design of a novel HTS coreless induction motor for high-speed operation. IEEE Trans. Appl. Supercond. 28, 1–5 (2018)
33. Arish, N., Ardestani, M., Hekmati, A.: Optimum structure of rotor slot for a 20 kW HTS induction motor. Physica C: Supercond. Appl. 582, 1353829 (2021)

Smart Devices

Rib Waveguide Plasmonic Sensor
for Lab-on-Chip Technology

Daniel Almeida[1,2,3]($\boxtimes$), João Costa[2,3], Alessandro Fantoni[2,3], and Manuela Vieira[1,2,3]

[1] School of Science and Technology, NOVA University of Lisbon, Caparica, Portugal
dg.almeida@campus.fct.unl.pt
[2] UNINOVA-CTS, Caparica, Portugal
{jcosta,afantoni}@deetc.isel.ipl.pt
[3] ISEL - Instituto Superior de Engenharia de Lisboa, Instituto Politécnico de Lisboa, Lisbon, Portugal
mv@isel.ipl.pt

Abstract. A prompt medical diagnosis is of major importance, starting the appropriate treatment earlier results in better outcomes and faster recovery times. Plasmonic biosensors based on photonic integrated circuits (PIC) are potential candidates in the development of lab-on-chip (LOC) technology, allowing digitalization of results and virtualization of laboratorial procedures in the detection of important biomarkers. These sensors have the advantages of high sensitivity and faster analysis when compared with traditional laboratorial methodologies. We study the possibility of exciting a surface plasmon, using low-cost fabrication methods and techniques based on amorphous silicon compounds, rib waveguide geometry and dimensions compatible with plasma-enhanced chemical vapor deposition (PECVD) and ultraviolet (UV) lithography. Results of Finite-Difference Time-Domain (FDTD) simulation of the plasmon excitation and sensor response are presented and discussed.

Keywords: Plasmonics · Lab-on-Chip · Amorphous silicon · Photonic integrated circuit

1 Introduction

Clinical assays are fundamental diagnostic tools employed to detect disease markers on samples of human tissue and fluids. Conventional techniques require expensive laboratory equipment and trained personnel, making the process complex, expensive and time-consuming. Lab-on-chip (LOC) technology, based on compact optical devices, such as photonic integrated circuit (PIC) biosensors, can be designed to detect several biomarkers (e.g. proteins, nucleic acids, drugs, pathogens and human cells) [1], paving the way to the development of Point-of-Care (PoC) diagnostic platforms. Studies demonstrate that these highly integrated sensors can be employed in the diagnosis of several diseases and health conditions, such as viruses [2], cancers [3] and acute kidney injury

L. M. Camarinha-Matos (Ed.): DoCEIS 2022, IFIP AICT 649, pp. 187–196, 2022.
https://doi.org/10.1007/978-3-031-07520-9_17

[4]. Early biomarker detection contributes to improving patient prognosis. State-of-the-Art photonic biosensors are able to detect analytes in a few minutes [5] and can achieve very high sensitivities [1], with detection limits between 10^{-4} and 10^{-6} RIU (refractive index units) or even less [1, 6–8].

The success of PoC testing platforms is dependent on the development of technologies which are easily adapted to the detection of various analytes with high sensitivity and suitable for low-cost large scale deployment. Surface Plasmon Resonance sensors based on the Kretschmann configuration [9] are an example of a technology which excels on sensitivity and adaptability to different analytes. On the negative side, the equipment is too expensive and bulky for mass deployment in PoC applications. There is much interest in solutions that avoid large or expensive components, such as motor rotation stages and prisms, and which are based on low-cost materials and fabrication processes. In recent studies a large diversity of photonic sensor architectures comprising waveguides have been reported, the vast majority of sensors lay inside one of the following categories: 1) Plasmonic sensors based solely on waveguides [10–12]; 2) Interferometric sensors, Fig. 1, exploring surface plasmon resonance [13–15], the evanescent wave effect [16] or the interference between two modes (bimodal waveguides) [17]; 3) Sensors employing one or more ring resonators [18, 19], Figs. 1; 4) Sensors featuring cavities [20, 21].

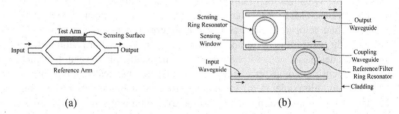

(a)   (b)

Fig. 1. Top view of two photonic sensor configurations (simplified). (a) Mach-Zehnder Interferometer (MZI) implementation based on waveguides, comprising Y-junction splitter and combiner. (b) An example of ring resonator topology, the Vernier-cascade sensor [22], this configuration comprises three waveguides and two ring resonators, the filter ring resonator and input waveguide are totally covered by the cladding.

The trend has been to reduce the form factor of the photonic circuits, to achieve higher integration, leveraged by sub-micrometer lithographic processes [19, 21, 23–25], however, there is a major drawback in size reduction, which are the increased manufacturing costs. A possible alternative are larger photonic devices, which can be produced at lower costs [26]. Despite current trends, multi-micron sensor devices have been proposed in the last decade [16, 17], these designs are based on rib waveguides. Considering the State-of-the-Art in biosensing, the following research question is proposed:

- What could be a suitable method to develop a low-cost, highly sensitive, compact and efficient sensor system that can be suitable to the detection of various biomarkers in point-of-care medical applications?

Sub-micron waveguides have the advantage of higher integration, however, when compared with multi-micron waveguides, the former have the disadvantages of higher losses and higher sensitivity to fabrication imperfections [26]. Multi-micron waveguides can be fabricated using low-cost processes with lower spatial resolutions, such as Plasma-Enhanced Chemical Vapor Deposition (PECVD) combined with ultraviolet (UV) lithography. Multi-micron rib waveguides have some advantages when compared with other waveguide types (e.g. strip waveguides), in terms of light coupling efficiency, losses and production costs, making them suitable for biosensing applications [16]. Large cross-section rib waveguides can be designed to support single-mode (SM) operation [27–29], resulting in reduced light coupling loss when interfaced with optical fibers [30] and lower losses due to side-wall roughness [31].

Hydrogenated amorphous silicon (a-Si:H) and its compounds, hydrogenated amorphous silicon carbide (a-SiC:H) and hydrogenated amorphous silicon nitride (a-SiN:H), can be deposited by PECVD at lower temperatures (typically, between 200 °C–400 °C) [32], reducing fabrication costs. By controlling the compound percentages, it is possible to fine tune the material structure and optical properties, like for example the refractive index [33], allowing the integration of several components, such as power splitters, interferometers, waveguides and photodetectors.

In this research, finite-difference time-domain (FDTD) and Finite Element Method (FEM) simulations are performed to study a SM rib waveguide surface plasmon resonance sensor. The photonic circuit is of low complexity and can be fabricated with inexpensive materials, such as silicon dioxide (SiO_2) and nitrogen-rich a-SiN:H, the sensitive layer is made of a thin silver layer (Ag), with 40 nm thickness. The device can be fabricated using low-cost methods such as PECVD and UV lithography, also benefiting from better light coupling efficiency, due to its larger cross-section. The operating wavelength is 405 nm, the same used in high-definition optical discs, in the limit of the visible spectrum.

2   Contribution to Technological Innovation for Digitalization and Virtualization

Industry 4.0 is a concept devised to the industrial domain, comprising individualization and virtualization [34], implemented by new technologies for automation and data exchange. This concept applied to the health domain is called Health 4.0 [35]. The six principles of Industry 4.0 [34] are: 1) Interoperability; 2) Virtualization; 3) Decentralization; 4) Real-Time Capability; 5) Service Orientation; 6) Modularity. Biosensors and LOC technology contribute to all seven principles of Health 4.0:

Interoperability can be achieved by aggregation and integration of the different devices and services, being a major step towards the generation of meaningful information [35]. Data fusion combines information collected from different sensors to more accurately assess the patient's health conditions [36], helping medical staff in the establishment of a personalized treatment.

With point-of-care analytical platforms, the clinical assay procedure can be partially virtualized, because the laboratory is "contained within a single device" and result interpretation can be made by computational algorithms, contributing to a significant reduction of the workload and the physical size of the lab.

Decentralization is accomplished due to the portability of the LOC platform, enabling clinical assays to be conducted *in-loco*, by a single doctor, nurse or analyst, the service is personalized, meaning healthcare can shift from centralized to a customized patient-oriented service.

Biosensors are extremely fast and typically can provide results within minutes [5], significantly contributing for real-time diagnosis. Due to the increased access to clinical assays, appropriate disease follow-up and prevention measures can be taken, so the probability of serious episodes and hospital admission lowers significantly.

The sensors' output is converted into the digital domain, allowing interfacing with latest generation networks (i.e. 5G) and cloud technologies, which are enablers for service orientation in the health domain [35]. The concept of modularity is also applicable to PoC equipment for medical assays, considering that the equipment features one or more receptacles were biosensor "cartridges" can be inserted or removed. Following this approach, LOCs can adapt to detect different analytes, the sensor "cartridges" can also be periodically upgraded or replaced if malfunctioning.

Another principle was added later: Safety, security and resilience [35]. In order to minimize the risks for the patients, it is important to assure the reliability and resilience of the system, by improving the biosensor's sensitivity and selectivity.

Conventional medical diagnostics rely primarily on the symptomatology, being prone to fail due to inadequate reporting or lack of symptoms on initial stages of disease [36]. Machine learning (ML), artificial intelligence (AI) and the internet of things (IoT) have the potential to be applied with biosensors, allowing real-time monitoring [37].

3 Theoretical Background and Sensor Configuration

The sensor developed in this study is based on a SM silicon-on-insulator (SOI) rib waveguide, having an a-SiN:H core deposited over a SiO_2 substrate, Fig. 2. The plasmonic section is covered by a thin silver (Ag) layer. It differs from the work of Fantoni *et al.* [12], because it is focused on a multi-micron design, made possible by a rib geometry, different waveguide materials and operating wavelength.

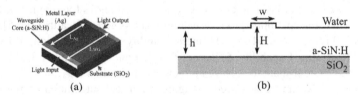

Fig. 2. Sensor design based on the rib waveguide. (a) Tridimensional model, L_{WG} and L_{Ag} represent waveguide and silver layer lengths, respectively. (b) Transversal section, w represents rib width, H rib height and h slab height.

3.1 Single-Mode Rib Waveguide Dimensioning

It is desirable to design waveguides for SM propagation in order to maximize power efficiency. Rib waveguide SM operation was the focus of several studies [27–29]. Rib waveguide geometry is characterized by three main parameters, rib width (w), rib height (H) and slab height (h), Fig. 2. To guarantee the design is compatible with low-cost lithographic and deposition processes (UV and PECVD), the width of the rib (w) should be equal to or greater than 1 μm, so it was set at 1.5 μm, to allow a small margin. Etch depth (D) was defined as 0.1 μm, the maximum r value was set at 0.9. Expression (1) establishes the relationship between rib waveguide design parameters and SM operation [28, 29], the expression is valid for $0.5 \leq r < 1$. By replacing h in $r = h/H$ by $H - D$, the rib height (H) can be obtained from (1):

$$w/H \leq \alpha + r \cdot \left(1 - r^2\right)^{-1/2}. \tag{1}$$

Parameter α is 0 when considering the Effective Index Method (EIM), Pogossian *et al.* [28] or 0.3 according to Soref *et al.* [27]. Following the more conservative approach of null α, the resulting rib height value is 0.82 μm, implying a slab height value of 0.72 μm, which were the dimensions used in this study.

3.2 Surface Plasmon Polariton (SPP) Excitation

Surface Plasmon Polaritons can only be excited by TM guided modes. In order to excite the SPP the effective refractive index difference between the plasmonic mode and the waveguide fundamental TM mode must be small. SPP complex refractive index as a function of angular frequency is given by (2):

$$n_{\text{eff SPP}}(\omega) = \sqrt{\frac{\varepsilon_d(\omega)\varepsilon_m(\omega)}{\varepsilon_d(\omega) + \varepsilon_m(\omega)}}, \tag{2}$$

where ω is the angular frequency in rad/s, $\varepsilon_d(\omega)$, $\varepsilon_m(\omega)$ correspond to the complex permittivity function of the sample medium and metal, respectively.

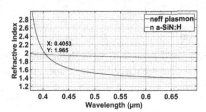

Fig. 3. Effective refractive index of the SPP (real component), represented in blue, refractive index of a-SiN:H with Si/N < 1 (real component), represented in red. The intersection point shows an ideal SPP excitation wavelength of 405 nm and a refractive index of 1.965.

From (2) and considering that the effective refractive index of the waveguide's fundamental mode is similar to the index of the core material, the intersection point is found in Fig. 3. The resulting wavelength of 405.3 nm is ideal to excite the SPP from the fundamental TM mode of the waveguide. Results assume the sample medium is water, the metal layer is silver (refractive index from Jiang *et al.* [38]) and the waveguide material is a-SiN:H with Si/N ratio under 1 (refractive index from Charifi *et al.* [39]). The intersection point occurs for a refractive index of 1.965.

4   Results

4.1 Modal Analysis

In Fig. 4, the major electric and magnetic XY field distributions are depicted, on the top of the rib a small field intensity is present, this effect makes plasmon excitation possible. The mode's effective refractive index is 1.949, the extinction coefficient is 2.8×10^{-12}, because the material is considered non-dispersive.

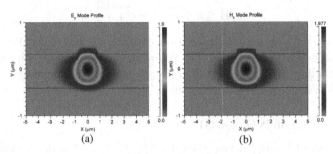

Fig. 4. Fundamental TM mode of the rib waveguide obtained in FEM simulation. (a) E_y and (b) H_x fields. Layers are delimited by black lines (from top to bottom, water, a-SiN:H and SiO_2).

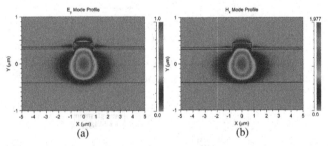

Fig. 5. FEM simulation results of the coupling between the fundamental TM mode and the SPP. (a) E_y and (b) H_x fields. Layers are delimited by black lines (from top to bottom, water, silver, a-SiN:H and SiO_2).

In Fig. 5, it is possible to notice the coupling between the fundamental TM mode of the rib waveguide and the surface plasmon mode, in this region of the sensor a thin silver layer with 40 nm thickness is deposited over the waveguide's core. The plasmonic field is visible over the center of the silver layer placed on top of the waveguide's rib. The effective refractive index of the mode is approximately 1.948. The deviation from the predicted refractive index of 1.965 (Fig. 3) is under 0.9%.

In Fig. 6, the vertical cuts of the major electric and magnetic fields are represented, the higher peaks represent the waveguide fundamental TM mode, which is confined within the waveguide's core. Minor peaks are also visible, which correspond to the SPP propagating over the silver layer.

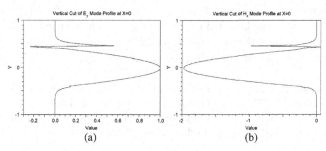

(a)   (b)

Fig. 6. Vertical cut of: (a) E_y and (b) H_x fields, the characteristic plasmon field profile is present on the top, showing coupling between the waveguide TM mode and SPP mode.

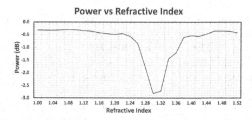

Fig. 7. Transmitted power as a function of the sample medium refractive index.

4.2 Sensor's Response

The sensor's response was simulated for a waveguide length (L_{WG}) of 12 μm and a silver layer length (L_{Ag}) of 10 μm, Fig. 2. FDTD simulations were performed for sample medium refractive index values between 1 and 1.52. The fundamental TM mode is coupled to the input of the waveguide and power is measured at the output.

In Fig. 7, for refractive index values between 1.29 and 1.31, a large dip is observable in the sensor's response, output power is under -2.7 dB, confirming the sensing behavior. The attenuation from the baseline is 2.2 dB.

5 Conclusions and Future Work

A plasmonic sensor based on a rib waveguide was designed and simulated. The waveguide geometry and multi-micron size allows light coupling from optical fibers, requiring only a plane-convex lens termination to converge the light beam. Due to the large size of the sensor, simple design and constituting materials (a-SiN:H), low-cost fabrication techniques can be employed, such as PECVD and UV lithography.

The sensitivity window covers the refractive index of human body fluids making it interesting to biosensing platforms. The dip in the power of the transfer function is still modest leaving room for improvement. Since the sensor operates with visible light (405 nm), testing is facilitated. This wavelength is also used in high-definition optical disks. Further studies are necessary to establish the optimal metal and waveguide lengths. Equally important is the impact of the silicon-to-nitrogen ratio of a-SiN:H. Discovering the ideal proportion is fundamental to achieve the best plasmon excitation scenario. It is also necessary to improve the a-SiN:H model with k values based on experiments conducted at visible light wavelengths (400 nm to 700 nm).

Acknowledgments. Research supported by FCT - Fundação para a Ciência e Tecnologia, through grant SFRH/BD/07792/2021 and projects PTDC/NAN-OPT/31311/2017, FCT/MCTES: UIDB/00066/2020, and by Instituto Politécnico de Lisboa, through project IPL/2021/wavesensor_ISEL and project IPL/2021/MuMiAS-2D_ISEL.

References

1. Kazanskiy, N.L., Khonina, S.N., Butt, M.A., Kaźmierczak, A., Piramidowicz, R.: State-of-the-art optical devices for biomedical sensing applications—a review. Electron. **10**, 1–29 (2021). https://doi.org/10.3390/electronics10080973
2. Shrivastav, A.M., Cvelbar, U., Abdulhalim, I.: A comprehensive review on plasmonic-based biosensors used in viral diagnostics. Commun. Biol. **4**, 1–12 (2021). https://doi.org/10.1038/s42003-020-01615-8
3. Soler, M., Estevez, M.C., Villar-Vazquez, R., Casal, J.I., Lechuga, L.M.: Label-free nanoplasmonic sensing of tumor-associate autoantibodies for early diagnosis of colorectal cancer. Anal. Chim. Acta. **930**, 31–38 (2016). https://doi.org/10.1016/j.aca.2016.04.059
4. Albeltagy, E.S., Abdul-Mohymen, A.M., Taha, D.R.A.: Early diagnosis of acute kidney injury by urinary YKL-40 in critically ill patients in ICU: a pilot study. Int. Urol. Nephrol. **52**(2), 351–361 (2020). https://doi.org/10.1007/s11255-019-02364-2
5. Soler, M., Huertas, C.S., Lechuga, L.M.: Label-free plasmonic biosensors for point-of-care diagnostics: a review. Expert Rev. Mol. Diagn. **19**, 71–81 (2019). https://doi.org/10.1080/14737159.2019.1554435
6. Soler, M., Lechuga, L.M.: Principles, technologies, and applications of plasmonic biosensors. J. Appl. Phys. **129**, 111102 (2021). https://doi.org/10.1063/5.0042811
7. Diao, B., et al.: Diagnosis of acute respiratory syndrome coronavirus 2 infection by detection of nucleocapsid protein. medRxiv. (2020). https://doi.org/10.1101/2020.03.07.20032524
8. Gauglitz, G.: Critical assessment of relevant methods in the field of biosensors with direct optical detection based on fibers and waveguides using plasmonic, resonance, and interference effects. Anal. Bioanal. Chem. **412**(14), 3317–3349 (2020). https://doi.org/10.1007/s00216-020-02581-0
9. Kretschmann, E., Raether, H.: Radiative decay of nonradiative surface plasmons excited by light. Z Naturforsch A. **23**, 2135–2136 (1968)
10. Yuan, D., Dong, Y., Liu, Y., Li, T.: Design of a high-performance micro integrated surface plasmon resonance sensor based on silicon-on-insulator rib waveguide array. Sensors (Switzerland). **15**, 17313–17328 (2015). https://doi.org/10.3390/s150717313
11. Jabbarzadeh, F., Habibzadeh-Sharif, A.: High performance dielectric loaded graphene plasmonic waveguide for refractive index sensing. Opt. Commun. **479**,(2021)

12. Fantoni, A., Costa, J., Fernandes, M., Vygranenko, Y., Vieira, M.: Theory and FDTD simulations of an amorphous silicon planar waveguide structure suitable to be used as a surface plasmon resonance biosensor. Opt. Pura Apl. **53**, 1–8 (2020). https://doi.org/10.7149/OPA. 53.2.51032

13. Lee, D.E., Lee, Y.J., Shin, E., Kwon, S.H.: Mach-Zehnder interferometer refractive index sensor based on a plasmonic channel waveguide. Sensors (Switzerland) **17**, 12–16 (2017). https://doi.org/10.3390/s17112584

14. Lotfi, F., Sang-Nourpour, N., Kheradmand, R.: High-sensitive plasmonic sensor based on Mach-Zehnder interferometer. Opt. Laser Technol. **137**, 106809 (2021). https://doi.org/10. 1016/j.optlastec.2020.106809

15. Gupta, R., Labella, E., Goddard, N.J.: An optofluidic Young interferometer sensor for real-time imaging of refractive index in μTAS applications. Sens. Actuat. B Chem. **321**, 128491 (2020). https://doi.org/10.1016/j.snb.2020.128491

16. Yuan, D., Dong, Y., Liu, Y., Li, T.: Mach-Zehnder interferometer biochemical sensor based on silicon-on-insulator rib waveguide with large cross section. Sensors (Switzerland) **15**, 21500–21517 (2015). https://doi.org/10.3390/s150921500

17. Jung, H.S.: A study on the design of integrated-optic biosensor based on the power coupling of two modes utilizing Si3N4 rib-optical waveguides. In: 2020 International Conference on Numerical Simulation of Optoelectronic Devices (NUSOD), pp. 91–92 (2020). https://doi. org/10.1109/NUSOD49422.2020.9217690

18. Butt, M.A., Khonina, S.N., Kazanskiy, N.L.: Plasmonic refractive index sensor based on metal–insulator-metal waveguides with high sensitivity. J. Mod. Opt. **66**, 1038–1043 (2019). https://doi.org/10.1080/09500340.2019.1601272

19. Chou Chao, C.T., Chou Chau, Y.F., Chiang, H.P.: Highly sensitive metal-insulator-metal plasmonic refractive index sensor with a centrally coupled nanoring containing defects. J. Phys. D. Appl. Phys. **54**, 115301 (2021). https://doi.org/10.1088/1361-6463/abce7f

20. Rakhshani, M.R., Mansouri-Birjandi, M.A.: High-sensitivity plasmonic sensor based on metal-insulator-metal waveguide and hexagonal-ring cavity. IEEE Sens. J. **16**, 3041–3046 (2016). https://doi.org/10.1109/JSEN.2016.2522560

21. Luo, S., Li, B., Xiong, D., Zuo, D., Wang, X.: A high performance plasmonic sensor based on metal-insulator-metal waveguide coupled with a double-cavity structure. Plasmonics **12**(2), 223–227 (2016). https://doi.org/10.1007/s11468-016-0253-y

22. Martens, D., Bienstman, P.: Comparison between Vernier-cascade and MZI as transducer for biosensing with on-chip spectral filter. Nanophotonics. **6**, 703–712 (2017). https://doi.org/10. 1515/nanoph-2016-0181

23. Rahmatiyar, M., Danaie, M., Afsahi, M.: Employment of cascaded coupled resonators for resolution enhancement in plasmonic refractive index sensors. Opt. Quant. Electron. **52**(3), 1–19 (2020). https://doi.org/10.1007/s11082-020-02266-z

24. Butt, M.A., Kazanskiy, N.L., Khonina, S.N.: Highly integrated plasmonic sensor design for the simultaneous detection of multiple analytes. Curr. Appl. Phys. **20**, 1274–1280 (2020). https://doi.org/10.1016/j.cap.2020.08.020

25. Danaie, M., Shahzadi, A.: Design of a high-resolution metal–insulator–metal plasmonic refractive index sensor based on a ring-shaped SI resonator. Plasmonics **14**(6), 1453–1465 (2019). https://doi.org/10.1007/s11468-019-00926-9

26. Zilkie, A.J., et al.: Multi-micron silicon photonics platform for highly manufacturable and versatile photonic integrated circuits. IEEE J. Sel. Top. Quant. Electron. **25**, 1-3 (2019). https:// doi.org/10.1109/JSTQE.2019.2911432

27. Soref, R.A., Schmidtchen, J., Petermann, K.: Large single-mode rib waveguides in GeSi-Si and Si-on-SiO2. IEEE J. Quantum Electron. **27**, 1971–1974 (1991). https://doi.org/10.1109/ 3.83406

28. Pogossian, S.P., Vescan, L., Vonsovici, A.: The single-mode condition for semiconductor rib waveguides with large cross section. J. Light. Technol. **16**, 1851–1853 (1998). https://doi.org/10.1109/50.721072

29. Ziyang, M., Li, L., Hongtao, L., Xiaowu, N.: Theoretical study of weakly-guided large-mode-area rib waveguides: single-mode condition, birefringence, and supermode generation. Opt. Quant. Electron. **48**(12), 1–11 (2016). https://doi.org/10.1007/s11082-016-0828-z

30. Solehmainen, K., Aalto, T., Dekker, J., Kapulainen, M., Harjanne, M., Heimala, P.: Development of multi-step processing in silicon-on-insulator for optical waveguide applications. J. Opt. A Pure Appl. Opt. **8**, S455 (2006). https://doi.org/10.1088/1464-4258/8/7/S22

31. Cassan, E., Laval, S., Lardenois, S., Koster, A.: On-chip optical interconnects with compact and low-loss light distribution in silicon-on-insulator rib waveguides. IEEE J. Sel. Top. Quant. Electron. **9**, 460–464 (2003). https://doi.org/10.1109/JSTQE.2003.814185

32. Costa, J., Almeida, D., Fantoni, A., Lourenço, P.: Performance of an a-Si:H MMI multichannel beam splitter analyzed by computer simulation. Silicon Photonics XVI, SPIE. **11691**, 1169106 (2021). https://doi.org/10.1117/12.2583028

33. Vieira, M.A., Vieira, M., Louro, P., Silva, V., Costa, J., Fantoni, A.: SiC multilayer structures as light controlled photonic active filters. Plasmonics **8**, 63–70 (2013). https://doi.org/10.1007/s11468-012-9422-9

34. Chute, C., French, T.: Introducing care 4.0: an integrated care paradigm built on industry 4.0 capabilities. Int. J. Environ. Res. Public Health. **16**, 2247 (2019). https://doi.org/10.3390/ijerph16122247

35. Thuemmler, C., Bai, C.: Health 4.0: How Virtualization and Big Data are Revolutionizing Healthcare. Springer, Cham (2017). https://doi.org/10.1007/978-3-319-47617-9

36. Haick, H., Tang, N.: Artificial intelligence in medical sensors for clinical decisions. ACS Nano **15**, 3557–3567 (2021). https://doi.org/10.1021/acsnano.1c00085

37. Qazi, S., Raza, K.: Smart biosensors for an efficient point of care (PoC) health management. In: Smart Biosensors in Medical Care, pp. 65–85. Academic Press (2020)

38. Jiang, Y., Pillai, S., Green, M.A.: Realistic silver optical constants for plasmonics. Sci. Rep. **6**, 1–7 (2016). https://doi.org/10.1038/srep30605

39. Charifi, H., Slaoui, A., Stoquert, J.P., Chaib, H., Hannour, A.: Opto-structural properties of silicon nitride thin films deposited by ECR-PECVD. World J. Condens. Matter Phys. **06**, 7–16 (2016). https://doi.org/10.4236/wjcmp.2016.61002

An Energy-Efficient Wideband Input-Buffer for High-Speed CMOS ADCs

David Leonardo$^{(\boxtimes)}$ and João Goes

School of Science and Technology, NOVA University of Lisbon, Campus de Caparica,
2829-516 Caparica, Portugal
d.leonardo@campus.fct.unl.pt

Abstract. Input buffers (IBs) for driving analog-to-digital converters (ADCs) in direct down-conversion radio frontends are normally operated with supply voltages higher than the nominal, mainly due to bandwidth (BW) and dynamic linearity constraints. Therefore, several voltage-regulators are required as well as the need of having I/O devices capable of handling such voltages. An energy-efficient input buffer architecture is presented in this paper and fairly compared to other existing IB realizations using a standard 1.2-V 130-nm CMOS technology as reference. The proposed new architecture presents better dynamic performance, and it can be readily used to drive moderate-resolution ADCs without requiring either a higher supply voltage or any non-standard I/O devices.

Keywords: ADC · Input buffer · CMOS · High linearity · High bandwidth · Direct conversion · Harmonic distortion · Intermodulation distortion

1 Introduction

Moderate resolution ADCs (10-to-12 bits) with sampling-rates of several GHz (1-to-8 GHz) and dissipating low power are in high demand for the next generation of communication systems. In fact, the input bandwidths (BW) requirements of the ADCs have continuously increased allowing down-convert signals directly from radiofrequency (RF) multi-GHz bands. This is a common practice to either reduce or eliminate the need for analog mixers and complex filters. For 5 G receivers, for instance, ADCs with resolutions of 10-bit and sampling speeds in the range of 1–2 GHz are often employed [1].

With faster ADCs, these operations can move forward, into the digital domain, and carried out in software. Therefore, in modern radio-receiver systems, the ADC is closer to the antenna. As a result, the required input signal BW of the sample-and-hold (S/H) circuit in the frontend of the ADC cannot be directly and efficiently driven by the low-noise amplifier (LNA) without rising significantly the power dissipation of the whole receiving chain. Therefore, as it is shown in Fig. 1, a high-performance voltage input-buffer (IB) should be added between the wideband LNA and the ADC to properly interface these two main building-blocks. Due to the fast sampling-rate (Fs) of the ADC

© IFIP International Federation for Information Processing 2022
Published by Springer Nature Switzerland AG 2022
L. M. Camarinha-Matos (Ed.): DoCEIS 2022, IFIP AICT 649, pp. 197–205, 2022.
https://doi.org/10.1007/978-3-031-07520-9_18

a relatively short time (a few hundreds of picoseconds) is available for input signal tracking. During this window, the ADC driver must fully charge the large sampling capacitor with low noise and distortion.

In order to not degrade the overall dynamic performance of the entire receiving chain, the IB must reach excellent dynamic performance in terms of BW, linearity, and energy-efficiency. Consequently, the design of these (IBs) guarantee that the dynamic specifications of the ADC are not significantly degraded. Due to this reason, most of the existing solutions for these IBs require supply voltages higher than the nominal (core supply) values of the technology and, consequently, additional voltage regulators.

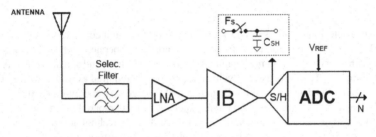

Fig. 1. Direct-conversion receiver system.

In this paper, a novel wideband IB architecture is proposed. When compared with other existing solutions and using the same comparison conditions, our architecture presents an extended BW, better dynamic performance and higher energy-efficiency, and it can be readily used to drive moderate-resolution ADCs without requiring either a higher supply voltage or any non-standard I/O devices.

2   State of the Art of Input Buffer Architectures

2.1   The Source-Follower (SF) and Cascade SF

Due to its simplicity, the source-follower (SF), shown in Fig. 2(a), is the first design option for voltage buffers. The output voltage extracted on the source of a common-drain (CD) device (M1) is almost a perfect copy of its gate voltage if body-effect is eliminated [2]. Therefore, and despite the simplicity, the voltage buffer is an effective solution when nominal power-supply is not a major concern.

This design has, however, a few limitations that have been analyzed and optimized, over the years, in the literature. Limitations in the non-zero output resistance have been studied in [2–4]. Linearity issues with this design were studied in [5], as well as studies to overcome the level-shifting and offset at the output [3].

Figure 2(b) shows the cascade source-follower (CSF) as early presented in [8]. This approach is used to keep the input common-mode voltage (V_{CMI}) close to the output common-mode voltage (V_{CMO}). In the design if $V_{GS2} \approx V_{SG1}$ then the $V_{CMO} \approx V_{CMI}$. However, small changes in the process, voltage and temperature (PVT) of the operating design may incur in changes of V_{GS} [8].

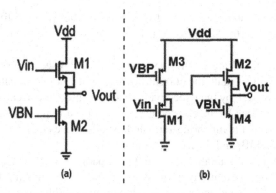

Fig. 2. (a) Source-follower, SF; (b) Cascade source-follower, CSF.

2.2 Super Source-Follower (SSF)

Since most of the deep-submicron technologies operate with low positive power supply voltages (≤ 1.2 V) the simple SF and CSF voltage buffers may have a larger output resistance than the one needed to drive large capacitive loads [3, 4]. Hence, in some cases, a super source-follower (SSF), as shown in Fig. 3, is used as an improved version of the traditional SF. In fact, this architecture can lower the output resistance of this buffer significantly, through the negative feedback implemented through common-source (CS) transistor M2 [3, 4]. However, due to the feedback in voltage-mode, it usually presents some bandwidth resonance in frequencies close to the cutoff frequency.

Nevertheless, this SSF buffer represents a significant improvement of the traditional SF, especially for heavy and switched capacitive loads, since it has a lower output resistance and the feedback loop on M2 corrects some of the non-linearity of the V_{GS} signal dependency of CD device M1.

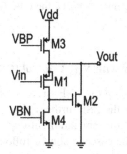

Fig. 3. Super source-follower (SSF).

2.3 Current-Feedback Input Buffer (CFIB)

The current-feedback input buffer (CFIB), as shown in Fig. 4, differs from the SSF since its feedback is in current-mode rather than in voltage-mode. Similar to the SSF, this current-mode negative feedback also maximizes the dynamic linearity of the SF and CSF architectures [6]. Moreover, it is better suited for operation with lower supply voltages.

The voltage at the drain of the main device M1 is used to regulate the V_{GS} of device M2. This will regulate the current flowing on the common-gate device M2 that is mirrored and fed-back by the wide-swing dynamic cascode-current-mirror composed by M3A and M4A. This feedback is controlled by the current mirroring factor (e.g., 1: K where K represents the mirroring-ratio and usually made equal to 2, 3 or 4) between devices M3A and M3B, and devices M4A and M4B.

To reach a larger and an almost flat BW, the parasitic capacitances in the current-mode feedback-loop (particularly at the gate terminals of mirroring devices M3A and M3B) need to be minimized and properly compensation. With proper compensation, the AC current required to charge these parasitic capacitors is kept at its minimum value [6], while the feedback is still fast enough to improve (extend) the overall signal BW.

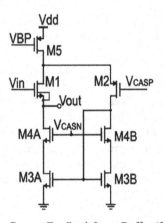

Fig. 4. Current Feedback Input Buffer (CFIB).

2.4   Cascade Source-Follower with V_{GS} Control (CSF-VC)

Figure 5 shows the basic concept of the CSF circuit with V_{GS} control (CSF-VC) [8]. A global negative-feedback loop in the CSF further reduces the output resistance and keeps $V_{GS2} \approx V_{SG1}$, reducing both the constant and input-dependent components of the offset. Transistors M1 and M2 form the cascade source-follower. The gate and source of the PMOS transistor M3 are connected to the source and gate of NMOS device M2, allowing M3 to sense the V_{GS} of M2. Transistors M1 and M3 form a differential pair with current-mirror load M4 and M5. If $V_{GS2} \neq V_{SG1}$, the gate voltage of M9 is adjusted to change the current through M2 until V_{GS2} is approximately equal to V_{SG1}. A major aspect of this circuit is that it uses, simultaneously, local negative-feedback and local feedforward in the source followers to set the gain almost equal to unity and global feedback, thus reducing the gain and offset errors. Since global feedback is applied to a circuit with a small gain error, the BW of the circuit is significantly increased compared to circuits relying on global feedback only to overcome gain errors. An additional compensation capacitor Cc needs to be added between the gate and the drain of transistor M9 for proper stabilization.

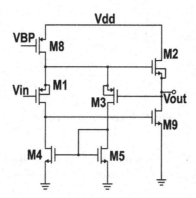

Fig. 5. Cascade Source Follower with VGS sensing (CSF-VC).

3 Proposed Input Buffer (IB) Circuit

The schematic of the proposed IB architecture is shown in Fig. 6. The main ideas behind our voltage buffer are: *i*) avoid the use of cascode structures at the output branch of the buffer circuit in order to maximize the output-swing and improve linearity; *ii*) implement all the necessary local feedback-loops, either positive or negative, in current-mode due to the reduced nominal power-supply. Common-drain (CD) devices M1 and M2 form a CSF and transistor M7 is in a common-gate (CG) configuration.

This IB uses two separated main current-mode feedback-loops. Similarly to the CFIB (removing the cascode device at the output branch), the first feedback-loop is implemented by the CG device M7 together with a wide-swing high-output impedance current-mirror comprising transistors M4 and M8-M11. When the voltage at the gate of M2 increases, the current increases. With this increase of the drain current, the voltage at the drain of M2 will decrease, decreasing the V_{GS} of M7 (V_{CASP} is a DC constant voltage biasing the CG device M7) and the current flowing through M7. The reduction in current in M7 will further decrease the gate voltage in M4. This first feedback-loop provides a local positive-feedback to guarantee additional bandwidth by quickly increase V_{out} when the input increases.

The second (negative) feedback-loop starts at the gate of M4, M9 and M14. When the voltage at this gate terminal decreases, then the current also decreases, since V_{GS} is reduced. This will increase the drain voltage of M14, decreasing the drain current of M12 and M5 (M12 and M5 form a basic current-mirror) feeding the main CD input device M1.

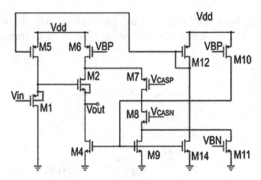

Fig. 6. Proposed Input Buffer.

Using MATLAB™ tool for Symbolic Analysis of Analog Circuits the transfer function (TF) at low-frequencies, and tolerating an error of the order of 10%, is given by:

$$\text{DC Gain} = \frac{g_{m1} \cdot (g_{m4} + g_{m9})}{g_{m1} \cdot (g_{m4} + g_{m9}) + g_{m4} \cdot (g_{ds1} + g_{ds5})} \tag{1}$$

showing that the first stage feedback loop is the most important regarding low-frequency (DC) gain.

4 Simulation Results

The proposed IB has been designed and optimized employing a fully-differential structure and in a standard 1.2-V, 130-nm CMOS process node. Only standard devices have been employed. All IBs have been simulated in DC, AC, and using transient-noise simulations, in the same load conditions and with the same input signal (600 mVpp-differential). Hence, although the described IBs have different attenuations of the input signal at lower frequencies (DC gain), the output signal is kept similar for all topologies, in order to allow fair comparisons among all IBs. Moreover, all CD devices have been biased in the same operating bias condition in all the simulated IBs (i.e., in moderate inversion with $V_{DSsat} \sim 100$ mV) and the (switched) capacitive load has been normalized to 1 pF.

The frequency (AC) simulation results of the proposed IB demonstrate that the peaking at higher frequencies, which occurs in both circuits (SSF and the CFIB), is reduced in the proposed topology by employing the second current-mode negative feedback-loop. Figure 6 shows the frequency response of each feedback-loop independently. Note that there are two resonances around the same frequency. Figure 7 shows the overall (combined) simulated frequency response of the system where it is possible to see that the peaking is not that noticeable.

Transient-noise simulations have been performed in order to calculate the fast-Fourier-transform (FFT) of the output signal. The FFT results shown in Fig. 9 have been then used to calculate all key performance parameters regarding the dynamic linearity (THD and SFDR) and the signal-to-noise ratio (SNR).

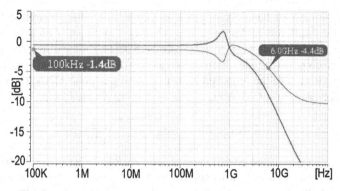

Fig. 7. Simulated frequency response of the two feedback-loops.

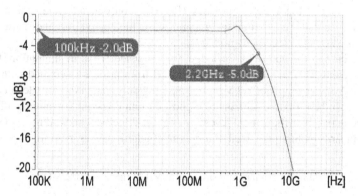

Fig. 8. Simulated frequency response of the proposed IB.

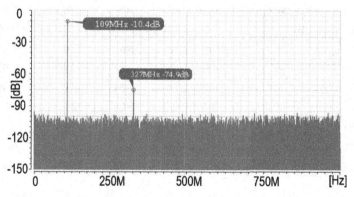

Fig. 9. Simulated FFT of the output signal (4096 bins and coherent sampling).

Similar simulations have been carried out of all the other IB architectures (also employing fully-differential designs), in order to compare them with the proposed IB. Table 1 shows the simulated key performance parameters for the different IBs.

In order to compare the energy-efficiency among the different IB solutions, and since the target application of the proposed IB is to drive high-speed ADCs, the well-known Walden figure-of-merit (FOM-W) has been used in the adapted form:

$$\text{FOM} - \text{W} = \frac{\text{Power}}{2^{\frac{\text{SNDR}-1.76}{6.02}} \cdot 2 \cdot \text{BW}} \tag{2}$$

to account for the dissipated power, the signal bandwidth (BW) and both, the noise and the dynamic linearity (the signal-to-noise-plus-distortion-ratio, SNDR, taking into consideration both, the total-harmonic-distortion, THD, and the simulated transient noise). In case of the FOM-W, the lower the number the better the efficiency of the IB.

As stated in the Introduction section, since the IB will be interfacing between the LNA and the ADC, it must reach excellent dynamic performance in terms of BW, linearity (SNDR), and energy-efficiency (Power). Consequently, the design of these (IBs) guarantee that the dynamic specifications and the key performance parameters of the ADC are not significantly degraded.

To the best of the authors knowledge, the proposed IB is, in simulation, the most energy-efficient IB (reaching 1.83 fJ) among all from prior art, supplied with a single and nominal power supply of 1.2 V and comprising only standard (core) devices. Notice that, although the proposed IB has the highest current consumption among all, since it uses more active branches, it achieves the highest effective bandwidth (2.2 GHz) and the best linearity without the need of any type of additional compensation.

Table 1. Simulation results in 1.2-V 130-nm standard CMOS.

	SF [2]	CSF [8]	CFIB [6]	CSF-VC [8]	Proposed IB
Current consumption (mA) @ 1.2 V	2.0	2.6	3.0	2.8	**5.5**
Bandwidth (GHz) @ $C_{LOAD} = 1\text{pF}$	1.5	1.7	1.0	1.2	**2.2**
Input signal frequency (MHz)	109	109	109	109	**109**
Systematic offset (dB)	−121	−105	−106	−87	**−95**
$V_{CMI} = V_{CMO}$	No	Yes	No	Yes	**Yes**
HD2 (dB)	−80	−85	−84	−74	**−97**
HD3 (dB)	−55	−61	−54	−60	**−69**
IM3 (dB)	70	66	57	72	**65**
SFDR (dB)	55	61	54	57	**69**
SNDR (dB)	50	53	49	51	**60**
FOM-W (fJ)	3.10	2.51	7.82	4.83	**1.83**

In order to compare the energy-efficiency among the different IB solutions, and since the target application of the proposed IB is to drive high-speed ADCs, the well-known

Walden figure-of-merit (FOM-W) has been used in the adapted form:

$$\text{FOM} - \text{W} = \frac{\text{Power}}{2^{\frac{\text{SNDR}-1.76}{6.02}} \cdot 2 \cdot \text{BW}} \tag{2}$$

to account for the dissipated power, the signal bandwidth (BW) and both, the noise and the dynamic linearity (the signal-to-noise-plus-distortion-ratio, SNDR, taking into consideration both, the total-harmonic-distortion, THD, and the simulated transient noise). In case of the FOM-W, the lower the number the better the efficiency of the IB.

As stated in the Introduction section, since the IB will be interfacing between the LNA and the ADC, it must reach excellent dynamic performance in terms of BW, linearity (SNDR), and energy-efficiency (Power). Consequently, the design of these (IBs) guarantee that the dynamic specifications and the key performance parameters of the ADC are not significantly degraded.

To the best of the authors knowledge, the proposed IB is, in simulation, the most energy-efficient IB (reaching 1.83 fJ) among all from prior art, supplied with a single and nominal power supply of 1.2 V and comprising only standard (core) devices. Notice that, although the proposed IB has the highest current consumption among all, since it uses more active branches, it achieves the highest effective bandwidth (2.2 GHz) and the best linearity without the need of any type of additional compensation.

5 Conclusions

An energy-efficient input buffer architecture was presented in this paper and fairly compared to other existing IB realizations using a standard 1.2-V and 130-nm CMOS technology as reference. The proposed new architecture presents a better dynamic performance (fom, noise and distortion), it has a wider input signal BW and it can be readily used to drive moderate-resolution ADCs without requiring either a higher supply voltage or any non-standard I/O devices.

References

1. Dermit, D., et al.: A 1.67-GSps TI 10-Bit Ping-Pong SAR ADC With 51-dB SNDR in 16-nm FinFET. IEEE Solid-State Circ. Lett. **3**, 150–153 (2020)
2. Farag, F.A.: High performance CMOS buffer amplifier with offset cancellation. In: Saudi International Electronics, Communications and Photonics Conference, pp. 1–4 (2013)
3. Gray, P.R., Meyer, R.G., Hurst, P.J., Lewis, S.H.: Analysis and Design of Analog Integrated Circuits, 4th edn. Wiley, Hoboken (2001)
4. Kong, Y., Xu, S., Yang, H.: An ultra low output resistance and wide swing voltage follower. In: International Conference on Communications, Circuits and Systems, pp. 1007–1010 (2007)
5. Rapakko, H., Kostamovaara, J.: On the performance and use of an improved source-follower buffer. IEEE Trans. Circ. Syst. I: Regul. Pap. **54**(3), 504–517 (2007)
6. Vaz, B., et al.: A 13b 4GS/s digitally assisted dynamic 3-stage asynchronous pipelined-SAR ADC. In: IEEE International Solid-State Circuits Conference (ISSCC), pp. 276–277 (2017)
7. Fan, X., Chan, P.K.: Analysis and design of low-distortion CMOS source followers. Trans. Circ. Syst. I Regul. Pap. **52**(8), 1489–1501 (2005)
8. Xing, G., Lewis, S.H., Viswanathan, T.R.: A unity-gain buffer with reduced offset and gain error. In: IEEE Custom Integrated Circuits Conference 2006, pp. 825–828 (2006)

Novel Graphene Electrode for Electromyography Using Wearables Based on Smart Textiles

Manuel Humberto Herrera Argiró[1,2]([⊠]), Cláudia Quaresma[1], and Hugo Plácido Silva[2]

[1] NOVA School of Science and Technology and LIBPhys, Largo da Torre, 2825-149 Caparica,
Portugal
m.argiro@campus.fct.unl.pt
[2] PLUX - Wireless Biosignals, S.A., Av. 5 de Outubro, n. 70 - 2, 1050-059 Lisbon, Portugal

Abstract. Studies show that biofeedback increases patient proprioception in physical rehabilitation training, improving outcomes; surface Electromyography (sEMG) is particularly appealing as it enables accurate progress evaluation and instant feedback. Furthermore, extending the rehabilitation processes to patients' homes has been shown to increase the quality of the recovery process. This led research to move towards telerehabilitation, however, usability remains an issue in sEMG biofeedback, mainly because of the electrode materials. This work proposes a novel electrode, designed using a Shieldex Technik-Tex P130+B conductive fabric substrate, spray-coated with graphene to reduce the contact impedance with the skin. Experimental evaluation was performed in a population of 16 subjects with ages ranging from 20 to 50 years; results show up to 97% correlation and less than 3 dB (in average) degradation of the signal quality comparatively to standard pre-gelled Ag/AgCl electrodes.

Keywords: Graphene · Dry electrodes · Electromyography · Wearables

1 Introduction

In this work we propose and evaluate novel graphene-based e-textile electrodes, to be used in rehabilitation as an alternative to the gold standard. The needs for rehabilitation are increasing; as reported by the World Health Organization (WHO), at least one in every three people in the world will need rehabilitation at some point during their disease or injury. Also, musculoskeletal disorders are typically associated with pain, and limitations in mobility, dexterity, and overall level of function[1].These conditions may affect joints, bones, and/or multiple body systems [1]. Biofeedback has been shown to improve outcomes in rehabilitation, with surface Electromyography (sEMG) being a particularly appealing modality due to the possibility of objectively measuring muscle

---

[1] https://www.who.int/teams/noncommunicable-diseases/sensory-functions-disability-and-reh
abilitation/global-estimates-of-the-need-for-rehabilitation.

L. M. Camarinha-Matos (Ed.): DoCEIS 2022, IFIP AICT 649, pp. 206–213, 2022.
https://doi.org/10.1007/978-3-031-07520-9_19

functions in real time [2]. Recent work proves that complementing the rehabilitation protocols performed at the clinic, with autonomous work done by patients at home, can accelerate recovery and prevent relapse [3, 4]. The usability of sEMG data acquisition devices is a major barrier, leading to the development of wearables [4]. Emphasis has been given to smart textiles; however, limitations persist on the signal pickup electrodes, which are single-use and disposable [5].

2 Related Work

The popularity of sEMG rehabilitation has led to the creation of highly integrated wearables with dry electrodes. These can constitute one step further in the digitalization and virtualization of human physiology, in particular muscle signals. The Trigno Wireless EMG (Delsys Inc., MA, USA) is an example that uses 99.9% silver (Ag) rods as electrodes, having been extensively used in upper limb assessment (e.g., O. W. Samuel *et al.* in [6]). Still, smart textiles can offer greater convenience and higher usability to end-users [7]. In smart textiles, low electrical resistance is achieved by integrating conductive materials between the fibres of the fabric. This has led researchers to evaluate e-textiles as a way of improving usability of sEMG devices. In [5] Lycra with a surface resistance $< 1\Omega.\square^{-1}$ is tested, concluding that a satisfactory performance is achieved in sEMG acquisition comparatively with standard Ag/AgCl electrodes (although with higher baseline noise). The Mbody 3 system (Myontec Oy, Kuopio, Finland) uses silver coated yarns integrated in a garment as electrode; these have already shown promising results in upper and lower body muscle rehabilitation. The topical nature of our research is further reinforced by the recent work of Alizadeh-Meghrazi *et al.* [8], in which conductive silicone rubber yarn is applied to a textile substrate to create a washable smart garment for sEMG.

3 Proposed Approach

3.1 Graphene e-Textile

Graphene has been explored in previous work for producing e-textiles [9–11]; research suggests that electrodes could be made by spraying graphene on a textile, as a way of endowing the material with conductive properties [12]. Typically, non-conductive fabrics are used as substrate, sprayed, or submerged into a graphene solution, conferring conductive properties to the material. Instead, we use Shieldex® Technik-Tex P130+B conductive fabric as substrate (Table 1), which is then coated with graphene. This decreases the resistance of the exposed fabric, further reducing the skin contact impedance. Our multilayer e-textile electrode was produced by spray coating, using a 0.3 mm nozzle ejecting air at 3 bars. The graphene-based ink used in this process was supplied and applied by Graphenest® (Aveiro, Portugal). As per the details provided by the company, the (wet) graphene content is placed between 5–10 wt.% however, due to intellectual property rights, the exact formulation was not fully disclosed. After the coating, a layer of dielectric material is also applied to expose only a circular surface with a diameter of 10 mm of graphene that will be in contact with the skin (i.e., the electrode). This process was made through screen-printing with a silk mesh fabric of 16t-90/40 Mesh. Figure 1 depicts the electrode.

Table 1. Main electrical, mechanical, and dimensional properties of the standard Pre-Gelled Ag/AgCl electrodes used in regular clinical practice and of the material used in our work.

Property	Pre-gelled Ag/AgCl	Shieldex® Technik-tex P130+B
Raw material	Conductive self-adhesive hydrogel + Coated polymer	Polyamide (78%) + Elastomer (22%)
Metal plated	Ag/AgCl coated polymer	99.9% pure silver
Metal content		26.5 ± 2% silver
Electrical resistivity	220 Ω	<2 Ω.□$^{-1}$
Stretch	None/Polypropylene (PP) transparent substrate	Double stretch/Elongation warp 155–205%/weft 85–125%
Total thickness	1 mm (adapter excluded)	0.55 mm ± 15%

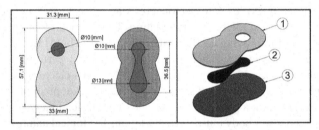

Fig. 1. Proposed electrode dimensional drawing (*left*) and layer forming (*right*). 1. Dielectric screen-printed coating; 2. Graphene sprayed coating; 3. Conductive fabric base subtract layer.

3.2   Electrode Assembly

In our envisioned target form factor, the electrode, sensor, and data acquisition system are all placed on a wearable elastic armband. The graphene-based e-textile (Sect. 3.1) has a thin and flat surface that, depending on the placement with respect to the body surface, may not always ensure a stable contact. Moreover, an interface with the sEMG sensor leads is needed. To address these two aspects, our electrode design includes other mechanical elements beyond the e-textile. With the goal of improving the skin contact, a flexible silicone spacer was designed for placement between the electrode and the elastic armband. In addition, a metallic snap (for textile use) is crimped to the e-textile, enabling to interface the electrode with any standard sEMG sensor lead. Figure 2 (*right*) illustrates the electrode assembly; as per the SENIAM recommendations for sEMG[2], two electrodes were sewn to the elastic armband in a fixed position with a 20 mm inter-electrode spacing. The direct connection between electrode and sensor lead in our design, minimizes stretching on the conductive parts of the textile during the armband placement. As seen in Fig. 2 (*centre*), the conductive substrate was partially exposed due to the manufacturing process, thus being a potential noise source. We addressed this

---

[2] http://www.seniam.org/.

issue by applying SYLGARD™ 184 Silicone Elastomer from DOW®[3], which works as encapsulant preventing unintended contact with the skin. This solution was tested by other researchers with positive results [8]. The composite was prepared using 10 parts of base compound to 1.2 parts of catalyser, mixed manually for 30 s, and degassed at 1 bar of pressure for 120 s. Curing was done for 48 h at room temperature between 20 to 25 °C, the result is shown in Fig. 2 (*right*). It is important to highlight that the electrodes show surface cracks, potentially caused by a poor adhesion between the graphene ink and the substrate (Fig. 2 - *left*). Nevertheless, the work herein presented is a proof of concept, reason for which we decided to continue with the validation of the proposed approach as a way of identifying further improvement points.

4   Experimental Evaluation

4.1   Materials

An experimental setup was devised for concurrent data acquisition with our electrode and standard disposable electrodes. For the latter we selected the Kendall® H124SG (Cardinal Health, Inc, Dublin, OH, USA), composed of an Ag/AgCl coated polymer; the main characteristics are described in Table 1. These electrodes are primarily designed to monitor ECG signals, hence applicable also to record EMG signals, as demonstrated by Song *et al.* [13]. Two biosignalsplux Electromyography (EMG) sensors were used as sEMG analogue front-end (one for the standard electrodes and another for our graphene-based electrodes). Each sensor has an amplification gain of 1000, ±1.5 mV measurement range (with VCC = 3 V), 25–500 Hz pass-band filtering, input impedance > 100GΩ, and 100 dB Common Mode Rejection Ratio (CMRR); full specifications can be found in the sensor datasheet[4]. Data acquisition was performed with 16-bit resolution and at 1 kHz sampling rate, using a biosignalsplux Hybrid 8 system (PLUX, S.A., Lisbon, Portugal) through the OpenSignals recording software.

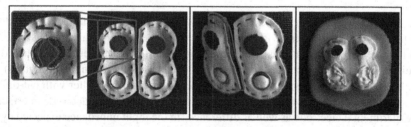

Fig. 2. Front view of the electrode (*left*) showing the electrode-skin interface zoomed and rear side of snap connector. Exposed zone (*centre*) of the conductive fabric after application on the band. Electrode after the encapsulant compound deposition (right).

---

[3] https://www.dow.com/en-us/pdp.sylgard-184-silicone-elastomer-kit.01064291z.html.

[4] https://support.pluxbiosignals.com/wp-content/uploads/2021/10/biosignalsplux-Electromy ography-EMG-Datasheet.pdf.

4.2 Protocol

Muscle activation was promoted through an experiment consisting of a single-limb dumbbell arm curl. Participants lifted their forearm against gravity until an elbow flexion of 90° was achieved, and to maintain this position for ≈5 s. This movement was repeated 5 times with dumbbells of 2, 4 & 6 kg. Similar experiments were already made by Pylatiuk et al. [14] while evaluating their wearable device. Electrodes were placed at the *biceps brachii* according to the SENIAM guidelines (see footnote 3); although in our study we used the elbow to place the reference electrode instead of the wrist. This was done because the elbow bone is closer to the anatomical location in which our setup is placed, while still providing an electrically neutral tissue [15].

In terms of experimental procedure, first we attach the reference electrode and then secure the armband. Participants maintain a standing position with the armband (with the electrodes) surrounding the *biceps brachii*; the inter-electrode distances are kept at 20 mm following again the SENIAM guidelines. sEMG data is simultaneously acquired using the Kendall® H124SG and our graphene-based electrodes, to provide a way to compare both signals in a synchronous way. Each electrode pair is therefore placed at the same distance from the muscle belly to enable a fair comparison.

4.3 Population

A total of 16 subjects (11 women) were enrolled, ages between 20 and 50 years old, with no associated pathology. Participation was done on a volunteering basis, having as inclusion criteria an age >18 years old. Exclusion criteria included having physical impairments that would be aggravated by the protocol and belonging to a population group considered to be vulnerable. To make the sample more heterogeneous, we have subjects who exercise regularly, alongside people with a more sedentary lifestyle.

5 Results

Raw data collected with the experimental setup (Sect. 4.1) and defined protocol (Sect. 4.2) was pre-processed to enable an event-based numerical analysis of EMG onset segments. Given that noise can contaminate the signal between the sensor and the acquisition system (e.g., powerline noise introduced through the connection cables), the data is digitally filtered using a 2nd order Butterworth band pass filter with cut-off frequencies between of [10; 450] Hz. As a result of both a poor skin-electrode interface of the experimental electrode as well as differences in the input impedance expected by the EMG sensor, which is factory adapted to the disposable electrode impedance to achieve a standardized signal amplitude, we were already expecting that the signal amplitude from our electrode is significant smaller than the gold standard; this effect can be visualized in Fig. 3 (*left*). However, the signal morphology is quite similar. This means that despite the slight variations in the electrode-electrolyte interface, due to differences in the materials in contact with the skin, the signals are still similar.

Onset detection and EMG activation delineation is based on the method by Bonato et al. [16]. First the filtered signal is rectified (i.e., the absolute value is determined);

afterwards, smoothing is performed through convolution with a scaled cosine shape Hanning window of 200 ms. The onset and offset detection thresholds are computed as follows: $Onset_{th} = \mu$ and $Offset_{th} = \mu - k\cdot\sigma$. Where μ represents the average value of the smoothed signal, σ is the standard deviation and k is a scale factor to ensure that the $Offset_{th}$ level is not under the baseline noise level. To bring consistency to the experiment, the scale factor is selected within a range of [0.75; 0.9], where the lowest value is applied to the more "baseline noisy" signals and the highest values to the less noisy ones. Delineation of EMG activation segments is performed through binarization of the smoothed signal; 1 is assigned to samples in which $Onset_{th} < x < Offset_{th}$ and 0 is

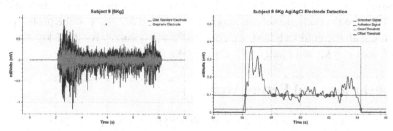

Fig. 3. Comparison of EMG signal acquisitions (*left*), where the darker signal (*background*) corresponds to the standard electrode and the lighter (*front*) corresponds to our graphene-based electrode. Binarization and detection of the activation (*right*) showing the acquisition of the gold standard electrode, for the same burst shown at Fig. 3 (*left*).

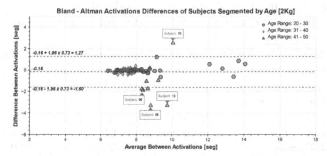

Fig. 4. Bland-Altman plot of the difference between activation times derived from sEMG acquired with both electrodes, highlighting intra-subject variability examples.

Table 2. Average Signal-to-Noise Ratio (SNR) for the standard and proposed electrodes.

Load	Mean SNR for Ag/AgCl $\mu \pm \sigma$ [dB]	Mean SNR for Graphene $\mu \pm \sigma$ [dB]	Mean scale factor $\mu \pm \sigma$	EMG activation window correlation (% $\pm \sigma$)
2 kg	23.10 ± 3.48	22.85 ± 3.61	0.95 ± 0.09	89.07 ± 0.05
4 kg	27.50 ± 2.23	24.71 ± 4.43	0.97 ± 0.05	97.13 ± 0.02
6 kg	30.28 ± 2.16	27.93 ± 4.66	0.98 ± 0.05	95.56 ± 0.03

assigned otherwise. Figure 3 (*right*) shows an example of this process. The results of the delineation step were validated through visual inspection, which, despite being a time-consuming task, allows the curation of the EMG activation segments hence providing accurate ground-truth information for comparison. After the curation, the time instants of each EMG activations are determined, and feature extraction is performed. To check if the detections are comparable, we applied a linear regression to the sample recorded for each of the loads used in the study (2, 4 & 6 kg) between the events detected by both electrodes. Using a Bland-Altman plot, to compare the difference between the activations times is shown in Fig. 4 within the 95% confidence band. We can observe that only 6 of 80 events in total, are out the confidence interval.

Through the difference between the number of activations inside the confidence interval against the outliers, we can obtain the *detection accuracy* of the prototype comparatively with the gold standard; we obtain a 92.5% accuracy for the 2 kg experiment, a 97.5% for the 4 kg and finally 95% for the 6 kg (Table 2).

6   Conclusions and Future Work

Preliminary results show that the proposed prototype has acceptable performance, nevertheless further work is needed on the manufacturing process, due to descaling of the graphene coating. It is important to highlight that an amplitude attenuation is introduced by the electrode (Fig. 3 - *left*), reason for which the front-end design to acquire the signal needs to be adjusted in future work. On the other hand, besides the similarity in morphology of the signals from both acquisitions, it is mandatory to perform a more detailed study of the frequency content. Future work will be focused on refining and tuning the coating process, seeking to mitigate the surface cracking issues detected in the electrode assembly.

These findings further pave the way for the development of wearable devices based on smart textiles for remote rehabilitation. In this context the medical accuracy is not needed, because the main goal is to give coarse feedback to the patient about the muscle activation during the exercise.

Acknowledgments. This work was partially funded by PLUX, S.A., by Fundação para a Ciência e Tecnologia (FCT) grants "NOVA I4H" (PD/BDE/150858/2021) and UIDB/50008/2020, and by Portugal 2020 grant "SMART-HEALTH-4-ALL" (POCI-01-0247-FEDER-046115 & LISBOA-01-0247-FEDER-046115).

References

1. Cieza, A., Causey, K., Kamenov, K., Hanson, S., Chatterji, S., Vos, T.: Global estimates of the need for rehabilitation based on the Global Burden of Disease study 2019: a systematic analysis for the Global Burden of Disease Study 2019. Lancet **396**, 2006–2017 (2020)
2. Basmajian, J.: Research foundations of EMG biofeedback in rehabilitation. Biofeedback Self Regul. **13**, 275–298 (1988)
3. Cottrell, M., Galea, O., O'Leary, S., Hill, A., Russell, T.: Real-time telerehabilitation for the treatment of musculoskeletal conditions is effective and comparable to standard practice: a systematic review and meta-analysis. Clin. Rehabil. **31**, 625–638 (2017)

4. Lemos, A., Oliveira, C., Telo, G., da Silva, H.P.: Bridging the clinic-home divide in muscular rehabilitation. In: Biofeedback, pp. 137–144. InTech (2018)
5. Silva, H., Scherer, R., Sousa, J., Londral, A.: Towards improving the usability of electromyographic interfaces. In: Pons, J.L., Torricelli, D., Pajaro, M. (eds.) Converging Clinical and Engineering Research on Neurorehabilitation. BB, vol. 1, pp. 437–441. Springer, Heidelberg (2013). https://doi.org/10.1007/978-3-642-34546-3_71
6. Samuel, O.W., et al.: A novel time-domain descriptor for improved prediction of upper limb movement intent in EMG-PR system. In: Proceedings of the Annual International Conference of the IEEE Engineering in Medicine and Biology Society (EMBC), pp. 3513–3516 (2018)
7. Silva, H.P.: The Biosignal C.A.O.S.: reflections on the usability of physiological sensing for human-computer interaction practitioners and researchers. In: Ibáñez, J., González-Vargas, J., Azorín, J.M., Akay, M., Pons, J.L. (eds.) Converging Clinical and Engineering Research on Neurorehabilitation II. BB, vol. 15, pp. 807–811. Springer, Cham (2017). https://doi.org/10.1007/978-3-319-46669-9_132
8. Alizadeh-Meghrazi, M., et al.: A mass-producible washable smart garment with embedded textile EMG electrodes for control of myoelectric prostheses: a pilot study. Sensors 22, 666 (2022)
9. Kowalczyk, D., et al.: Electrically conductive composite textiles modified with graphene using sol-gel method. J. Alloys Compd. 784, 22–28 (2019)
10. Liu, J., Liu, M., Bai, Y., Zhang, J., Liu, H., Zhu, W.: Recent progress in flexible wearable sensors for vital sign monitoring. Sensors 20, 4009 (2020)
11. Zheng, Y., et al.: High-performance wearable strain sensor based on graphene/cotton fabric with high durability and low detection limit. ACS Appl. Mater. Interfaces. 12, 1474–1485 (2020)
12. Samanta, A., Bordes, R.: Conductive textiles prepared by spray coating of water-based graphene dispersions. RSC Adv. 10, 2396–2403 (2020)
13. Song, M.-S., Kang, S.-G., Lee, K.-T., Kim, J.: Wireless, Skin-mountable EMG sensor for human–machine interface application. Micromachines 10, 879 (2019)
14. Pylatiuk, C., et al.: Comparison of surface EMG monitoring electrodes for long-term use in rehabilitation device control. In: Proceedings of IEEE ICORR, pp. 300–304 (2009)
15. Luca, C: Surface electromyography: detection and recording. DelSys (2002)
16. Bonato, P., D'Alessio, T., Knaflitz, M.: A statistical method for the measurement of muscle activation intervals from surface myoelectric signal during gait. IEEE Trans. Biomed. Eng. 45, 287–299 (1998)

Control and Digital Platforms

PLC as the Main Controller for Additive Manufacturing Machines

Gerson Fabio da Silva[1]([⊠]), Marcosiris Amorim de Oliveira Pessoa[1],
Paulo Eigi Miyagi[1], Ahmad Barari[2], and Marcos Sales Guerra Tsuzuki[1]

[1] Department of Mechatronics and Mechanical Systems Engineering, Escola Politécnica da Universidade de São Paulo, Av. Prof. Mello Moraes, 2231, São Paulo, SP 05508-030, Brazil
{gerson.fabio,marcosiris,pemiyagi,mtsuzuki}@usp.br
[2] Department of Mechanical and Manufacturing Engineering, Ontario Tech University, 2000 Simcoe Street North, Oshawa, ON L1G 0C5, Canada
ahmad.barari@ontariotechu.ca

Abstract. Additive manufacturing (AM) is the process of manufacturing a physical object, layer by layer, from a 3D digital model. Despite the advantages of using this technology, its adoption, especially by users with fewer resources, is still limited by the high cost of machines, raw materials, and the complexity of the process. To make this technology more accessible, increasing the cost-effectiveness of the machines, this work analyzes the feasibility of using a single programmable logic controller (PLC) as the main controller of an additive manufacturing machine, as an alternative to the CNC and PLC structure used in most of the applications of this type. Through a PLC programming structure, it was possible to load an instruction file in G code generated by a market slicer program, convert it into axis position commands, and verify that the deposition trajectory was executed.

Keywords: Additive manufacturing · Fused filament fabrication · Wire arc additive manufacturing · Direct energy deposition · PLC · Position axis control · Industry 4.0

1 Introduction

Additive manufacturing is a building process that consists of producing parts from a 3D digital model, progressively adding thin layers of raw material [1–4]. There are seven types of technologies that employ the concept of additive manufacturing [4], and among them are material extrusion (MEX), which is the process in which the material is selectively dispensed through a nozzle or orifice, and directed energy deposition (DED), where a source of thermal energy is used to fuse the material, melting it as it is deposited [5, 6]. In both processes, the layer deposition trajectory is controlled by mechatronic systems that can be machines equipped with dedicated boards or with a computerized numerical controller (CNC) that, from a sequence of commands, provides simultaneous control of machine axes, resulting in the trajectory in a three-dimensional Cartesian plane

© IFIP International Federation for Information Processing 2022
Published by Springer Nature Switzerland AG 2022
L. M. Camarinha-Matos (Ed.): DoCEIS 2022, IFIP AICT 649, pp. 217–224, 2022.
https://doi.org/10.1007/978-3-031-07520-9_20

[7]. This system approach has been widely adopted on machines utilized in conventional production processes for a long time. Another device typically used with CNC is the programmable logic controller (PLC).

PLC is a universal microprocessor-based device designed to control the operation of various machines, devices, or process lines. Its cyclic program memory circuit is a characteristic that distinguishes it from other computer-based controllers [8, 9]. With the advancement of technology, PLCs began to integrate axis positioning control functionality through sophisticated control loops, making it possible to create applications that involve more flexible motion control. Furthermore, they have a high degree of connectivity with other devices, being able to use different communication protocols, allowing their use in automation and modularized control systems capable of making data available through a local or global network, making them a fundamental device for the implementation of the concept of industry 4.0 in industries [10].

This work analyzes the feasibility of using PLC as an alternative to CNC to generate and control the trajectory of the layer deposition in an additive manufacturing machine, MEX or DED type, and, in an integrated way, to control all the intrinsic aspects of the process. This work is organized as follows: Sect. 2 relates this work with the context of technological innovation for digitalization and virtualization; Sect. 3 presents the necessary system hardware and software architecture to make the tests; Sect. 4 presents the methodology used in the tests, and the last section discusses the results and the future research directions.

2 Contribution to Technological Innovation for Digitalization and Virtualization

The entire additive manufacturing process, whether for the construction of a simple prototype or a part with highly complex geometry, necessarily starts from the part's digital model. It is not possible to think of additive manufacturing without digitalization. Another critical point is that the processes are complex. They require a high degree of knowledge as there are an infinity of parameters to be adjusted to produce the part correctly, which demands time and cost in its development. Therefore, virtualization tools, such as the digital twin that allows manufacturers to make more accurate predictions, rational decisions, and informed plans [11–13], are being increasingly used to validate production parameters, thus reducing the time and costs associated with a trial-and-error process in the physical process. The use of the PLC as a single controller of an additive manufacturing machine allows, in addition to greater flexibility and modularization of the application, the integration and virtualization of the entire manufacturing process; they are the fundamentals of Industry 4.0 [14–16]. In addition, the constant growth of competitiveness in the market has led industries to a continuous process of adaptation to remain competitive. Despite additive manufacturing being a disruptive technology that has caused a paradigm shift in production processes, its access is still restricted to large companies, partly due to the high costs of implementing this technology and partly due to the shortage of skilled labor. Using the machine approach with a single PLC as a controller reduces machine costs, allowing the generalization of the application, its development, and sharing, making it increasingly possible for smaller companies to digitize their processes and maintain a competitive position in the market.

3   System Architecture

The additive manufacturing process consists of well-defined steps and is common to all technologies used. The first step is to model the part produced using computer-aided design CAD software [17], thus generating a 3D digital file. Typically, additive manufacturing machine builders provide the manufacturing process parameterization software that slices the model and generates another file with a sequence of instructions encoded in a language known as G-code [18], specifying how the movement of the machine axes should be to perform the layer deposition trajectory. After its production, the part will be removed and can go through a post-processing process, which can be the removal of building support, a heat treatment, or a polishing. Finally, the part is inspected for verification of its geometric characteristics. Computerized Numerical Control can easily interpret the instructions from a G-code file as it is a native language for it. However, to use this file in a PLC, a whole programming structure must be developed. The structure proposed (see Fig. 1) must be able to load the file, check its consistency, interpret it, and convert the instructions into axis movement commands.

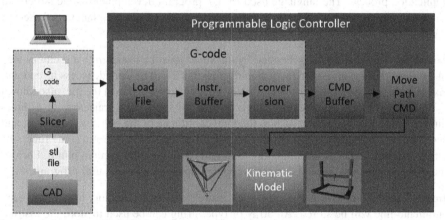

Fig. 1. System architecture proposed of a PLC as a controller for additive manufacturing machines.

Another important point is that the CNC is natively capable of converting a positioning instruction in the Cartesian plane, such as linear interpolation, into coordinated and synchronous movements of electric motors. In other words, it is enough to configure the type of kinematics that will be used, and the CNC cyclically calculates what the movement in revolutions per minute of the electric motors connected to each axis should be for the interpolation to be performed. The entire transform calculation must be carried out through the user program if the used PLC does not have this functionality integrated into its system.

3.1   Hardware

To use a PLC as a controller of an additive manufacturing machine, hardware and software architecture will be presented. For the hardware architecture, the PLC needs to have a communication interface (ethernet, OPC UA, etc.) that allows loading the file in G-code from an external device (personal computer via local or global network) to a memory area and that allows it to be accessed by the user program that is running. It can also be checked the possibility of using a physical port such as USB or SD card to transfer the file to the PLC's internal memory. Another characteristic that the PLC must have is the ability to establish a closed control loop with the drive unit, responsible for moving the axes motors, through well-defined communication protocols. For the positioning control loop to be as precise as possible, it is essential that the PLC supports an isochronous real-time (IRT) communication protocol with the drive system [19].

3.2 Software

As PLCs do not have a system architecture prepared for reading and executing G-code language instructions, all steps, from reading the file to the commands for the axes, must be developed via a user program. For the tests carried out, a modularized structure was adopted for the user program, with specific functions for each step of the application process. The language used for the program development is the structured control Language (SCL), which is a high-level textual programming language based on PASCAL and conforms to DIN EN-61131-3 (IEC 61131-3).

LoadFile. The G-code file generated by the slicer must be loaded into a memory area of the PLC. The LoadFile function should allow this file to be loaded, access its content, and sequentially fill a buffer of instructions. Each instruction line in the file, also known as instruction blocks, defines the characteristics of the point's trajectory in a three-dimensional Cartesian plane, such as the final coordinate of the trajectory, velocity, and acceleration. In addition, other commands can be configured to perform some functions on the machine, such as activating the laser and turning on the vacuum pump. Each of these commands must have its respective logic implemented in the user program.

InstructionBuffer. This part of the architecture refers to the memory area where each command line will be stored. An array of type String can be used to store the instructions. G-code files for additive manufacturing applications usually have thousands of instruction lines. Each line corresponds to a small path that makes up the layer profile and that makes up a set of many layers that will form the final part. Therefore, it becomes prohibitive to try to use a fixed size of memory to store all the instruction lines of the G-code file. A buffer must be created with a reasonable number of elements. Each instruction that has already been executed must be removed from the buffer to make room for a new.

Conversion. The biggest challenge of this application is the conversion of instructions in string format for the positioning commands intrinsic to the PLC firmware. First, we must interpret each command line in the instruction buffer and identify which PLC command the instruction refers to. Then this command must be inserted into a sequential list of commands that the PLC executes and monitors. Once command execution begins, there must be mechanisms in the system that allow monitoring this execution to determine when the following command can be executed or if there was a problem and the movement had to be stopped.

Path Commands Buffer. Refers to the memory area where motion commands interpreted by the conversion function will be stored and executed sequentially (FIFO).

Axes Movement Commands. The movement commands stored in the command buffer will be sequentially executed, and the movement state monitored in this function. The library used for axis control functions, such as axis enable, reference, absolute positioning, linear interpolation, etc., is based on PCLopen Motion Control Function blocks standardization that standardizes application libraries for a wide variety of different PLCs [20].

Kinematic Model. This structure item refers to the mathematical model that represents the kinematics of the machine. It is responsible for receiving the axes positioning and movement commands based on a three-dimensional Cartesian system and converting them into movements of the electric motors so that the specified trajectory is performed because of the coordinated and synchronized movement of the set of engines. Some PLCs come with this model integrated into their system (see Fig. 2); it is ready and is only necessary to configure the desired mechanical system. Otherwise, it must be implemented via a user program, which can considerably increase the complexity of the application.

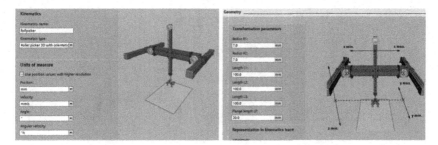

Fig. 2. Siemens PLC S7 1500T integrated Roller Picker 3D kinematic model.

4   Method

To verify the feasibility of using PLC as the central controller of an additive manufacturing machine, a Siemens S7 1500T PLC will be used together with TIA Portal V17, an engineering platform for the configuration and parameterization of devices and software development for automation systems. For the application simulation, the software S7-PLCSim Advanced 4.0 will be used, which allows the simulation of the PLC programs in a virtual controller. For the software structure, a library available for this specific PLC model and developed primarily for machine tools will be used, with some adaptation, to carry out the tests.

The first step in the process is to digitally model the part to be produced. A digital model of a piece made available as an open source was chosen. The extension of the model file is of type stl, which is an extension widely used in additive manufacturing processes and has the representation of the surface of the digital model in a mesh of small triangles [21].

As a slicer, the Ultimaker Cura software was used, which is also an open-source project. In this software, the digital model file was loaded and, with the basic parameter settings, the file with the instructions in G-code was generated [22]. The file was transferred from the PC to the nonvolatile PLC memory accessing the internal PLC web server through the Ethernet protocol.

The S7-1500T PLC series uses the concept of "technology objects" (TO) in motion control and industrial automation applications (see Fig. 3). TOs are programming units that create an interface between the various elements of the machine and the user program. They are independent objects with their own parameters. For an additive manufacturing machine based on a Cartesian system application, synchronous axis technology objects were created and configured with respect to the synchronized axes of the plane, X, Y, and Z, and connected to the kinematic model technology object.

A library available for applications that use this type of PLC with machine tools will be used for control software, which should be adapted to work as an additive manufacturing application. In addition, relevant logic must be implemented with respect to other intrinsic functions of this application.

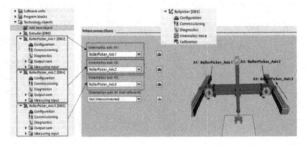

Fig. 3. Axes and kinematic model technology objects configuration.

5   Results and Conclusion

The proposed structure was commissioned and tested entirely in a virtualized way through the PLCSIM Advanced software that creates an instance of a virtual network card on the PC, allowing the TIA Portal development software to connect to the controller's virtual CPU through an IP address. The PLC's internal webserver was enabled and accessed via a web browser to load the G-code file into the PLC's virtual non-volatile memory.

The first observation is regarding the available memory size for storing the G-code file on the PLC, which must be sufficient to store large files. The file generated by the slicer needed to be manipulated. Some commands generated by the slicer software, Ultimaker Cura 3D, were removed or ignored when interpreting the code by the library functions because they were not applicable to a DED or FFF industrial additive man-ufacturing application. The positioning commands described by the G-code program were all interpreted and executed by the application, resulting in the expected trajectory of each layer. Through the trace tool integrated into the Tia Portal V17 platform and real-time position monitoring of the X, Y, and Z axes, it was possible to confirm the coordinated movement of the axes of the mechanical model faithfully representing the instructions generated by the slicer. Therefore, we conclude that the proposed software and hardware structure can be used to control the axes of an additive manufacturing machine.

As future work, a specific additive manufacturing application library will be developed in order to leverage the PLC programming flexibility, its hardware connectivity, and its integration capacity with both IIoT and cloud systems, which means a library that allows the machine to connect to a computing edge device, which can process the g code conversion algorithm saving PLC processor resources, and to connect directly to a cloud platform to share data generated from the process. A digital twin will also be implemented to interact with the application to enhance the tests, provide a better understanding of the axis's dynamics, and to make possible the integration and tests of new functionalities.

Acknowledgments. The authors would like to thank the Brazilian governmental agencies CAPES, CNPq and FAPESP, and Siemens Infraestrutura e Indústria for their partial support of this work.

References

1. Brown, A.C., De Beer, D.: Development of a stereolithography (STL) slicing and G-code generation algorithm for an entry level 3-D printer. In: 2013 Africon, pp. 1–5. IEEE (2013)
2. DebRoy, T., et al.: Additive manufacturing of metallic components – process, structure and properties. Prog. Mater Sci. **92**, 112–224 (2018)
3. Oliveira, J., Santos, T., Miranda, R.: Revisiting fundamental welding concepts to improve additive manufacturing: from theory to practice. Prog. Mater Sci. **107**, 100590 (2020)
4. Wang, C., Tan, X., Tor, S., Lim, C.: Machine learning in additive manufacturing: state-of-the-art and perspectives. Addit. Manuf. **36**, 101538 (2020)
5. Gardan, J.: Additive manufacturing technologies: state of the art and trends. Int. J. Prod. Res. **54**(10), 3118–3132 (2016)
6. Standard, A., et al.: Standard terminology for additive manufacturing technologies. ASTM International F2792-12a (2012)
7. Nguyen, T.K., Phung, L.X., Bui, N.-T.: Novel integration of CAPP in a G-code generation module using macro programming for CNC application. Machines **8**(4), 61 (2020)
8. Rullan, A.: Programmable logic controllers versus personal computers for process control. Comput. Ind. Eng. **33**(1–2), 421–424 (1997)
9. Barkalov, A., Titarenko, L., Mazurkiewicz, M.: Programmable logic controllers. In: Foundations of Embedded Systems. Studies in Systems, Decision and Control, vol 195, pp. 145–162. Springer, Cham (2019). https://doi.org/10.1007/978-3-030-11961-4_6
10. Langmann, R., Rojas-Pena, L.F.: A PLC as an industry 4.0 component. In: 201613th International Conference on Remote Engineering and Virtual Instrumentation (REV), pp. 10–15 (2016)

11. Fuller, A., Fan, Z., Day, C., Barlow, C.: Digital twin: enabling technologies, challenges and open research. IEEE Access **8**, 108952–108971 (2020)
12. Tao, F., Zhang, H., Liu, A., Nee, A.Y.: Digital twin in industry: state-of-the-art. IEEE Trans. Industr. Inf. **15**(4), 2405–2415 (2018)
13. Wei, Y., Hu, T., Wang, Y., Wei, S., Luo, W.: Implementation strategy of physical entity for manufacturing system digital twin. Robot. Comput. Integra. Manuf. **73**, 102259 (2022)
14. Culot, G., Orzes, G., Sartor, M., Nassimbeni, G.: The future of manufacturing: a delphi-based scenario analysis on industry 4.0. Technol. Forecast. Soc. Change **157**, 120092 (2020)
15. Jandyal, A., Chaturvedi, I., Wazir, I., Raina, A., Haq, M.I.U.: 3D printing–a review of processes, materials and applications in industry 4.0. Sustain. Oper. Comput. **3**, 33–42 (2022)
16. Oztemel, E., Gursev, S.: Literature review of industry 4.0 and related technologies. J. Intell. Manuf. **31**(1), 127–182 (2020)
17. Iqbal, M., Hashmi, M.S.: Design and analysis of a virtual factory layout. J. Mater. Process. Technol. **118**(1–3), 403–410 (2001)
18. Shin, H.S., Lee, H.I., Jang, E.S.: An effective data structure for a 3D printing slicer API. In: 2016 IEEE International Conference on Consumer Electronics-Asia (ICCE-Asia), pp. 1–4. IEEE (2016)
19. Berardinelli, G., Mahmood, N.H., Rodriguez, I., Mogensen, P.: Beyond 5G ireless IRT for industry 4.0: design principles and spectrum aspects. In: 2018 IEEE Globecom Workshops (GC Workshops), pp. 1–6. IEEE (2018)
20. Contreras, J., Rubio, J., Martínez, A.: PLC based control of robots using PLCopen motion control specifications. In: Moreno, H.A., Carrera, I.G., Ramírez-Mendoza, R.A., Baca, J., Banfield, I.A. (eds.) Advances in Automation and Robotics Research. LACAR 2021. Lecture Notes in Networks and Systems, vol. 347, pp. 109–120. Springer, Cham (2022). https://doi.org/10.1007/978-3-030-90033-5_13
21. Szilvśi-Nagy, M., Matyasi, G.: Analysis of STL files. Math. Comput. Modell. **38**(7–9), 945–960 (2003)
22. Wüthrich, M., Gubser, M., Elspass, W.J., Jaeger, C.: A novel slicing strategy to print overhangs without support material. Appl. Sci. **11**(18), 8760 (2021)

Dynamic and Efficiency Study Applied to Automotive Vehicles

Sergio André[1,2], Nelson Santos[1,2,5(✉)], Gonçalo O. Duarte[1,4], Paulo Almeida[1,2], Pedro M. Fonte[1,2,3], and Rita Pereira[1,2,3]

[1] ISEL – Instituto Superior de Engenharia de Lisboa, Instituto Politécnico de Lisboa (IPL), Rua Conselheiro Emídio Navarro 1, 1959-007 Lisbon, Portugal
{sergio.andre,nelson.santos,goncalo.duarte,paulo.almeida,
pedro.fonte,rita.pereira}@isel.pt
[2] LCEC, Rua Conselheiro Emídio Navarro 1, 1959-007 Lisbon, Portugal
[3] ISRC, Rua Dr. António Bernardino de Almeida, 431, 4200-072 Porto, Portugal
[4] Centre for Innovation, Technology and Policy Research (IN+), Instituto Superior Técnico, Universidade de Lisboa, Lisbon, Portugal
[5] INESC-ID, Rua Alves Redol, 1000-029 Lisbon, Portugal

Abstract. This paper addresses a simulation system based on an Electromechanical Stewart Platform (ESP) used to analyze a vehicle driving dynamic, allowing to emulate forces and accelerations that passengers or cargo are subject to. The ESP interacts with a driving simulation platform, where the drivers' action on wheel and pedals are used as input on the driving simulation software. The software is being built to provide the correspondent movement to the ESP, and visual feedback on the driver behavior. The inclusion of virtual reality into the system will enhance the physical effect felt by the user, resulting in a more realistic driving simulator when compared with the conventional ones. This system can be an efficient, flexible, agile, and sustainable solution to provide driver training, for professional drivers, providing initial training on the vehicle motion behavior, as well as for continuous training, by including information on energy use and emission outcomes.

Keywords: Stewart platform · Virtual reality · Driving simulators · Comfort

1 Introduction

The existing driving simulators allow a visual perception of the road and driving conditions, however usually they do not provide feedback from the resulting longitudinal and lateral accelerations that occur in real vehicles. The inclusion of a 6 degrees-of-freedom simulation platform provides a realistic sensorial perception of the automotive vehicle dynamic behavior to the user.

The possibility to include this type of platform adds a layer on the perceptive dynamics of the vehicle on the driving simulator. This is of particular interest for heavy-duty vehicle drivers training. For bus drivers, riding comfort is of major importance since some of the passengers are standing and not seated. Therefore, the vehicle dynamics

© IFIP International Federation for Information Processing 2022
Published by Springer Nature Switzerland AG 2022
L. M. Camarinha-Matos (Ed.): DoCEIS 2022, IFIP AICT 649, pp. 225–232, 2022.
https://doi.org/10.1007/978-3-031-07520-9_21

applied in the six degrees-of-freedom (6 DOF) platform contributes to training on undesirable driving behaviors on the perspective of passenger comfort. Moreover, real-time driving consumption can be included in the simulator, allowing to evaluate real-time undesired driver behaviors, the vehicle movement, and its energy impact.

2   Relationship with Technological Innovation for Digitalization and Virtualization

The proposed simulation system encompasses the interconnection between hardware and software developed to provide a realistic sensorial effect to the user. The hardware is defined by an ESP, with 6 DOF, which actuators are induction motors with mechanical movement conversion from rotation to linear displacement, driven by electronic power converters. The software allows the incorporation of vehicle dynamics, according with drivers' actions on wheels and pedals, used as software inputs. The realistic enhancement of the proposed simulator, when compared with conventional simulators, is attained by a conjunction between movements provided by drivers' actions on the ESP and a corresponding image that gives visual feedback on driver behavior, such as warnings on hard acceleration, deceleration, or excessive fuel usage, for example. Including virtual reality into this system contributes for increasing the simulator flexibility, making it more agile and efficient in classroom drivers training, namely for professional drivers. Even in a continuous training context, the proposed simulator contributes for drivers and system efficiency improvement, by including information and data of used energy, such as fuel, and the emissions. It is also important to underline that with this approach the driver can integrate the relations between his actions on the vehicle, that are traduced in vehicle dynamics and, in real-time, receive indicators on energy, emissions outcomes and, with the 6 DOF ESP, also feedback on comfort. This innovative approach allows to provide complete training under classroom.

3   Related Literature

First simulators were developed to be applied in aerospace industry as flight simulators and have approximately 7 decades of existence. Automobile driving simulators first developments are dated from de early 1980's. Nowadays there are several driving simulators that can range from a simple structure and low-cost, to high-level structure based on expensive parallel manipulators, used for different applications, such as drivers' behavior analysis, vehicles technology study, safety study and drivers' training [1]. Some well-known simulators are high-level systems and result from intensive research and development work, such as NADS, TUTOR [2], Simulator III [3] and others [4, 5] developed by universities or research institutions.

Driving behavior studies includes the assessment of passengers' comfort, the road profile, and conditions [6], driving performance and economic driving techniques [7], improvement of driving safety and warning systems [8].

The energy and emission impacts associated to vehicle dynamics can be assessed using the Vehicle Specific Power (VSP) methodology [9]. This method is widely used for light and heavy-duty vehicles and allows to evaluate energy and environmental impacts of specific vehicles in specific routes, under any driving condition, based on a combination of speed, acceleration, and road grade [10] which can be obtained from a driving simulator.

It has been shown that driver training can contribute to improve eco-driving, by reducing fuel consumption, or non-comfort events, such as hard decelerations, whether by providing real-time feedback or just by classroom eco-driving sessions [11]. However, other studies underline that without real-time feedback, drivers tend to increase the percentage of time in undesirable events [12, 13]. Moreover, acceleration with strong power demand, stop, acceleration with moderate power demand, mostly contribute to energy efficiency and emission outcomes [14]. Also, passenger comfort uses some of these metrics, namely hard acceleration, hard start, hard deceleration, and hard stop [13].

All the parameters required to provide real-time feedback to the driver can be obtained from the simulator and used to build energy, emission, and comfort indicators, as well as providing the vehicle movement using the 6 DOF platform.

The proposed simulator is high-level, portable and less expensive when compared with other existent high-level simulators, offering a dynamic response in line with the drivers' sensorial perceptions and allowing to develop studies on driving efficiency. In addition, the proposed system shows promising results in what concerns to the interface between human and virtual environment, achieved by the synchronization between the platform and the human sensorial effects.

4 System Characterization

To virtualize a vehicle as a driver or passenger, the entire system must be able to transmit sensations identical to a real-world situation. The entire system considers the visual, auditory, tactile and motion perception to offer a complete experience to the user for easy identify discomfort or danger scenarios. Figure 1 presents an automotive vehicle virtualization scheme.

The system is composed by hardware and software with computational processing in real time using different communication protocols between all the interface components, increasing the complexity of the simulator control, making it essential to reach a synchronization between the visual perception and the movement of the platform according to the vehicle models.

In Fig. 1 Real-time feedback on comfort indicators can be provided using literature data, obtained from real-world bus operation, such as hard acceleration, hard start, hard deceleration, and hard stop [13]. All these indicators can be built based on data provided from the simulator, such as longitudinal speed and acceleration. The system inputs result from human actions provided by the driver, which receives sensorial effects from the system. This type of indicators based on longitudinal variables is easier for the driver to understand. However, work will be carried to include lateral acceleration indicators, which can also be obtained from the simulation tool, combined with the vehicle mathematical model.

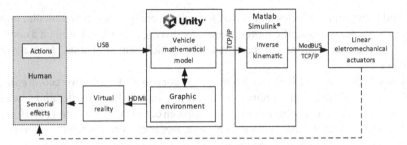

Fig. 1. Automotive vehicle virtualization scheme.

In the literature there are multiple ways to implement graphical environments [15]. For the implementation proposed in this study, software *Unity* was used. *Unity* is a cross-platform graphical game engine development software that supports different programming languages and multiple 3D object formats [15]. Herein, the usage of *Unity* in combination with software *Blender* for object drawing allows to produce the graphical environment. An example of the implemented graphic environment is present in Fig. 2.

Fig. 2. Graphical environment of drivers' view.

The vehicle dynamics is implemented using the models incorporated in the objects from *Unity*, and the C# code controls the torque applied to the wheel components. The *Unity* engine will compute all data and calculate the next position of the automotive, updating all the graphics.

The ESP consists of a parallel manipulator with 6 legs, each one formed by 2 joints connecting the base to the main element as shown in Fig. 3(a). A universal joint is mounted between the final element and the prismatic joint. From there, another universal joint is connected to the base. This configuration allows rotation movements such as roll, pitch and yaw and translation movements such as heave, surge, and sway. The heave defines the elevation movement allowing emulate vertical accelerations due irregularities in the road. The surge movement defines the forward and the backward translation in longitudinal axis to emulate the starting and the braking accelerations. The sway defines the lateral translation movement and emulate the accelerations to the left and right. Figure 3(a) depicts the ESP used in this work and Fig. 3(b) is a representation used to obtain the spatial coordinates.

The roll is the rotational movement along the longitudinal axis and emulates the oscillations due to the vehicle's suspensions. The pitch emulates the orography of the road, and the yaw emulates the direction of the road.

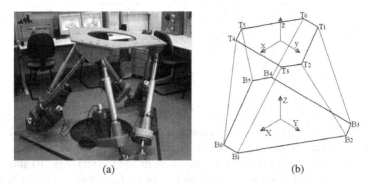

(a)   (b)

Fig. 3. ESP; (a) laboratorial implementation; (b) schematical representation.

Driver sends inputs to the system, such as, steering wheel angle, acceleration, and gear position. The vehicle mathematical model calculates the position of the vehicle in the graphical environment, and *Matlab*® provides to the ESP the translational movement (p_x, p_y and p_z) and rotational movement (α, β and γ). Equation (1) calculates the inverse kinematics and (2) the coordinates of the joints. Following Fig. 3(b) is possible to obtain the length of each actuator (L_1, L_2, L_3, L_4, L_5 and L_6) using Eq. (3). The displacement of the ESP legs is carried out by linear actuators with asynchronous motors and correspondent drivers with position control.

The combination of the 6 DOF movement with a head mounted display (HMD) gives a full immersive environment to the user. *Unity* software was carefully chosen to allow an easily integration of the HMD device, and at the same time, control the hardware in the loop (ESP) by providing data to *Matlab Simulink*®, however others open-source software can be used, such as *Octave* or *Python*. Moreover, it is possible with this software and the HMD device to track the position of the user's hands and virtualize it in the virtual steering wheel giving a more realistic environment to the user.

$$T_{BASE}^{TOP} = \begin{bmatrix} \cos\beta\cos\gamma + \sin\alpha\sin\beta\sin\gamma & -\cos\beta\sin\gamma + \sin\alpha\sin\beta\cos\gamma & \cos\alpha\sin\beta & p_x \\ \cos\alpha\sin\gamma & \cos\alpha\cos\gamma & -\sin\alpha & p_y \\ -\sin\beta\cos\gamma + \sin\alpha\sin\beta\sin\gamma & \sin\beta\sin\gamma + \sin\alpha\cos\beta\cos\gamma & \cos\alpha\cos\beta & p_z \\ 0 & 0 & 0 & 1 \end{bmatrix} \quad (1)$$

$$\begin{bmatrix} X_{Ti} \\ Y_{Ti} \\ Z_{Ti} \\ 1 \end{bmatrix} = T_{BASE}^{TOP}(p_x, p_y, p_z, \alpha, \beta, \gamma) \begin{bmatrix} x_{Ti} \\ y_{Ti} \\ z_{Ti} \\ 1 \end{bmatrix} \quad (2)$$

$$L_1 = \sqrt{(X_{T3} - X_{B1})^2 + (Y_{T3} - Y_{B1})^2 + (Z_{T3} - Z_{B1})^2}$$

$$L_2 = \sqrt{(X_{T2} - X_{B2})^2 + (Y_{T2} - Y_{B2})^2 + (Z_{T2} - Z_{B2})^2}$$

$$L_3 = \sqrt{(X_{T1} - X_{B3})^2 + (Y_{T1} - Y_{B3})^2 + (Z_{T1} - Z_{B3})^2}$$

$$L_4 = \sqrt{(X_{T6} - X_{B4})^2 + (Y_{T6} - Y_{B4})^2 + (Z_{T6} - Z_{B4})^2} \qquad (3)$$

$$L_5 = \sqrt{(X_{T5} - X_{B5})^2 + (Y_{T5} - Y_{B5})^2 + (Z_{T5} - Z_{B5})^2}$$

$$L_6 = \sqrt{(X_{T4} - X_{B6})^2 + (Y_{T4} - Y_{B6})^2 + (Z_{T4} - Z_{B6})^2}$$

It is very important that the ESP platform is precisely synchronized with the HMD. As the human body is expecting some accelerations associated to the visual events, the lack of synchronism can provoke some dizziness or motion sickness. To allow that, a bidirectional communication with sampling rate of 60 Hz between *Matlab Simulink*® and *Unity* is implemented, being the position of the vehicle in the graphical environment controlled by the pedals and steering wheel controller considering the feedback from the ESP.

5 Preliminary Experimental Results

To evaluate the response of the platform and verify the comfort of the driver or passengers, an inertial sensor was installed to check the feedback of the movements according to the mathematical model of the vehicle and the characteristics of the simulated route. With the measurement of lateral (sway), longitudinal (surge) and vertical (heave) acceleration, it is possible to evaluate the perception of the user and to study the limits of comfort, by synchronizing ESP movements and the graphical environment. Being this a preliminary study, only some system responses are here detailed. As an example, in Fig. 4 is depicted the response of the ESP to a surge, sway and heave movement for a positive step of 0.2 m in relation to the reference stand position.

The limitations of the ESP are determined by measuring the movements and analysing the data, allowing to validate which vehicle models can be used in the simulator for the comfort study. The measurement limits of ESP movement are presented in Table 1. Comparing these results with the limits presents in [13] it can be concluded that the ESP is able to simulate some vehicles such as a bus.

Table 1. Measurement limits of ESP movements.

Movement	Limits	Acceleration
Surge	±0.26 m	3.6 m/s^2
Sway	±0.22 m	3.5 m/s^2
Heave	±0.30 m	2.3 m/s^2

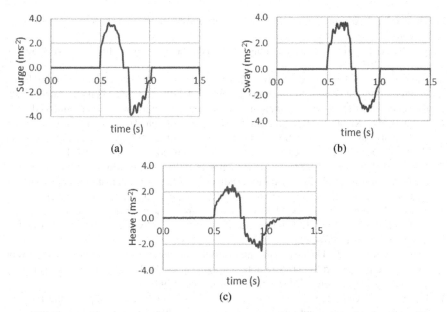

Fig. 4. Maximum acceleration experimental results: (a) surge; (b) sway; (c) heave.

6   Conclusions and Future Work

The proposed simulation system based on the ESP can emulate the dynamics of a passenger bus. Also, it allows to include the visual environment enhancing driver perceptions and analyze passengers comfort experiences accordingly with the road conditions and driver actions.

The experimental setup described provides a useful research tool to study driving comfort in laboratory environment with the ability to measure comfort parameters in real time in different road courses.

Combining the ESP and the graphical environment with head mounted display allows for immersive classroom driver training, also providing feedback on energy, emissions, and comfort indicators.

Future work will focus on the development and refinement of virtual reality graphical scenarios including a variety of daily living events, tune and develop strategies for synchronization between movements and the graphic environment and study and comparing driving efficiency simulator with real driving situations.

Acknowledgments. This work was supported by Portuguese national funds through IPL – Instituto Politécnico de Lisboa under Project IPL/2021/TrackDyman_ISEL.

References

1. Wang, Y., Zhang, W., Wu, S., Guo, Y.: Simulators for driving safety study – a literature review. In: Shumaker, R. (ed.) ICVR 2007. LNCS, vol. 4563, pp. 584–593. Springer, Heidelberg (2007). https://doi.org/10.1007/978-3-540-73335-5_63

2. The National Advanced Driving Simulator at University of Iowa. http://www.nads-sc.uio wa.edu
3. VTI, Swedish National Road and Transportation Research Institute. http://www.vti.se/templa tes/Page_3257.aspx
4. Suda, Y., et al.: Validation of the universal driving simulator with interactive traffic simulation. In: Proceedings of Driving Simulation Conference Asia/Pacific 2006, Tsukuba, Japan (2006)
5. University of Michigan Transportation Research Institute. http://www.umtri.umich.edu
6. Fuzhong, W., Xiaoli, L.: Research on the simulation of vehicle ride comfort with random road inputs based on ADAMSNiew. In: Proceedings of 2010 International Conference on Computer Design and Applications (ICCDA 2010), Fukuoka, Japan, pp.187–191 (2010)
7. Bogoni, T.N., Pinho, M.S.: Use of a simulator to assess the application of economic driving techniques by truck drivers. In: Proceedings of 2012 IEEE International Conference on Systems, Man, and Cybernetics (SMC), Seul, Korea, pp. 3020–3026. IEEE (2012)
8. Novak, M., Votruba, Z., Svitek, M., Bouchner, P.: Improvement of bus and truck driving safety. In: Proceedings of 2006 IEEE International Conference on Systems, Man and Cybernetics, Taipei, Taiwan, pp. 310–315 (2006)
9. Jiménez-Palacios, J.: Understanding and quantifying motor vehicle emissions with vehicle specific power and TILDAS remote sensing. Thesis (Ph.D.) Massachusetts Institute of Technology, Department of Mechanical Engineering (1999)
10. Duarte, G.O., Gonçalves, G.A., Farias, T.L.: Analysis of fuel consumption and pollutant emissions of regulated and alternative driving cycles based on real-world measurements. Transp. Res. Part D **44**, 43–54 (2016)
11. Strömberg, H.K., Karlsson, I.C.M.: Comparative effects of eco-driving initiatives aimed at urban bus drivers - results from a field study. Transp. Res. Part D **22**, 28–33 (2013)
12. Rolim, C., Baptista, P., Duarte, G., Farias, T., Shiftan, Y.: Quantification of the impacts of eco-driving training and real-time feedback on urban buses driver's behaviour. Transp. Res. Procedia **3**, 70–79 (2014)
13. Duarte, G.O., Gonçalves, G.A., Farias, T.L.: Vehicle monitoring for driver training in bus companies – application in two case studies in Portugal. Transp. Res. Part D **18**, 103–109 (2013)
14. Ericsson, E.: Independent driving pattern factors and their influence on fuel-use and exhaust emission factors. Transp. Res. Part D: Transp. Environ. **6**(5), 325–345 (2001)
15. Wang, S., Mao, Z., Zeng, C., Gong, H., Li, S., Chen, B.: A new method of virtual reality based on Unity3D. In: 18th International Conference on Geoinformatics, Beijing, China, pp. 1–5 (2010)

Digital Platform for Environmental and Economic Analysis of Wire Arc Additive Manufacturing

Samruddha Kokare[1](✉), Radu Godina[1], and João P. Oliveira[1,2]

[1] UNIDEMI, Department of Mechanical and Industrial Engineering, NOVA School of Science and Technology, Universidade NOVA de Lisboa, 2829-516 Costa da Caparica, Portugal
s.kokare@campus.fct.unl.pt

[2] CENIMAT/I3N, Department of Materials Science, NOVA School of Science and Technology, Universidade NOVA de Lisboa, 2829-516 Costa da Caparica, Portugal

Abstract. Additive Manufacturing (AM) is gaining attraction due to its benefits such as the ability to fabricate complex shapes, reduced material waste, minimal tooling among others. Wire Arc Additive Manufacturing (WAAM) is an AM process that presents novel opportunities in the fabrication, repair, and refurbishment of products. Nowadays with increased awareness regarding sustainability, assessment of WAAM based on its environmental and economic performance is essential. The popular methods for environmental and economic assessment are Life Cycle Assessment (LCA) and Life Cycle Costing (LCC) respectively. Both these methods are data and time-intensive requiring knowledgeable personnel for their implementation. The objective of this paper is to reduce the time, labour, and costs concerning LCA and LCC procedures by digitalizing them. This paper presents a digital platform where LCA and LCC analyses of WAAM products can be obtained by a user just by entering the geometrical specifications of a product and process parameters.

Keywords: Wire arc additive manufacturing · Life cycle assessment · Life cycle costing · Sustainability · Digitalization

1 Introduction

The industrial sector is resource intensive, accounting for 37% of the global energy use and responsible for about 24% of the global CO_2 emissions, according to a report by International Energy Agency (IEA) [1]. Increased customer consciousness about the environment and emergence of tougher environmental legislations have pushed the manufacturers to develop sustainable products [2]. Nowadays, adoption of additive manufacturing (AM) is gaining attention due to its ability to fabricate complex shapes and better material utilization [3]. One emerging AM process is Wire Arc Additive Manufacturing (WAAM), where a metal wire is melted using an electric arc and deposited

© IFIP International Federation for Information Processing 2022
Published by Springer Nature Switzerland AG 2022
L. M. Camarinha-Matos (Ed.): DoCEIS 2022, IFIP AICT 649, pp. 233–243, 2022.
https://doi.org/10.1007/978-3-031-07520-9_22

layer by layer. WAAM has a promising sustainability potential as it requires lesser material removal and shorter lead times compared to conventional subtractive manufacturing processes [4]. The environmental and economic sustainability of the WAAM can be evaluated using Life Cycle Assessment (LCA) and Life Cycle Costing (LCC) methodologies respectively. In LCA, the environmental impact of a product is calculated based on the resources and energy consumed over its life cycle. LCC involves economic evaluation of a product over its life cycle. However, conducting LCA and LCC analyses is a time and labour-intensive task, where the environmental and economic data needs to be collected from various sources and an expert is needed to perform such analyses. This makes the application LCA and LCC methodologies costly.

Digitalization of LCA and LCC methodologies using predictive models that require minimum human effort and expertise can help in reducing the costs of LCA and LCC methodologies. Therefore, the aim of this paper is to digitalize and virtualize the LCA and LCC procedures for WAAM. This paper presents a digital platform where LCA and LCC analyses of WAAM products can be performed by a user just by entering the geometrical specifications of a product and process parameters. This paper is structured as follows: Sect. 2 links this work with digitalization and virtualization. Section 3 presents the previous work on LCA and LCC studies of AM processes. In Sects. 4 and 5, the LCA and LCC models are explained in depth respectively while Sect. 6 demonstrates the digital platform for LCA and LCC of WAAM. Finally, the conclusions are discussed in Sect. 7.

2   Relation to Digitalization and Virtualization

The fourth industrial revolution or Industry 4.0 is leveraging digitalization across the whole life cycle of the products. Digitalization in manufacturing can be accomplished by digitalization of its supply, production, and delivery operations [5]. This is achieved using the principle of virtualization, where the real-world data is transformed into digital simulation-based models [6]. In manufacturing, digitalization has found applications in different operations like sensing, control, modelling and simulation, predictive maintenance among others [7]. As mentioned in the previous section, sustainability of products is gaining attention in the industrial sector in response to the strict environmental regulations and growing environmental awareness among the consumers. Therefore, the environmental and economic assessment of products need to be performed using LCA and LCC methodologies respectively.

In this paper, the environmental and economic assessment activities are digitalized. Using the real-world experimental data, predictive LCA and LCC models for environmental impact and production cost calculations, respectively are developed. Using these models, a digital platform is developed where even a non-expert user with minimal background in LCA or LCC can get the environmental impacts and production costs of WAAM by entering the geometrical and process parameters (see Fig. 1). Therefore, this digital platform will help in reducing the time, effort and labour cost associated with the environmental and economic assessment of WAAM products. This platform can offer new opportunities for prediction and improvement of environmental and economic performance of WAAM products. The designers can simulate different parts to be fabricated in future and assess their environmental footprint and production costs digitally.

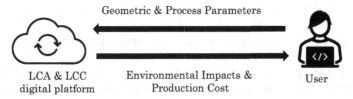

Fig. 1. Schematic representation of the digital platform for LCA and LCC of WAAM.

3 Related Work

Several LCA studies for different AM processes have been conducted in the past [8]. However, most of them are individual case specific studies and fewer studies focus on developing predictive LCA models that can be used to estimate the environmental performance of an AM process in advance. Bourhis et al. developed a predictive model to estimate the environmental impacts of manufacturing products by additive laser manufacturing (ALM) process [9]. Kellens et al. established parametric models to estimate the environmental footprint of Selective Laser Melting (SLM) process [10]. Meteyer et al. presented predictive models for material and energy consumption in binder jetting (BJ) process which then can be used to estimate the life cycle inventory data for LCA studies [11]. Yao and Huang integrated parametric LCA, LCC and optimization models to identify which parameters can affect the environmental impact and life cycle costs of emerging technologies including AM [12]. Ingarao et al. presented LCA models for aluminium parts made by AM, machining and forming routes [13]. Similarly, several studies based on cost modelling of different AM processes have been done in the past [14]. Ruffo [15], Rickenbacker [16] and Lindemann [17] have developed cost models for laser based AM processes. As far as WAAM is concerned, only a few studies performing LCA of WAAM [18–20] or its cost modelling [21] were reported.

Based on the above literature review, it was realized that LCA or LCC of any AM process is a data and time intensive process. One needs to record the amount resources and energy consumed during the process and collect their costs. Moreover, it needs to be carried out by an expert. This makes such assessments more costly. However, with growing emphasis on sustainable development, conducting LCA and LCC to understand environmental and economic aspects of a product/process is essential. Therefore, there is a need to develop predictive LCA and LCC models that can establish a relation between process/geometric parameters and environmental impacts/life cycle costs of AM processes. Digitalizing these models where a user without much knowledge about LCA and LCC methodologies can compute life cycle impacts and costs will further ease their adoption in early stages of product/process development. In this paper, analytical models are developed to predict the resource consumption, environmental impacts, and costs for producing components using WAAM process. Furthermore, a digital platform is developed where a user can enter geometric and process parameters to get the environmental impact and cost of WAAM production.

4 LCA Model

The goal of the LCA study is to determine the environmental impacts caused to due to manufacturing a part by WAAM process. The scope of this study has been limited to the production of a part geometry by WAAM process as illustrated in Fig. 2. The scope begins with raw material production where feed wire is produced by subjecting a billet to hot rolling followed by wire drawing. The feed wire, electricity and shielding act as inputs to WAAM process where the part is fabricated by depositing material layer by layer. After printing each layer, it is subjected to cooling while electric arc is turned off. Further, the part is subjected to CNC milling for post processing to achieve the required dimensions and tolerances.

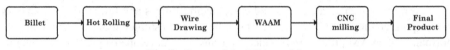

Fig. 2. Scope of the LCA model.

The WAAM process time can be divided into two categories: printing time ($t_{printing}$) and cooling time ($t_{cooling}$). The printing time is the time when the material is deposited while the machine is idle in cooling time and the printed layer is allowed to be cooled. The build rate (BR) of the WAAM process is calculated as follows:

$$BR = \left(\pi d_{wire}^2 \big/ 4\right) \times WFS. \tag{1}$$

where d_{wire} is the feed wire diameter and WFS is the wire feed speed.

The printing time is calculated by dividing the part volume (V_{part}) with the build rate.

$$t_{printing} = V_{part} \big/ BR. \tag{2}$$

The cooling time ($t_{cooling}$) is calculated by multiplying interlayer cooling time ($t_{cooling\ layer}$) with the total number of layers. The total number of layers is calculated by dividing the part height (h_{part}) with height of 1 layer (h_{layer}).

$$t_{cooling} = t_{coolinglayer} \times \left(h_{part} \big/ h_{layer}\right). \tag{3}$$

Therefore, the total time for WAAM process (t_{WAAM}) is the sum of printing and cooling times.

$$t_{WAAM} = t_{printing} + t_{cooling}. \tag{4}$$

The post-processing time i.e., CNC milling time ($t_{post-processing}$) is obtained by dividing the mass of the material removed by the material removal rate (MRR).

$$t_{post-processing} = (BTF - 1) \times m_{part} \big/ MRR. \tag{5}$$

where, BTF is the buy to fly ratio of WAAM and m_{part} is the final part weight. BTF ratio is the ratio of the final part weight after post-processing and the part weight before post-processing.

The inventory flows considered in WAAM process are raw material, electricity, shielding gas and the post-processing operation in the form of CNC milling. The amount of raw material ($m_{material}$) i.e., feed wire consumed in WAAM is calculated by multiplying BTF ratio of WAAM process and the mass of the final part (m_{part}) as follows

$$m_{material} = BTF \times m_{part}. \tag{6}$$

The environmental impact of raw material is calculated by multiplying the mass of material consumed by characterization factor of that material ($cf_{material}$) and is expressed in milli points (mPts).

$$EI_{material} = m_{material} \times cf_{material}. \tag{7}$$

Electricity is used for producing an electric arc which melts the feed wire in WAAM. The electricity consumed in part production (e_{part}) is computed by multiplying the power of the electric arc (P_{arc}) and time taken for printing ($t_{printing}$).

$$e_{part} = P_{arc} \times t_{printing}. \tag{8}$$

The environmental impact of the electricity consumed ($EI_{electricity}$) is calculated as a product of e_{part} and characterization factor for electricity ($cf_{electricity}$), as follows

$$EI_{electricity} = e_{part} \times cf_{electricity}. \tag{9}$$

The shielding gas is used during the process to protect the molten metal from interaction with atmospheric gases. The volume of shielding gas used in part manufacture is determined as a product of the gas flow rate (f_{gas}) and the printing time ($t_{printing}$).

$$g_{part} = f_{gas} \times t_{printing}. \tag{10}$$

The environmental impact of shielding gas (EI_{gas}) is given by multiplying g_{part} with the characterization factor for shielding gas (cf_{gas}).

$$EI_{gas} = g_{part} \times cf_{gas}. \tag{11}$$

Similarly, the environmental impact of CNC milling is determined as the product of amount of material removed and the characterization factor for CNC milling ($cf_{CNCmilling}$).

$$EI_{CNCmilling} = (BTF - 1)m_{part} \times cf_{CNCmilling}. \tag{12}$$

The total environmental impact of the production of a part (EI_{part}) is the sum of the environmental impacts of raw material, electricity, shielding gas and post-processing.

$$EI_{part} = EI_{material} + EI_{electricity} + EI_{gas} + EI_{CNCmilling}. \tag{13}$$

The characterization factors (cf) for individual inventory flows obtained from Ecoinvent 3 database [22] are listed in Table 1.

Table 1. Characterization factors of inventory flows based on Ecoinvent 3 database [22].

Element	Characterization factor (cf)	Unit
Steel Wire	157	mPts/kg
Electricity (Portuguese mix)	20.6	mPts/kWh
Shielding gas (Argon)	106	$mPts/m^3$
CNC milling	84.6	mPts/kg

To characterize the inventory of WAAM process experimentally, a single steel wall of 120 mm in length, 40 mm in height and 5 mm in thickness was fabricated using WAAM. The voltage was set to 21 V and a feed wire of 1 mm in diameter was used. The wire feed speed of 3 m/min, travel speed of 240 mm/min and layer height of 1.3 mm was used. The shielding gas flow rate was fixed at 15 l/min. The deposited mass was milled to required dimensions. The weight of the material deposited by WAAM was measured to be 260 g. The final weight of the wall after milling was recorded to be 134 g. Hence, the BTF ratio calculated was 1.96. It took 17 min to print the wall consuming 0.483 kWh of electricity. The cooling time was 64 min. Thus, the power of the electric arc calculated is 1.7 kW.

5   LCC Model

A LCC model for WAAM process is formulated using the guidelines given by IEC 60300-3-3 Dependability management–Part 3-3: Application guide–Life cycle costing standard [23]. The scope is limited to production phase and following cost elements are considered: machine cost, material cost, consumables cost, post-processing cost and labour cost. The machine cost ($C_{machine}$) includes the cost of WAAM machine tool (C_{mct}), its maintenance (C_{mt}) and tooling ($C_{tooling}$). The WAAM machine is assumed to be available for 3 shifts of 8 h a day, for 250 days a year with 80% availability for a depreciation period of 7 years. Therefore, the hourly cost of using machine (MCC_{1h}) is given as follows

$$MCC_{1h} = \left(C_{mct} + C_{mt} + C_{tooling} \right) / t_{available}. \tag{14}$$

The machine cost ($C_{machine}$) is computed by multiplying the hourly machine cost (MCC_{1h}) with the total time of the WAAM process (t_{WAAM}) as given by

$$C_{machine} = MCC_{1h} \times t_{WAAM}. \tag{15}$$

The material cost ($C_{material}$) is the cost of raw material i.e., the feed wire consumed in WAAM. It is determined as by multiplying the amount of wire consumed ($m_{material}$) and the cost of 1 kg wire (MC_{1kg}) as follows

$$C_{material} = m_{material} \times MC_{1kg}. \tag{16}$$

The consumables cost ($C_{consumables}$) is the cost of process consumables like electricity and shielding gas. It is calculated by the multiplying the amount of electricity (e_{part}) and shielding gas consumed (g_{part}) with their respective costs per unit (EC_{1kWh} & GC_{1m3}).

$$C_{consumables} = e_{part} \times EC_{1kWh} + g_{part} \times GC_{1m3}. \tag{17}$$

The post-processing cost (Cpost-processing) is the cost of post processing operation associated with WAAM i.e., CNC milling in our case. It is the product of hourly cost of post-processing operation (PPC_{1h}) and post processing time ($t_{post\text{-}processing}$).

$$C_{post\text{-}processing} = PPC_{1h} \times t_{post\text{-}processing}. \tag{18}$$

The labour cost is the cost of WAAM operator and is determined by multiplying hourly labour rate (LC_{1h}) and time required by the operator (t_{labour}).

$$C_{labour} = LC_{1h} \times t_{labour}. \tag{19}$$

The production cost ($C_{production}$) for a part is the sum of all the above costs.

$$C_{production} = C_{machine} + C_{material} + C_{consumables} + C_{post\text{-}processing} + C_{labour}. \tag{20}$$

The values of the above cost elements with their respective units and sources are presented in Table 2 below.

Table 2. Values of different cost elements used in this study.

Costs	Value	Unit	Reference
Machine tool cost	300000	€	Quotation
Machine cost	12	€/h	Calculated
Material cost	13	€/kg	Quotation
Electricity cost	0.13	€/kWh	[24]
Shielding gas cost	2.3	€/m3	Quotation
Post-processing cost	30	€/h	Quotation
Labour cost	15	€/h	[25]

6   Digital Platform for LCA and LCC: Example of a Part Geometry

Based on the above LCA and LCC models, a digital platform is developed where the user can compute the environmental impacts and production cost of a part that is intended to be fabricated by WAAM. In this section, a demonstration of LCA and LCC analysis of a part (see Fig. 3) to be manufactured by WAAM using the digital platform is presented. The part in consideration has a volume of 15 cm^3 and height of 13 mm. It has a wall thickness of 4 mm and a pocket of 9 mm depth.

The process parameters for WAAM and geometrical parameters of the part are entered in the input interface of the platform as indicated in Fig. 4. The wire feed speed and travel speed are set at 300 cm/min and 24 cm/min respectively. The steel wire of 1 mm diameter is employed as feed wire input. The shielding gas i.e., pure argon flow rate of 15 l/min is used. The interlayer cooling time of 120 s is being utilized and layer height is set at 1.3 mm. Based on these input parameters and the LCA and LCC models described previously, environmental, and economic analyses of the given part geometry are carried out on the digital platform. The results of analyses are displayed on the output interface, as depicted in Fig. 4.

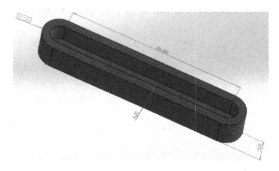

Fig. 3. Part to be manufactured by WAAM.

The environmental impact caused by production of the above part using WAAM process is 88.73 milli points (mPts). The production cost of this part is 20.60 €. The feed wire is the major contributor (52.52 mPts) to the total environmental impact followed by shielding gas (19.65 mPts). Labour is the main cost driver accounting for 8.09 € followed by the machine cost of 6.47 €. Therefore, using this digital platform, the ecological and economic performance of WAAM process can be predicted. This is helpful for designers and manufacturers, especially in the early phases of product development. Such platform can be used to simulate the environmental impact and costs of WAAM products, integrating the environmental and economic considerations in the design phase. Also, the platform is simple to use, and the user does not need extensive knowledge about LCA and LCC methodologies.

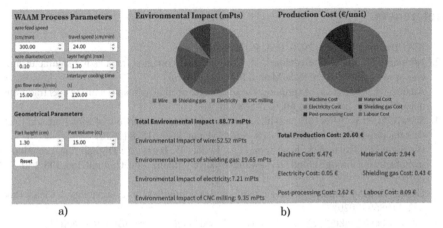

Fig. 4. a) Input interface b) Output interface of the digital platform.

However, it must be noted that currently the platform can be used only for WAAM process where steel wire is used as feed wire input. Efforts need to be done for compiling the environmental and cost data for other materials. The scope of this investigation needs to be extended further to the use, transport, and disposal life cycle stages. Furthermore, the interface of the digital platform lacks features like choosing between different feed wire materials and exporting the LCA and LCC results to the user. Future works will involve the expansion of this work to different materials and life cycle stages along with features to export the results.

7   Conclusions

A digital platform to conduct LCA and LCC analyses of WAAM process was developed in this paper. Analytical models to predict the environmental impact and production costs using process and geometrical parameters of a part design were developed. Using these models, a digital platform was created, where a user can calculate environmental impact and cost of WAAM process by entering process and geometrical parameters. This digitalization of LCA and LCC methodologies will reduce the time, effort, and cost of economic and environmental assessment of WAAM products. The current work involved modelling of environmental impacts and costs for the production of steel parts. Future works will incorporate the further life cycle stages of a product and inclusion of more raw materials. Additionally, advanced features such as exporting the results of the analyses need to be added in the digital platform.

Acknowledgements. The authors acknowledge Fundação para a Ciência e a Tecnologia (FCT-MCTES) for its financial support via the project UIDB/00667/2020 (UNIDEMI). This activity has received funding from the European Institute of Innovation and Technology (EIT) – Project Smart WAAM: Microstructural Engineering and Integrated Non-Destructive Testing. João P. Oliveira acknowledges the funding of CENIMAT/i3N by national funds through the FCT-Fundação para a Ciência e a Tecnologia, I.P., within the scope of Multiannual Financing of R&D Units, reference UIDB/50025/2020-2023.

References

1. IEA: Tracking Industry 2020. IEA, Paris (2020)
2. Nörmann, N., Maier-Speredelozzi, V.: Cost and environmental impacts in manufacturing: a case study approach. Procedia Manuf. **5**, 58–74 (2016)
3. Attaran, M.: The rise of 3-D printing: the advantages of additive manufacturing over traditional manufacturing. Bus. Horiz. **60**, 677–688 (2017)
4. Seow, C.E., et al.: Effect of crack-like defects on the fracture behaviour of wire + arc additively manufactured nickel-base Alloy 718. Addit. Manuf. **36**, 101578 (2020)
5. Borangiu, T., Trentesaux, D., Thomas, A., Leitão, P., Barata, J.: Digital transformation of manufacturing through cloud services and resource virtualization. Comput. Ind. **108**, 150–162 (2019)
6. Ghobakhloo, M.: Industry 4.0, digitization, and opportunities for sustainability. J. Clean. Prod. **252**, 119869 (2020)
7. Lu, Y., Shevtshenko, E., Wang, Y.: Physics based compressive sensing to enable digital twins of additive manufacturing processes. **31** (2021)
8. Saade, M.R.M., Yahia, A., Amor, B.: How has LCA been applied to 3D printing? A systematic literature review and recommendations for future studies. J. Clean. Prod. **244**, 118803 (2020). https://doi.org/10.1016/j.jclepro.2019.118803
9. Le Bourhis, F., Kerbrat, O., Dembinski, L., Hascoet, J.-Y., Mognol, P.: Predictive model for environmental assessment in additive manufacturing process. Procedia CIRP **15**, 26–31 (2014)
10. Kellens, K., Renaldi, R., Dewulf, W., Kruth, J., Duflou, J.R.: Environmental impact modeling of selective laser sintering processes. Rapid Prototyping J. **20**, 459–470 (2014)
11. Meteyer, S., Xu, X., Perry, N., Zhao, Y.F.: Energy and material flow analysis of binder-jetting additive manufacturing processes. Procedia CIRP **15**, 19–25 (2014)
12. Yao, Y., Huang, R.: A parametric life cycle modeling framework for identifying research development priorities of emerging technologies: a case study of additive manufacturing. Procedia CIRP **80**, 370–375 (2019)
13. Ingarao, G., Priarone, P.C., Deng, Y., Paraskevas, D.: Environmental modelling of aluminium based components manufacturing routes: additive manufacturing versus machining versus forming. J. Clean. Prod. **176**, 261–275 (2018)
14. Busachi, A., Erkoyuncu, J., Colegrove, P., Martina, F., Watts, C., Drake, R.: A review of additive manufacturing technology and cost estimation techniques for the defence sector. CIRP J. Manuf. Sci. Technol. **19**, 117–128 (2017)
15. Ruffo, M., Tuck, C., Hague, R.: Cost estimation for rapid manufacturing - laser sintering production for low to medium volumes. Proc. Inst. Mech. Eng. Part B: J. Eng. Manuf. **220**, 1417–1427 (2006)
16. Rickenbacher, L., Spierings, A., Wegener, K.: An integrated cost-model for selective laser melting (SLM). Rapid Prototyping J. **19**, 208–214 (2013)
17. Lindemann, C.F.W., Jahnke, U.: Modelling of laser additive manufactured product lifecycle costs. In: Laser Additive Manufacturing: Materials, Design, Technologies, and Applications, pp. 281–316. Elsevier Inc. (2017)
18. Bekker, A.C.M., Verlinden, J.C.: Life cycle assessment of wire + arc additive manufacturing compared to green sand casting and CNC milling in stainless steel. J. Clean. Prod. **177**, 438–447 (2018)
19. Priarone, P.C., Pagone, E., Martina, F., Catalano, A.R., Settineri, L.: Multi-criteria environmental and economic impact assessment of wire arc additive manufacturing. CIRP Ann. **69**, 37–40 (2020)

20. Campatelli, G., Montevecchi, F., Venturini, G., Ingarao, G., Priarone, P.C.: Integrated WAAM-subtractive versus pure subtractive manufacturing approaches: an energy efficiency comparison. Int. J. Precis. Eng. Manuf.-Green Technol. **7**(1), 1–11 (2019). https://doi.org/10.1007/s40684-019-00071-y
21. Facchini, F., De Chirico, A., Mummolo, G.: Comparative cost evaluation of material removal process and additive manufacturing in aerospace industry. In: Reis, J., Pinelas, S., Melão, N. (eds.) IJCIEOM 2018. SPMS, vol. 280, pp. 47–59. Springer, Cham (2019). https://doi.org/10.1007/978-3-030-14969-7_5
22. Ecoinvent: Ecoinvent 3 Database, Zurich (2021)
23. International Electrotechnical Commission: IEC 60300-3-3: 2017 Dependability management–Part 3-3: Application guide–Life cycle costing (2017)
24. Eurostat: Electricity price statistics. https://ec.europa.eu/eurostat/statistics-explained/index.php?title=Electricity_price_statistics. Accessed 20 Dec 2021
25. Statistica: Average hourly labor cost in selected European countries in 2020. https://www.statista.com/statistics/1211601/hourly-labor-cost-in-europe/. Accessed 20 Dec 2021

Author Index

Printed in the United States
by Baker & Taylor Publisher Services